COMPREHENSIVE TECTONICS

Comprehensive Tectonics considers building construction assemblies holistically to help you make architectural detailing decisions from the earth to the sky. Seven case studies from architecture firms such as Perkins + Will, Lake | Flato, and Olson Kundig Architects include more than 250 color images showing component details, building sections, wall sections, and floor plans. For each project, the architects explain their design intent and the reasons for their material and tectonic choices, to help you form your own strategies.

This book will provide you with assistance by its ease of use with legible keys, scales, and reference images. Its key insights about why the firm chose certain materials will allow you to create your own process for utilizing building construction assemblies. *Comprehensive Tectonics* aims to give you a more comprehensive overview of building construction assemblies to aid in the creation of well-designed and well-developed architecture.

Including a glossary and guide for how to determine assembly, this book makes a welcome desk reference, is an ideal addition for students in architecture integrated studios dealing with structures and materials, and is also a useful addition for professional architects.

Alexis Gregory is an Associate Professor at Mississippi State University in Mississippi State, Mississippi, USA.

"The successful translation of a design from idea to built reality is among the architect's most challenging and complex tasks. Through a series of detailed case studies, *Comprehensive Tectonics* by Alexis Gregory skillfully demystifies this process, explaining the priorities and decisions that inform the selection of materials and clearly illustrating their assembly from foundation to roof."

Scott Murray, Architect, Associate Professor, University of Illinois at Urbana-Champaign

"In the spirit of Ed Ford's *Details of Modern Architecture* series, the Birkhauser *Details* book series, and *Detail* magazine is Gregory's contemporary addition to the art and science of detailing. How a building turns a corner, touches the ground and reaches for the sky is presented through richly illustrated case studies that demonstrate that detailing has just as much design agency as form-making and that spatial polemics and means and methods are one and the same when making architecture."

Ryan E. Smith, Director & Professor, School of Design & Construction, Washington State University

COMPREHENSIVE TECTONICS

Technical Building Assemblies from the Ground to the Sky

Edited by Alexis Gregory

Routledge
Taylor & Francis Group

NEW YORK AND LONDON

First published 2020
by Routledge
52 Vanderbilt Avenue, New York, NY 10017

and by Routledge
2 Park Square, Milton Park, Abingdon, Oxon, OX14 4RN

Routledge is an imprint of the Taylor & Francis Group, an informa business

Library of Congress Cataloging-in-Publication Data
Names: Gregory, Alexis, editor.
Title: Comprehensive tectonics : technical building assemblies from the
    ground to the sky / edited by Alexis Gregory.
Description: New York : Routledge, 2019. | Includes bibliographical
    references and index.
Identifiers: LCCN 2019007874| ISBN 9781138925182 (hardback : alk. paper) |
    ISBN 9781138925199 (pbk. : alk. paper) | ISBN 9781315683881 (e-book :
    alk. paper)
Subjects: LCSH: Architecture—Details—Case studies. | Building materials—
    Case studies.
Classification: LCC NA2840 .C595 2019 | DDC 721/.04—dc23
LC record available at https://lccn.loc.gov/2019007874

ISBN: 978-1-138-92518-2 (hbk)
ISBN: 978-1-138-92519-9 (pbk)
ISBN: 978-1-315-68388-1 (ebk)

Typeset in Univers
by Swales & Willis Ltd, Exeter, Devon, UK

Contents

Foreword

Edward Ford

In 1929, Le Corbusier described, with prophetic certainty, what the building construction industry of the future would be like. We would dispose of the status quo and its archaic methodologies – the handcrafted chaos of the building site, the needless plethora of materials, the confusing diversity of components. In the future, everything would be simpler. Everything would be industrialized. Buildings would be made like cars from factory made components. This required a certain order of things based on the economics of mass production. Work at the site would be minimized. The parts would be selected from a limited number of rigidly standardized components, and the parts would be based on simple geometric forms – cubes, cones, cylinders, and prisms – to facilitate fabrication in assembly line production. The ultimate result would be a simple, uniform system of construction that could accommodate any program-a single family house or a large office. In fact, the system was almost here. A drawing at the same time, published in *Une maison or un palais*, shows that the section of Le Corbusier's Villa at Garches is the same as the section of his unbuilt League of Nations Office wing. The profiles are the same. The windows are the same repetitive, standardized units. Even the floor to floor heights, the structural bay size and for the most part the structure itself are the same.[1]

Le Corbusier was, of course, almost completely wrong. He was not wrong about certain trends – the increase in off-site fabrication, the specialization of labor or the tendency to use the same component, such as a standardized window, in a variety of applications – but he was wrong about the architectural implications of these trends. He was mostly wrong in thinking that building systems were moving toward simplicity and uniformity, that we would use fewer components and fewer systems and that buildings of very different program types would be built the same way. Ninety years later it is clear that precisely the opposite is the case. Building components have not become smaller in number. They are less multifunctional, more specialized and there are more of them. Many building components are made in standardized sizes but the standard sizes are so numerous they present no formal restrictions. The ways we build different program types – a house or an office for example – have radically diverged rather than becoming identical.

Over the last 20 years modern architects have developed an equally dogmatic prophesy of the construction of the future, one of a very different nature and, of course, it is a digital one. Not surprisingly, it is 180 degrees from the direction predicted by Le

Corbusier. According to the new prophets, digital technology will make possible an infinite variety of unique components. There are no economies in repetitive elements of the same size, quite the opposite. We will have an infinite variety of non-Euclidian geometries at our disposal with no adverse economic consequences. And then there are the robots. It is not difficult to find contemporary examples that contradict these premises, anecdotes of buildings with complex geometries and non-repetitive components whose cost, in the end, vastly exceeded the projections. These incidents are typically explained as the result of extraneous factors or by the assumption that when the digital revolution is completed all will be well, but at the moment there is little reason to believe these prophecies will be any more accurate than Le Corbusier's.[2]

But to the unbiased observer these two positions, Corbusier's and that of his digital counterparts, demonstrate something else. Both are examples of a way of thinking that is deeply embedded in the traditions of Modernism. On the one hand, technological changes may inspire changes in architectural form but they do not necessarily dictate them. But more critically the construction industry does not lend itself to simplistic generalizations, especially those regarding economies of material, of labor or of capital, and projecting apparent trends into the future with the assumption that they will increase in magnitude is a risky enterprise at best. In simple terms, architects are not very good at predicting the technological future. We are wrong most of the time. The history of our engagement with sustainability in all its manifestations provides a similar sequence – the identification of a technological trend, the exaggeration of the trend into a formal language and the production of a small number of prototypes that are duplicated only on a small scale. Since 1900 the architectural avant-garde has become dependent on metanarratives of historical inevitability that present us with certainties of the future against which we measure every design decision. It is a prime example of the type of thinking Karl Popper described and criticized in *The Poverty of Historicism* in 1957, "the theory that society will necessarily change but along a predetermined path that cannot change, through stages predetermined by inexorable necessity." Marxism and Fascism are the most prominent of these metanarratives and the most destructive. Popper argues the contrary, that, "there can be no prediction of the course of human history by scientific or any other rational methods."[3]

This brings us to the book that follows and presents a way of understanding and comparing the buildings that it contains. One of the more problematic aspects of the increased complexity of modern building – the specialization of parts and the multitude of components – has been its pedagogical effects. The logic of contemporary construction is simply harder to understand. The typical conventional set of contract documents is to the untrained layman and the uninitiated student not just a foreign language but a foreign country and provokes a variety of simple questions. Why is everything so complex? Why are there so many components? Why can't we use fewer pieces? Why can't the arrangement of these systems be less complex? So how, then, are we to go about teaching building construction? How are we going to conceptualize this mass of information into a coherent working methodology?

Pure pragmatism, treating each detail as an isolated, purely technical problem, is no answer, given the multiplicity of relatively equal choices in solving any constructional problem. It can be argued that we already have the answer. The construction industry has always been dependent on typologies – the assumption that a certain building types are likely to use certain systems – structural, mechanical, and exterior and interior enclosure systems in combination. A conspicuous example is the free-standing parking garage. Structural precast concrete is used as the primary structure in a relatively small number of the buildings built in the US, but the majority of freestanding long-span parking garages in the US are precast concrete. There are a variety of factors – long spans, exposed structure, maintenance – that make this economical. More complex examples of these typologies are less rigidly defined but easy to find. Of the office buildings built during the boom in central Manhattan of the 1980s, the vast majority were steel frame buildings of similar structural spans, bay sizes, floor to floor heights and to a degree mechanical systems. The recent glut of high rise apartments built in the same area follows a different but similarly limited typology – concrete frames, small bay sizes, lower floor to floor heights and different mechanical systems. I suspect that the decisions to use one of these types or another were not based on a rigorous and lengthy examination of various alternatives but rather drawn from a conventional wisdom based on long term experience.[4]

Building form, as the architect conceives it and describes it, is generated by what matters most. There may be local requirements or conditions – a regional tradition to be acknowledged, an urban context that must be respected, a sensitive environment that must be accommodated. Or there may be unique internal program requirements, perhaps an exhibit or performance space that requires accommodation, or major external conditions that need to be established – the provision of external/internal connections for psychological well-being or thermal disconnections for physical comfort.

But the same formal configurations can be understood in an analogous way – as variation of a constructional typology with a certain set of components. A common one in this text is the low-rise, steel-framed, non-residential building. Despite differences in appearance there are commonalities. They have a frame and a skin – sometimes several – a system of interior finish and services primarily a mechanical system, and we can say that the architect's task is to determine the relationship between them. The considerations described in the paragraph above will certainly affect these decisions but they may not determine them.

Some aspects of a system configuration, such as a structural bay, may be determined by program, e.g., an auditorium, but its configuration may be innate in the typology of the system. For example, many of the buildings here have equally spaced structural bays that fall within certain dimensional limits. But there are still a variety of decisions to be made. Is the frame exposed? Are the columns inside the internal partition or freestanding? Is it inside the exterior wall or outside? There are a variety of answers to all of these questions and many of these buildings answer the question differently in different locations. Each condition is again, determined by the environment, site, program, exterior but also the internal logic of the building system. The value of the text that follows is to provide an entry into this way of looking at buildings.

As to the technological future, it is important to realize that like those who I have criticized, I am also generalizing. I am also setting up historicist narratives and articulating my own after-the-fact prophesy – and making my own predictions, that buildings are becoming more complex, that systems are becoming more specialized and more numerous, that the building industry is becoming more national and international. But like all of these prophecies they are merely the projections of a trend. This could all change. It could all be reversed. It is just as possible that the future will see fewer parts, simpler components, multifunctional materials, local technology, and simpler building assemblies. As to how we should proceed, the answer is that we do not need to know the future, only to adhere the internal coherence of the task at hand and let history decide whether the architectural result is the paradigm of what is to come or just another experiment.

Notes

1   Le Corbusier. *Une Maison–Un Palais: "A La Recherche D'une Unité Architecturale."* (Paris: G. Crès et cie, 1929).

2   One of the many examples of this trend of thought is found in Mario Carpo, "Ten Years of Folding," in Greg Lynn, *Folding in Architecture* (Hoboken, NJ: Wiley Academy, 2004) pp. 12–19; EMBT's Parliament of Scotland is a conspicuous example of a building whose final cost vastly exceeded its estimate while making extensive use of digital technology.

3   Karl Popper, *The Poverty of Historicism* (London: Routledge & Kegan Paul, 1957/1974), p. 50, p. iv.

4   Regarding Precast: http://www.highconcrete.com/products/high-concrete-structures/parking-garages/

Preface

This case study book uses a holistic approach to study building construction assemblies. Information about why the architect chose certain materials combined with photographs and construction drawings will help readers understand the process for utilizing design decisions to create building construction assemblies. The main objective is to give readers a more comprehensive guide to building construction assemblies to aid in the creation of well-designed and well-developed architecture through building construction assemblies. The book operates as a handbook for undergraduate students and young architects, constructors, and other interested parties, and may be used in building construction assemblies classes and the design studio environment. It does this by using full building sections with appropriate scale, annotations, and symbols. This will work well for not only students in architecture and construction programs, but also nascent architects and constructors recently graduated from school, as well as intern architects, and others developing their knowledge of building construction assemblies. The projects in the book are from various regions around the United States and the world, so no specific region is targeted in the book. The projects were chosen to range in size and type, as well as to learn from some larger, well-known architecture firms, and some smaller, emerging firms. Another important aspect of the book is to use contemporary projects as the case studies to show readers current designs and building construction assemblies that they will be experiencing in professional practice.

Acknowledgements

Special thanks to my students, who inspired this book, and who helped me to complete it. I am also very thankful to my friends and family who gave much needed encouragement and advice while I was working on the book. I also greatly appreciate Edward Ford for taking the time to write the Foreword, and for inspiring me through his work to create a book on design and construction assemblies. Much appreciation to Wendy Fuller, for supporting my book idea and helping me make it happen, and to Trudy Varcianna for her patience and for answering my numerous, and varied questions during the development process. An additional thanks to Dr. Andrew Tripp, for being my sounding board and giving me the necessary feedback at the necessary time.

This book would not have been possible without the valuable work of the following former students who helped to create the overall design and format for the case study drawings:

Ashton Aime

Jacqueline Brooke Dorman

Chris Harper

Vanessa Holden

Edward Holmes V

Cody Smith

Contributors

The biggest thanks goes to all of the architecture firms and photographers who provided the materials needed to create this book. I would have not been able to realize this idea without your support, architectural designs, creative efforts, and willingness to share it all with me.

W. Scott Allen, Seven Valleys LLC, formerly with Perkins + Will

Allison Anderson, unabridged Architecture

John Anderson, unabridged Architecture

Benjamin Benschneider, Benjamin Benschneider Photography

Chris Burnside, Olson Kundig Architects

Ciara Cronin, Olson Kundig Architects

Francis Dzikowski, Francis Dzikowski Photography

Gabriela Frank, Olson Kundig Architects

Dennis Freeland, The Freelon Group (now part of Perkins + Will)

Mark Herboth, Mark Herboth Photography, LLC

Zena Howard, The Freelon Group (now part of Perkins + Will)

Robert Hoang, Lake | Flato Architects

Maria Java, Orcutt Winslow

Cindy Kenney, Orcutt Winslow

Brian Ledesma, Orcutt Winslow

Hank Mardukas, Hank Mardukas Photography

Toni Martin, The Freelon Group (now part of Perkins + Will)

Kristine Millar, Orcutt Winslow

Kirsten R. Murray, Olson Kundig Architects

Jeff Ocampo, Olson Kundig Architects

MacKenzie Otters, Olson Kundig Architects

Daria Pizzetta, H3 Hardy Collaboration Architecture

Will Randolph, Archimania

Chris Rogers, Point32

Victoria Saperstein, OTTO

Bryan Schabel, Perkins + Will – Chicago

Cecelia Smith, Lake | Flato Architects

James Smith, Olson Kundig Architects

James and Connor Steinkamp, Steinkamp Photography

Eugenia Uhl, Eugenia Uhl Photography

Todd Walker, Archimania

Introduction

Based on my more than ten years of experience in teaching building construction technology courses I have seen a gap in the technical literature that causes architecture and building construction students to struggle to understand the building construction detailing taught in lecture courses. The increased complexity of architectural design and construction has made it harder for students to grasp the vast nature of building construction assembly options. This inspired the development of a book to create a more comprehensive guide for students, and young professionals, to help them understand building construction detailing more holistically. The idea is based on Martin Heidegger's fourfold of the unity of earth, sky, mortals, and divinities and uses complete building projects to tell the story from the earth to the sky in building construction detailing.[1,2] The variety of building projects showcased in this book is important to introduce students to the wide variety of building typologies, and the numerous ways these typologies can be detailed and assembled.

Smaller-scale projects, such as the Hatiloo Theater in Memphis, Tennessee, by Archimania, allow students to grasp the scale of the project and to focus on the level of thought and detail that went into items such as the façade and ticket booth. Moderately scaled buildings like the Tenley-Friendship Library in Washington, DC by Perkins + Will (previously The Freelon Group) afford students an opportunity to see a more complex building and how issues of visibility, and also privacy, are achieved through assembly and detail decisions, not just spatial designs alone. Even larger scaled, and more intricate, projects like the renovation and addition for the Arizona State University Health Services Building in Tempe, Arizona, by Lake | Flato and Orcutt | Winslow introduce students to the importance of building reuse for both feasibility and sustainability. The detailing and assembly decisions demonstrate how an existing building and an addition can be seamlessly connected to function as one new structure. These projects, and the four additional ones explored in this book, help students understand that buildings have become more intricate, and their detailing and assembly more particular.

I have realized that students do not understand building construction assemblies without context, so *Comprehensive Tectonics: Technical Building Assemblies from the Ground to the Sky* aims to show students an entire project to provide some of that context. The projects discussed range from locations in the southeast coastal region of the United States to Seattle, Washington, and even Shanghai, China. This range of environments from the desert of Arizona to the swampy environs of Washington, DC give students a better grasp of how context, both in culture and climate, can inform building construction detailing.

Each chapter is told from the point-of-view of the architecture firm that designed and detailed the building to show readers how the design impacted the building construction detailing. Finding out how these decisions were made from the architecture firms is an important learning opportunity for students. Perkins + Will discusses the basis for the formation of the Shanghai Nature Museum, and how its atypical form came from a nautilus shell and is inspired by Chinese garden design. The Maritime and Seafood Museum in Biloxi, Mississippi, by H3 Hardy Collaboration Architecture was designed after the devastating destruction of Hurricane Katrina and incorporated FEMA's floodproofing requirements while still creating an open and inviting museum that has become a focal point for the area.

Rather than concentrate on a particular part of the building, this book aims to show all aspects of the building from the foundation to the roof. This is particularly important in understanding buildings like Art Stable in Seattle, Washington, by Olson Kundig, which was designed for a tight infill site that slopes 16' 2" from the main entrance on the west side of the building to the parking garage entry on the eastern side. Even one-story structures like the Waveland Business Incubator in Waveland, Mississippi, by unabridged Architecture must be understood holistically due to the important design decisions to use dogtrots, porches, and ramps to better engage the street while thinking about sustainability and resilience in another area greatly impacted by Hurricane Katrina.

The goals of the book are:

1   Introduce students to a variety of project scales and typologies.
2   Explore projects through a combination of descriptive text, photographs, and building construction assemblies to allow for analysis.
3   Help students learn to build their own process for understanding the relationship between design and the creation of building construction detailing.

The goals outlined above are intended to align with the problem-solving structure of architecture education and will allow students an ability to learn from the case studies to start making decisions on assembly and detailing for their own design studio projects. Students can analyze the case studies presented in this book and using the *Guide: How to Determine Assembly* with the assistance of their professors, embrace the "self-reflexive nature of the discipline" to realize the essential art of detailing as part of architectural design.[3]

This collection of projects has been utilized to showcase a variety of project scales and typologies to help students learn about the range of information that informs building construction detailing. Students do not understand the individual details on their own, but instead need them as a whole to grasp the depth of the design and detailing decisions. Selected drawings and photographs from each of the seven projects in this book were chosen to help students understand the drawings, in addition to the assemblies. The book organizes each project in the same manner through sections on the architect's design intent and reasoning behind material and tectonic choices, breakdown of major building components, floor plans, building sections, wall sections, and details. Additionally, consistent graphics are used to tie all drawings and images from the various projects together, as well as to make sure that the building construction detailing is clear and easy to understand for nascent architects and constructors. Students are being inundated by technological advances in both building assemblies and software to draw and develop those assemblies. The use of simple and consistent graphics will help students interpret and understand the drawings so that they can focus on the information on detailing and assemblies. Once students are able to use this book with the case studies and the *Guide: How to Determine Assembly*, they will better comprehend the relationship between the building structure, exterior skin, and how to develop that relationship in their own designs.

Simple in concept and rich in information, *Comprehensive Tectonics: Technical Building Assemblies from the Ground to the Sky* seeks to empower readers through a "comprehension of the parts of [buildings] as intimately interconnected and explicable only by reference to the whole."[4]

Notes

1   Heidegger, Martin. 1997. "Building, Dwelling, Thinking." In *Rethinking Architecture: A Reader in Cultural Theory*, edited by Neil Leach, 100–109. New York, NY: Routledge Taylor & Francis Group.

2   Nesbitt, Kate. 1996. "Introduction: Rappel a l'ordre, the Case for the Tectonic." In *Theorizing a New Agenda for Architecture: An Anthology of Architectural Theory*, edited by Kate Nesbitt, 517. New York, NY: Princeton Architectural Press.

3   Nesbitt, Kate. 1996. "Introduction: The Exercise of Detailing." In *Theorizing a New Agenda for Architecture: An Anthology of Architectural Theory*, edited by Kate Nesbitt, 495. New York, NY: Princeton Architectural Press.

4   http://www.oxforddictionaries.com/definition/american_english/holistic

Case Studies

1.1
Front entrance

Credit: Allison Anderson

1: Waveland Business Incubator

Waveland, MS, unabridged Architecture

Architect's Design Intent and Reasoning Behind Material and Tectonic Choices

The project is based on a "dogtrot" between enclosed spaces, a folk tradition in Mississippi architecture. Updating the vernacular in this project represented a pioneering effort based on sustainability to restore commercial uses within the flood-prone coastal zone where downtown Waveland, MS, lost every business and structure in Hurricane Katrina.

The Waveland Business Incubator was conceived in the Mississippi Renewal Forum as a catalyst for rebuilding the historic Main Street, with the challenge of placing commercial uses 6' 0" above the street. Porches and ramps make gradual level changes to reduce visual and physical barriers, and the traditional urban marketplace typology promotes multiple civic functions. The steel frame, color, and contemporary detailing sites this building form unequivocally in the present, but the presence of the past is evident in accommodating the rigors of the climate, its relationship to the street, and its deeply southern inspiration. Circulation is placed outside in response to tradition, but also to capture breezes and creates an active front porch to the street. Circulation was also placed outside the building envelope to eliminate the need to heat and cool circulation areas, and encourage people to spend time outside.

The initial concept for raised commercial space from the Mississippi Renewal Forum illustrated open retail at the grade level, with enclosed commercial space above to service the restaurants, kiosks, and markets located on the first level below. The completed design refined the initial program, but raised commercial functions out of the flood hazard zone for greater durability in the next storm and meet regulatory requirements. The structure now serves as the home to Studio Waveland, an artists' studio and gallery. It has transformed the downtown area, and the modern art reinforces the architecture in a perfect synergy.

This building contributes to a walkable, connected community, with ties to many neighborhood services, including a library, civic center, city hall, fire house, municipal fishing pier, churches, offices, and restaurants. Waveland had over 250 homes within half a mile walking distance before the storm, therefore this structure is oriented to the historic main street to promote a continuous urban environment to help replace some of what was lost. Large windows provide a connection between occupants and the street.

1.2
Ramp and canopy view
Credit: Allison Anderson

1.3
Stair detail at front entrance
Credit: Allison Anderson

1.4
Signage detail
Credit: Allison Anderson

1.5
Exterior view of café
Credit: Allison Anderson

1.6
Steel plate portal detail
Credit: Allison Anderson

1.7
East side of café
Credit: Allison Anderson

1.8
Interior view of front entrance
Credit: Allison Anderson

1.9
Interior view of café
Credit: Eugenia Uhl

1.10
Night view of front entrance
Credit: Allison Anderson

The transition to a higher elevation is made in small increments to make the steps easier to navigate, and the stairs themselves become seating for the theatre of the street.

The program includes 6,400 SF of tenant areas; a 1,500 SF shared resource center with reception, workroom, conference, and restrooms; and a café and full-service kitchen totaling 2,300 SF. These are grouped into three discrete structures, each with 360° exposure, to fill occupied spaces with views and daylight, reducing the need for artificial light and connecting occupants to the outdoors. The Waveland Business Incubator provides every regularly occupied space with views and light, including the café. Corners dematerialize to allow views around and through the spaces, encouraging conviviality and fostering connections between the structures.

The building was designed with durable materials that form the building's skin with steel framing, rigid insulation and a rainscreen of concrete board. A double roof system shades the building envelopes from heat gain and protects circulation spaces from weather. Principles of sustainability were incorporated to make the building last longer, use less electricity and water, and provide a healthy environment inside and out. Orientation and an insulated wall assembly contribute to a 30% improvement in energy performance from baseline while reclaimed concrete from damaged home slabs forms the base of the structure and contributes to the use of 45% recycled materials in this structure, including structural steel, metal studs, and metal roofing.

A thermally broken building envelope is made with 3″ thick rigid board insulation placed to the outside of the framing to enclose the metal studs. The roof on top of each pod uses the same rigid insulation to make a consistent barrier. In multi-tenant spaces, choosing zoned, high-efficiency mini-split systems also contributes to energy savings. The rainscreen includes a layer of waterproofing, painted black with UV-resistant coating, and concrete-board slats. Colors are drawn from the coastal context: blue, orange, and green from the vacation cottages and fishing camps nearby.

The compact building footprint preserves open space for storm water recharge and storage, incorporating vegetation to filter runoff. This is especially critical close to the Mississippi Sound and open water. The enclosed areas have organically shaped floor plates to shape exterior spaces in engaging and informal ways, and to funnel gulf breezes through the dogtrot. They also form a geometric contrast with the rectilinear plinth and canopy, breaking to frame special views of the water.

Passive solar strategies are driven by the double roof shells. The upper roof canopy provides shade, rain protection, and high reflectance of heat energy. The stack effect of the heated steel roof draws warm air up and through the porches, cooling people enjoying the outdoors. The curvilinear shape of the individual structures below creates a funnel, encouraging more air movement.

In southern towns a century ago, the dogtrot was the coolest place in the house. From rural cabins to upscale cottages, this vernacular way of building is used in this civic project to enliven the street. This space can be used for many things – concerts, parade-viewing, farmer's markets, and café seating. The porch is raised above the street in small steps to facilitate movement, and make the transition seem less like a barrier. This acts like an old-fashioned shoofly, which was rumored to keep the bugs away.

This structure uses 45% recycled materials, including aluminum for the storefront, structural steel columns and beams (about 85% recycled content from junked cars and other sources), and concrete (from slabs recovered after Katrina). The brightly-painted concrete board siding includes sawdust from wood shops and sawmills. The composite decking material incorporates recycled plastic bags and bottles. These humble materials combine to form durable surfaces that leave a lighter impact on the environment.

Daylighting reduces the need for artificial light during the daytime, when this building has the most intense use. This lowers the building's energy use, and reduces eyestrain from working under fluorescent lights. The generous windows also allow the relief of looking outside, focusing on the faraway, and enjoying a moment of distraction before getting back to work.

Buildings used to be built from materials available nearby, and Mississippi is rich in resources: timber from the forests, sand from the river bottoms to make concrete, clay to make bricks. This project uses 46% local materials: concrete, steel, and plywood, harvested or manufactured from sources within a 500-mile radius.

Critical components are selected to withstand extreme climate events, including higher wind pressures and potential storm surge. Steel framing for the upper roof is calibrated to resist uplift forces. The concrete base is hardened to prevent scouring from wave action. These climate adaptations offer durable service against new challenges.

Architects sometimes learn the sorrow of losing their work. Hurricane Katrina replaced three centuries of history in this town with a bleak dystopia stretching along the coastline for 250 miles. The physical context for new buildings offered unlimited possibilities. The Waveland Business Incubator is shaped by acknowledging the future rather than the limitations of the past; this future holds bigger storms and rising sea levels. Hurricane Katrina comprehensively bore witness to our failure to recognize the increasing threats of climate change. The great architecture of the South developed in response to hot, humid climates, but this history was washed away. We must respond to new climate challenges with enthusiasm and innovation.

Allison Anderson FAIA, LEED-AP
John Anderson AIA, LEED-AP

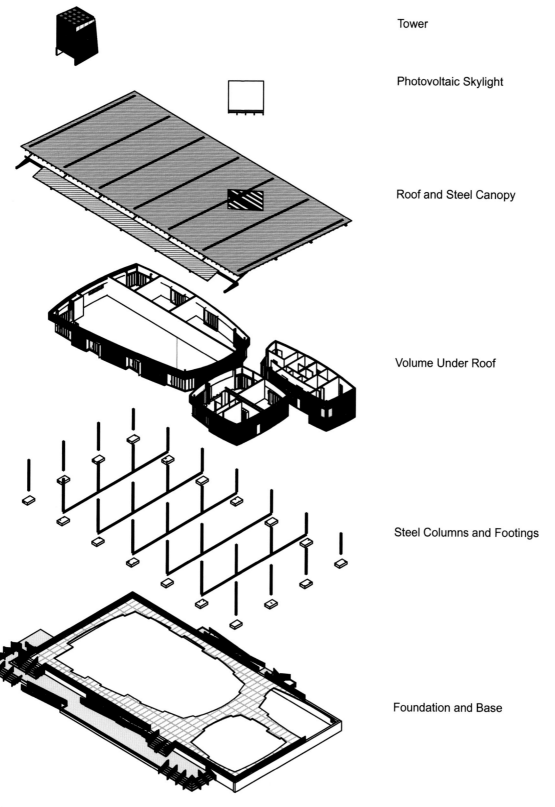

Tower

Photovoltaic Skylight

Roof and Steel Canopy

Volume Under Roof

Steel Columns and Footings

Foundation and Base

1.11
Breakdown of major building components
(Not to scale.)

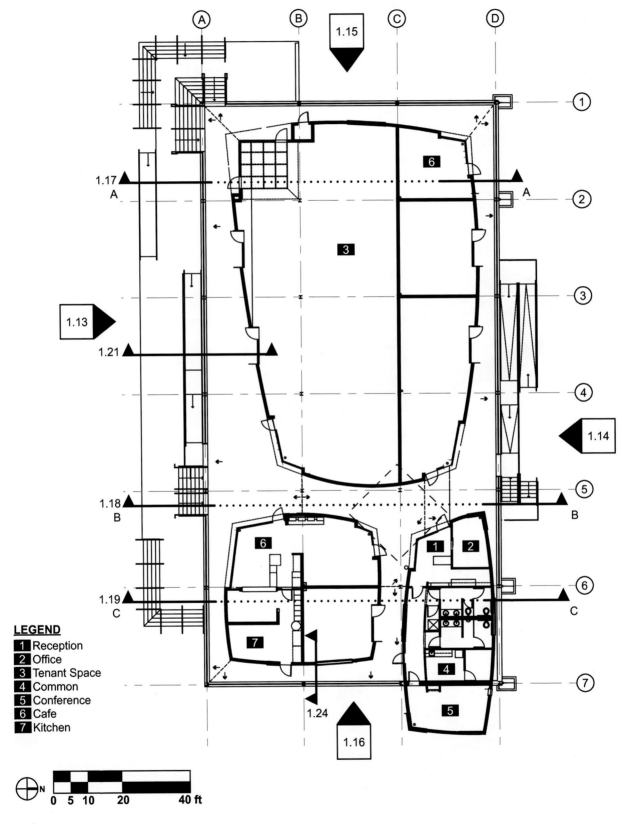

LEGEND
1 Reception
2 Office
3 Tenant Space
4 Common
5 Conference
6 Cafe
7 Kitchen

N   0 5 10   20   40 ft

1.12
Floor plan

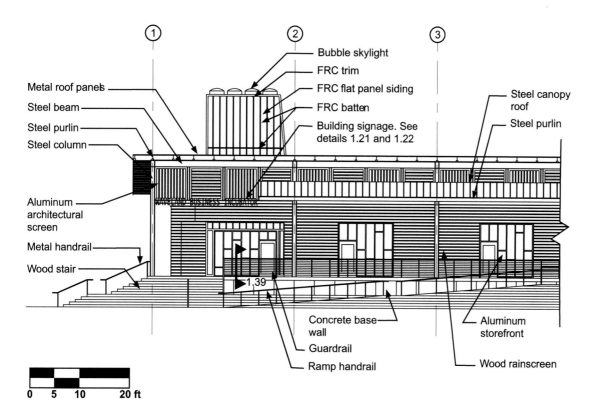

Bubble skylight

FRC trim

FRC flat panel siding

FRC batten

Building signage. See details 1.21 and 1.22

Metal roof panels

Steel beam

Steel purlin

Steel column

Steel canopy roof

Steel purlin

Aluminum architectural screen

Metal handrail

Wood stair

WAVELAND BUSINESS INCUBATOR

1.39

Concrete base wall

Guardrail

Ramp handrail

Aluminum storefront

Wood rainscreen

0 5 10 20 ft

1.13a
South elevation

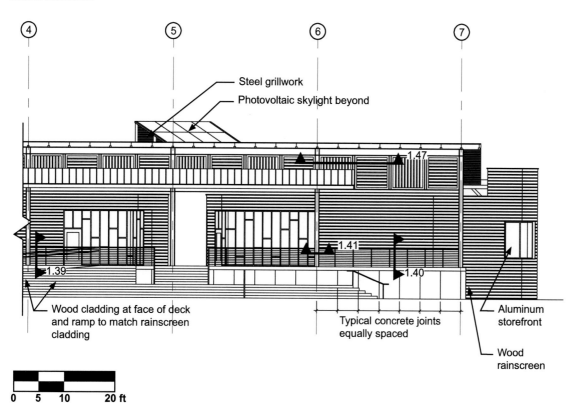

Steel grillwork

Photovoltaic skylight beyond

1.47

1.39

1.41

1.40

Wood cladding at face of deck and ramp to match rainscreen cladding

Typical concrete joints equally spaced

Aluminum storefront

Wood rainscreen

0 5 10 20 ft

1.13b
South elevation

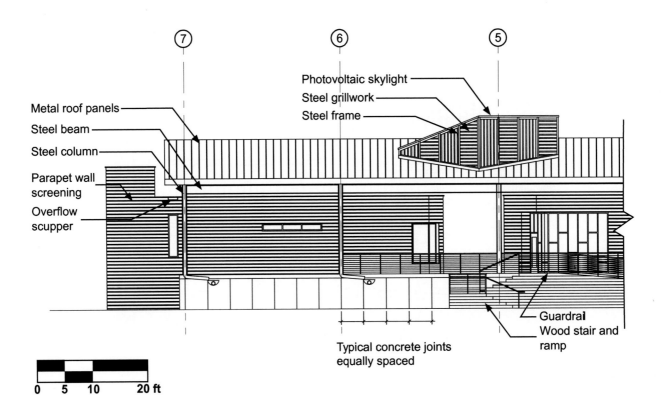

Photovoltaic skylight
Steel grillwork
Steel frame

Metal roof panels
Steel beam
Steel column
Parapet wall screening
Overflow scupper

Guardrail
Wood stair and ramp

Typical concrete joints equally spaced

0 5 10 20 ft

1.14a
North elevation

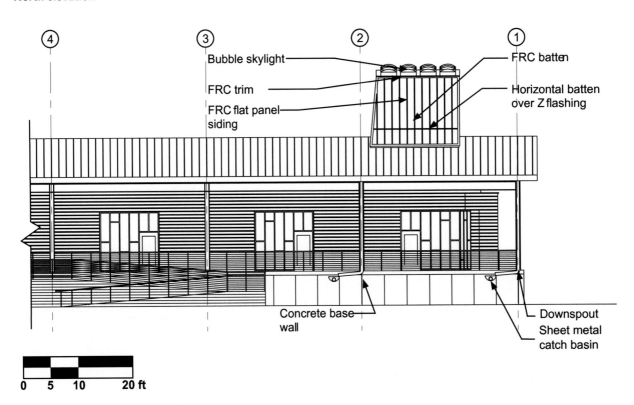

Bubble skylight
FRC trim
FRC flat panel siding

FRC batten
Horizontal batten over Z flashing

Concrete base wall

Downspout
Sheet metal catch basin

0 5 10 20 ft

1.14b
North elevation

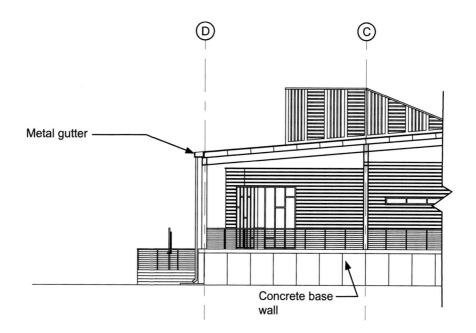

Metal gutter

Concrete base wall

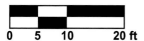

0   5   10   20 ft

1.15a
West elevation

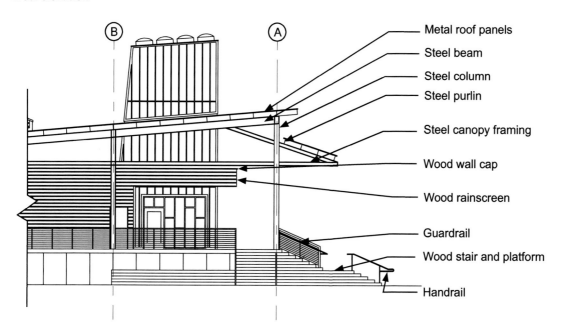

Metal roof panels

Steel beam

Steel column

Steel purlin

Steel canopy framing

Wood wall cap

Wood rainscreen

Guardrail

Wood stair and platform

Handrail

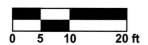

0   5   10   20 ft

1.15b
West elevation

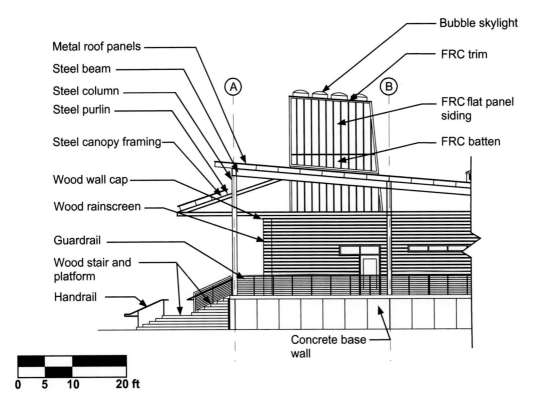

Metal roof panels

Steel beam

Steel column

Steel purlin

Steel canopy framing

Wood wall cap

Wood rainscreen

Guardrail

Wood stair and platform

Handrail

Ⓐ

Ⓑ

Bubble skylight

FRC trim

FRC flat panel siding

FRC batten

Concrete base wall

0   5   10   20 ft

1.16a
East elevation

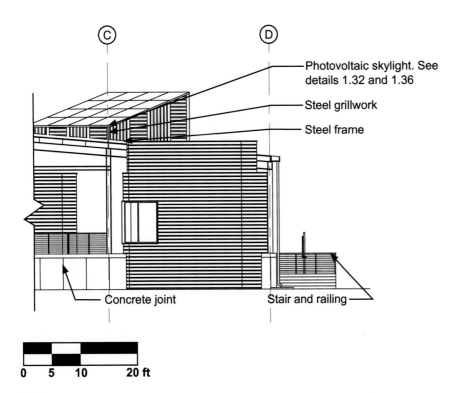

Ⓒ

Ⓓ

Photovoltaic skylight. See details 1.32 and 1.36

Steel grillwork

Steel frame

Concrete joint

Stair and railing

0   5   10   20 ft

1.16b
East elevation

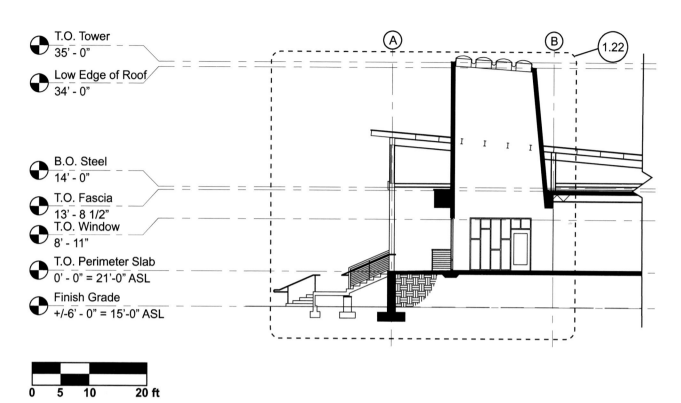

T.O. Tower
35' - 0"

Low Edge of Roof
34' - 0"

B.O. Steel
14' - 0"

T.O. Fascia
13' - 8 1/2"

T.O. Window
8' - 11"

T.O. Perimeter Slab
0' - 0" = 21'-0" ASL

Finish Grade
+/-6' - 0" = 15'-0" ASL

Ⓐ Ⓑ 1.22

0 5 10   20 ft

1.17a
North/south building section A-A

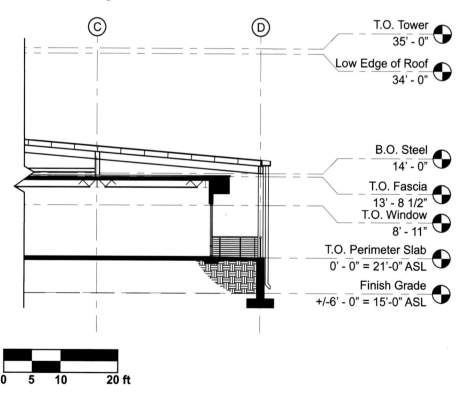

Ⓒ Ⓓ

T.O. Tower
35' - 0"

Low Edge of Roof
34' - 0"

B.O. Steel
14' - 0"

T.O. Fascia
13' - 8 1/2"

T.O. Window
8' - 11"

T.O. Perimeter Slab
0' - 0" = 21'-0" ASL

Finish Grade
+/-6' - 0" = 15'-0" ASL

0 5 10   20 ft

1.17b
North/south building section A-A

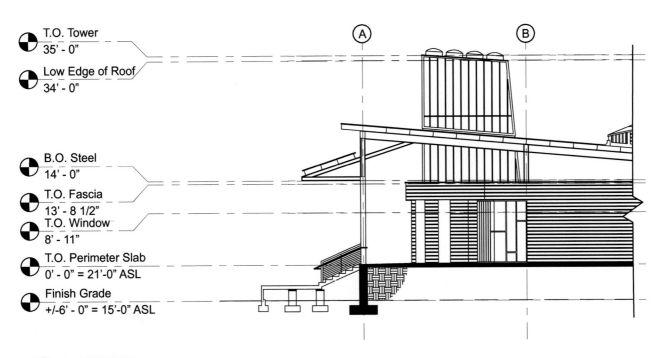

T.O. Tower
35' - 0"

Low Edge of Roof
34' - 0"

B.O. Steel
14' - 0"

T.O. Fascia
13' - 8 1/2"

T.O. Window
8' - 11"

T.O. Perimeter Slab
0' - 0" = 21'-0" ASL

Finish Grade
+/-6' - 0" = 15'-0" ASL

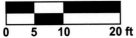

0   5   10   20 ft

1.18a
North/south building section B-B

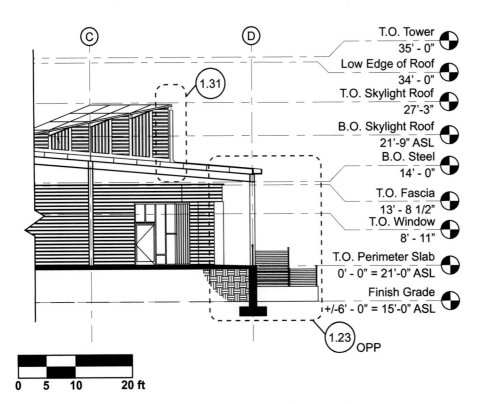

T.O. Tower
35' - 0"

Low Edge of Roof
34' - 0"

T.O. Skylight Roof
27'-3"

B.O. Skylight Roof
21'-9" ASL

B.O. Steel
14' - 0"

T.O. Fascia
13' - 8 1/2"

T.O. Window
8' - 11"

T.O. Perimeter Slab
0' - 0" = 21'-0" ASL

Finish Grade
+/-6' - 0" = 15'-0" ASL

1.23 OPP

0   5   10   20 ft

1.18b
North/south building section B-B

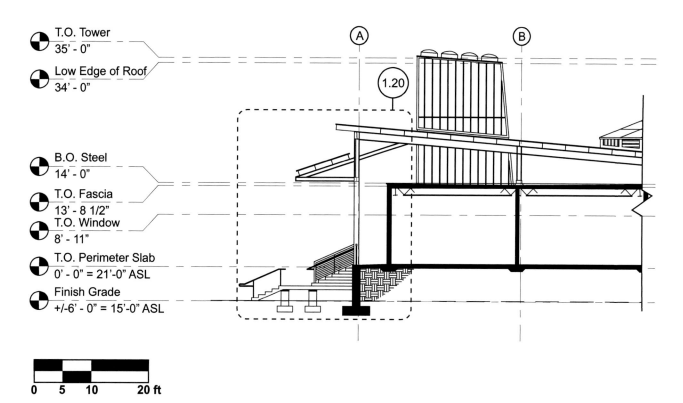

T.O. Tower
35' - 0"

Low Edge of Roof
34' - 0"

B.O. Steel
14' - 0"

T.O. Fascia
13' - 8 1/2"

T.O. Window
8' - 11"

T.O. Perimeter Slab
0' - 0" = 21'-0" ASL

Finish Grade
+/-6' - 0" = 15'-0" ASL

(A) (B) (1.20)

0   5   10   20 ft

1.19a
North/south building section C-C

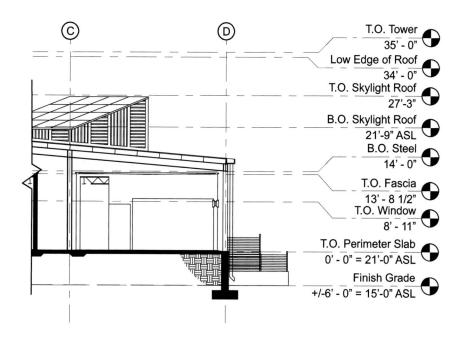

(C) (D)

T.O. Tower
35' - 0"

Low Edge of Roof
34' - 0"

T.O. Skylight Roof
27'-3"

B.O. Skylight Roof
21'-9" ASL

B.O. Steel
14' - 0"

T.O. Fascia
13' - 8 1/2"

T.O. Window
8' - 11"

T.O. Perimeter Slab
0' - 0" = 21'-0" ASL

Finish Grade
+/-6' - 0" = 15'-0" ASL

0   5   10   20 ft

1.19b
North/south building section C-C

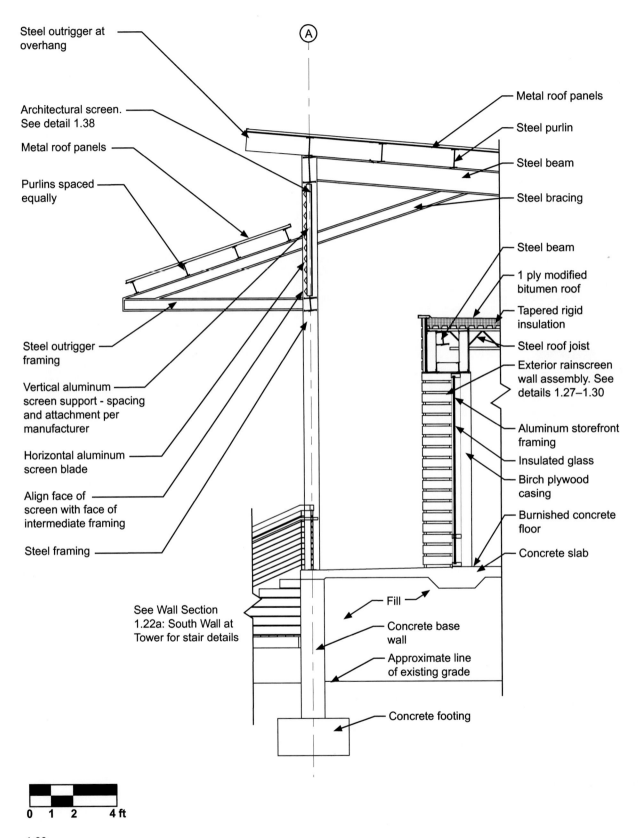

Steel outrigger at overhang

Architectural screen. See detail 1.38

Metal roof panels

Purlins spaced equally

Ⓐ

Metal roof panels

Steel purlin

Steel beam

Steel bracing

Steel beam

1 ply modified bitumen roof

Tapered rigid insulation

Steel roof joist

Exterior rainscreen wall assembly. See details 1.27–1.30

Aluminum storefront framing

Insulated glass

Birch plywood casing

Burnished concrete floor

Concrete slab

Steel outrigger framing

Vertical aluminum screen support - spacing and attachment per manufacturer

Horizontal aluminum screen blade

Align face of screen with face of intermediate framing

Steel framing

See Wall Section 1.22a: South Wall at Tower for stair details

Fill

Concrete base wall

Approximate line of existing grade

Concrete footing

0 1 2   4 ft

1.20
Wall section: south wall at cafe

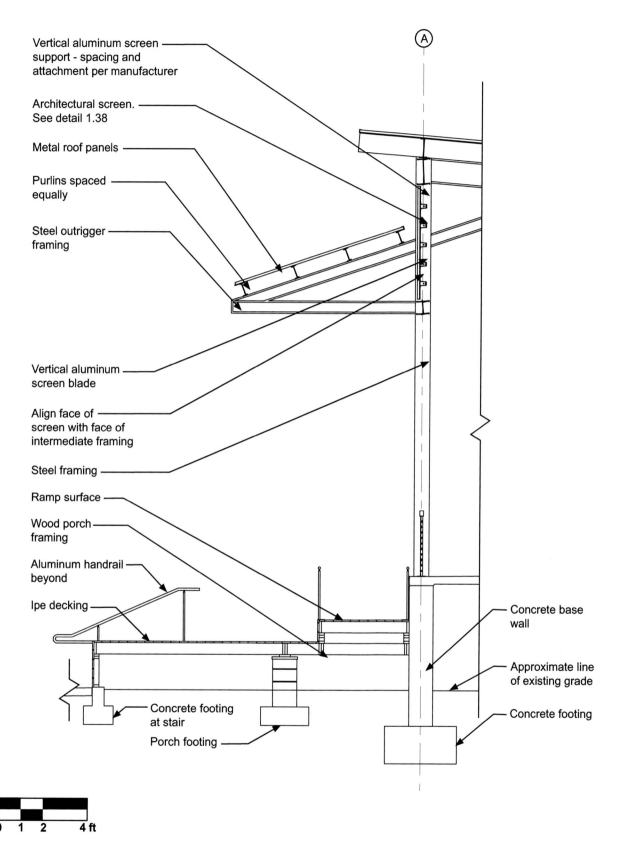

Vertical aluminum screen support - spacing and attachment per manufacturer

Architectural screen. See detail 1.38

Metal roof panels

Purlins spaced equally

Steel outrigger framing

Vertical aluminum screen blade

Align face of screen with face of intermediate framing

Steel framing

Ramp surface

Wood porch framing

Aluminum handrail beyond

Ipe decking

Ⓐ

Concrete base wall

Approximate line of existing grade

Concrete footing

Concrete footing at stair

Porch footing

0 1 2   4 ft

1.21a
Wall section: south wall at tenant Space – A

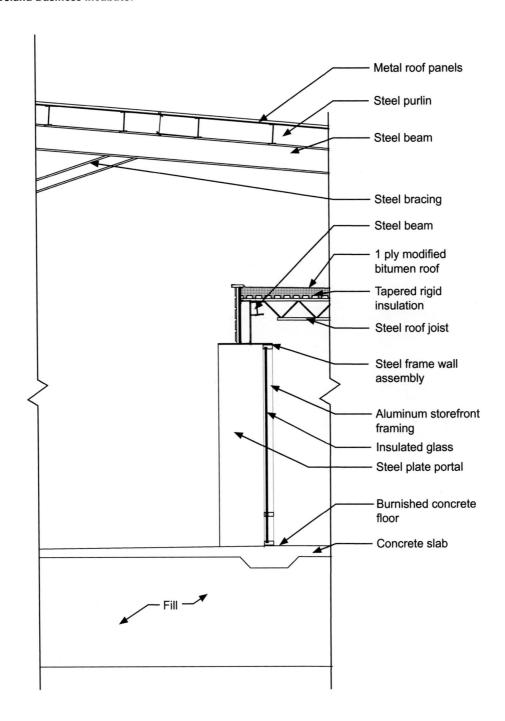

Metal roof panels

Steel purlin

Steel beam

Steel bracing

Steel beam

1 ply modified bitumen roof

Tapered rigid insulation

Steel roof joist

Steel frame wall assembly

Aluminum storefront framing

Insulated glass

Steel plate portal

Burnished concrete floor

Concrete slab

Fill

0 1 2 4 ft

1.21b
Wall section: south wall at retail – B

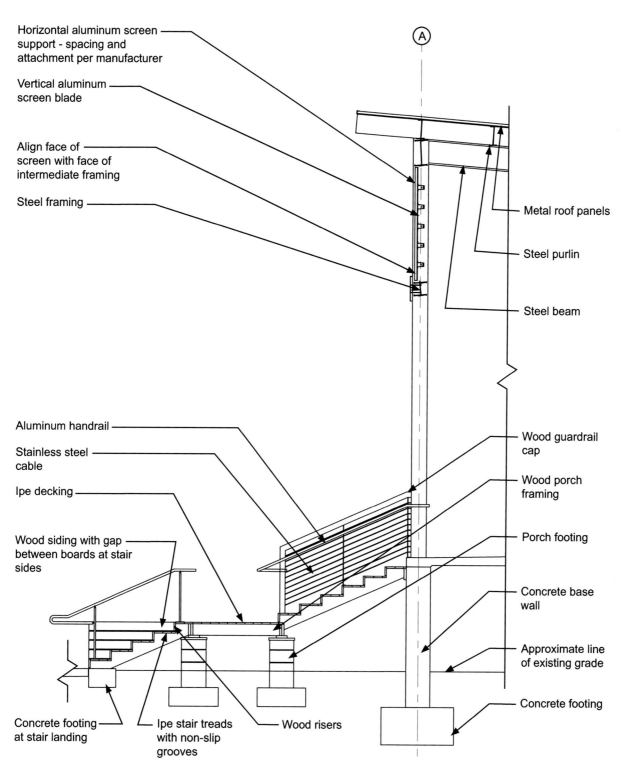

Horizontal aluminum screen support - spacing and attachment per manufacturer

Vertical aluminum screen blade

Align face of screen with face of intermediate framing

Steel framing

Metal roof panels

Steel purlin

Steel beam

Aluminum handrail

Stainless steel cable

Ipe decking

Wood siding with gap between boards at stair sides

Wood guardrail cap

Wood porch framing

Porch footing

Concrete base wall

Approximate line of existing grade

Concrete footing

Concrete footing at stair landing

Ipe stair treads with non-slip grooves

Wood risers

0 1 2 4 ft

1.22a
Wall section: south wall at tower – A

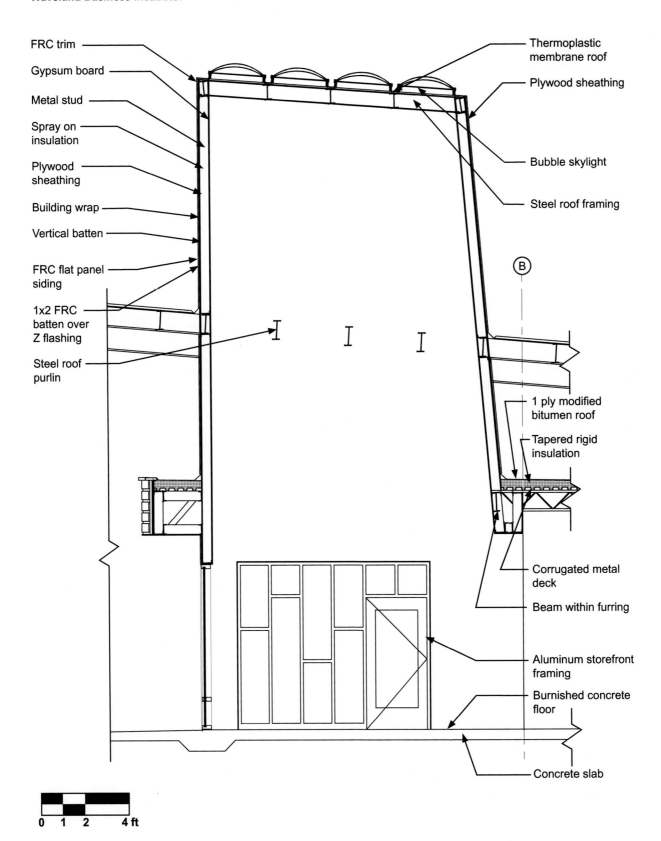

FRC trim

Gypsum board

Metal stud

Spray on insulation

Plywood sheathing

Building wrap

Vertical batten

FRC flat panel siding

1x2 FRC batten over Z flashing

Steel roof purlin

Thermoplastic membrane roof

Plywood sheathing

Bubble skylight

Steel roof framing

B

1 ply modified bitumen roof

Tapered rigid insulation

Corrugated metal deck

Beam within furring

Aluminum storefront framing

Burnished concrete floor

Concrete slab

0   1   2   4 ft

1.22b
Wall section: south wall at tower – B

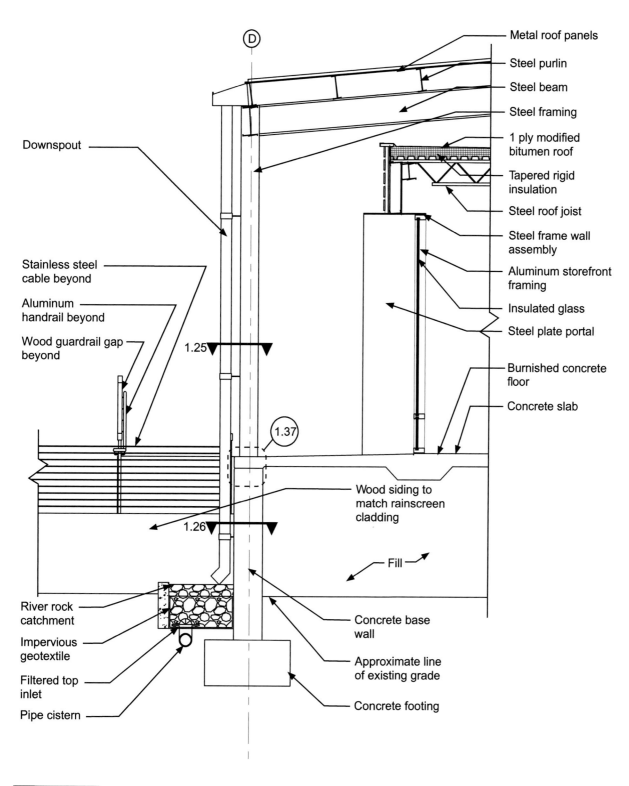

Ⓓ

Metal roof panels

Steel purlin

Steel beam

Steel framing

1 ply modified bitumen roof

Tapered rigid insulation

Steel roof joist

Steel frame wall assembly

Aluminum storefront framing

Insulated glass

Steel plate portal

Burnished concrete floor

Concrete slab

Downspout

Stainless steel cable beyond

Aluminum handrail beyond

Wood guardrail gap beyond

1.25

1.37

1.26

Wood siding to match rainscreen cladding

Fill

River rock catchment

Impervious geotextile

Filtered top inlet

Pipe cistern

Concrete base wall

Approximate line of existing grade

Concrete footing

0 1 2   4 ft

1.23
Wall section: north wall

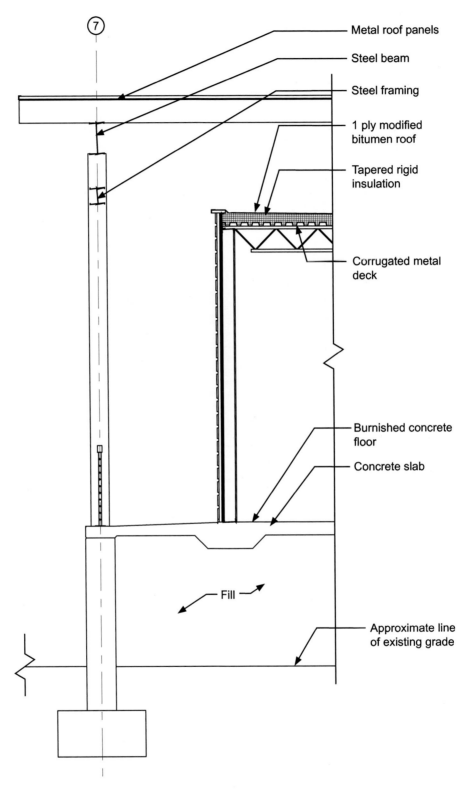

⑦

Metal roof panels

Steel beam

Steel framing

1 ply modified
bitumen roof

Tapered rigid
insulation

Corrugated metal
deck

Burnished concrete
floor

Concrete slab

Fill

Approximate line
of existing grade

0 1 2   4 ft

1.24
Wall section: east wall

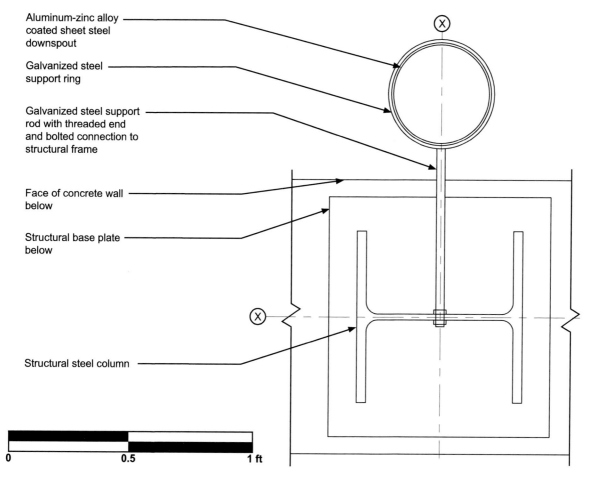

Aluminum-zinc alloy coated sheet steel downspout

Galvanized steel support ring

Galvanized steel support rod with threaded end and bolted connection to structural frame

Face of concrete wall below

Structural base plate below

Structural steel column

0   0.5   1 ft

1.25
Section detail: downspout at steel column

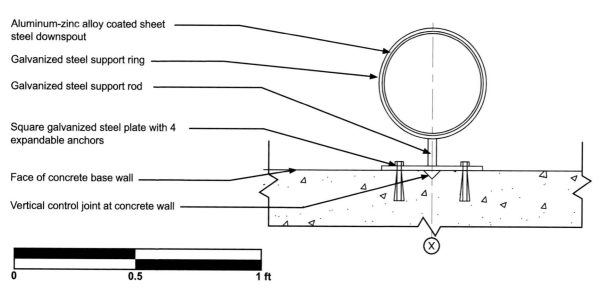

Aluminum-zinc alloy coated sheet steel downspout

Galvanized steel support ring

Galvanized steel support rod

Square galvanized steel plate with 4 expandable anchors

Face of concrete base wall

Vertical control joint at concrete wall

0   0.5   1 ft

1.26
Section detail: downspout at concrete wall

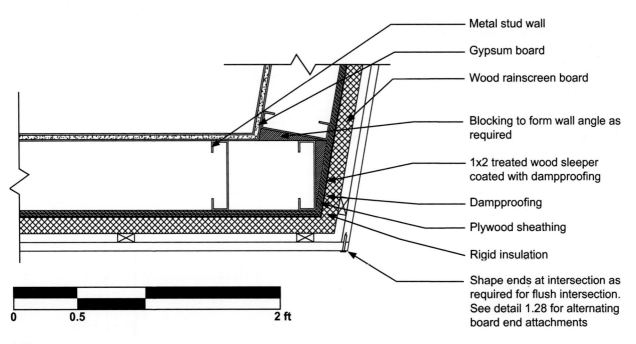

Metal stud wall

Gypsum board

Wood rainscreen board

Blocking to form wall angle as required

1x2 treated wood sleeper coated with dampproofing

Dampproofing

Plywood sheathing

Rigid insulation

Shape ends at intersection as required for flush intersection. See detail 1.28 for alternating board end attachments

0   0.5   2 ft

1.27
Plan detail: rainscreen wall

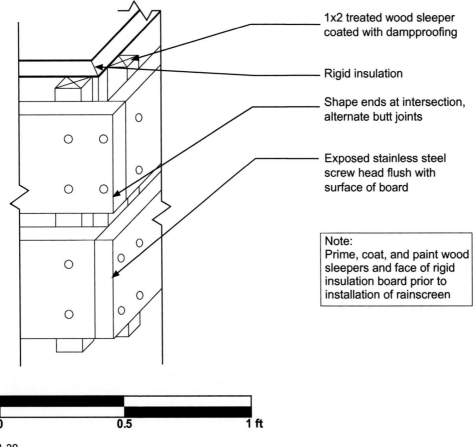

1x2 treated wood sleeper coated with dampproofing

Rigid insulation

Shape ends at intersection, alternate butt joints

Exposed stainless steel screw head flush with surface of board

Note:
Prime, coat, and paint wood sleepers and face of rigid insulation board prior to installation of rainscreen

0   0.5   1 ft

1.28
Detail: corner at rainscreen wall

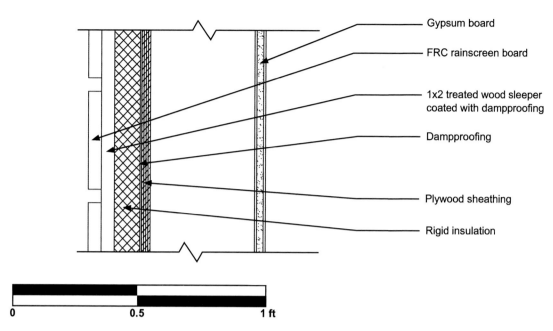

Gypsum board

FRC rainscreen board

1x2 treated wood sleeper
coated with dampproofing

Dampproofing

Plywood sheathing

Rigid insulation

0   0.5   1 ft

1.29
Section detail: rainscreen wall

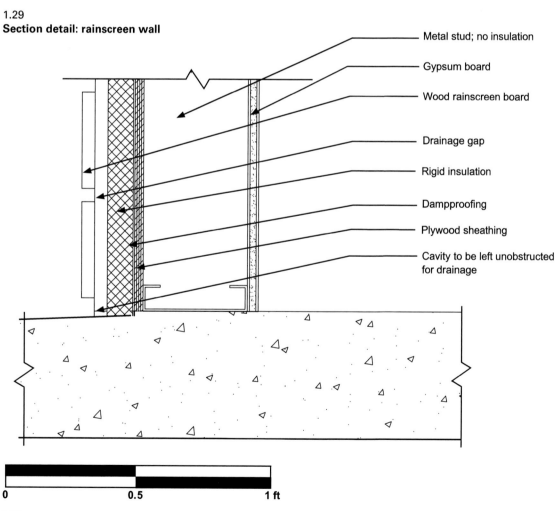

Metal stud; no insulation

Gypsum board

Wood rainscreen board

Drainage gap

Rigid insulation

Dampproofing

Plywood sheathing

Cavity to be left unobstructed
for drainage

0   0.5   1 ft

1.30
Section detail: wall base at rainscreen wall

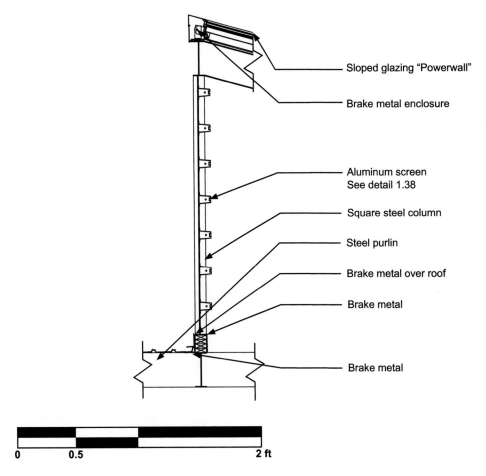

Sloped glazing "Powerwall"

Brake metal enclosure

Aluminum screen
See detail 1.38

Square steel column

Steel purlin

Brake metal over roof

Brake metal

Brake metal

0   0.5   2 ft

1.31
Section detail: photovoltaic skylight

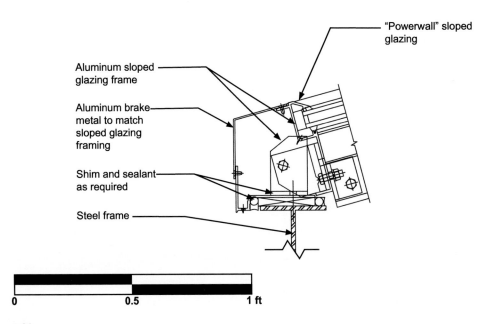

"Powerwall" sloped glazing

Aluminum sloped glazing frame

Aluminum brake metal to match sloped glazing framing

Shim and sealant as required

Steel frame

0   0.5   1 ft

1.32
Section detail: low side at photovoltaic skylight

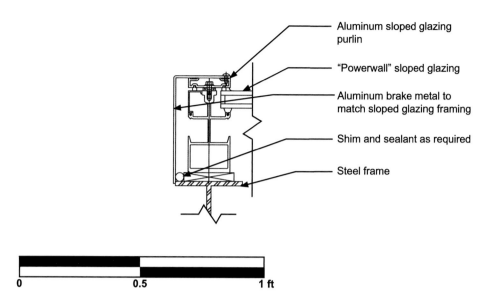

Aluminum sloped glazing purlin

"Powerwall" sloped glazing

Aluminum brake metal to match sloped glazing framing

Shim and sealant as required

Steel frame

0   0.5   1 ft

1.33
Section detail: rake end at photovoltaic skylight

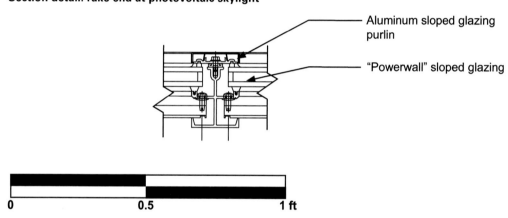

Aluminum sloped glazing purlin

"Powerwall" sloped glazing

0   0.5   1 ft

1.34
Section detail: purlin at interior photovoltaic skylight

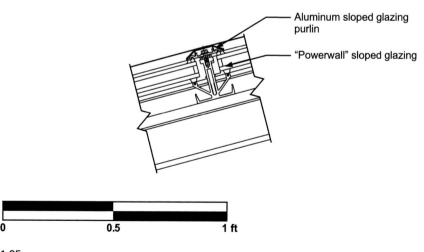

Aluminum sloped glazing purlin

"Powerwall" sloped glazing

0   0.5   1 ft

1.35
Section detail: interior purlin at slope

"Powerwall" sloped glazing

Aluminum sloped glazing frame

Aluminum brake metal to match sloped glazing framing

Shim and sealant as required

Steel frame

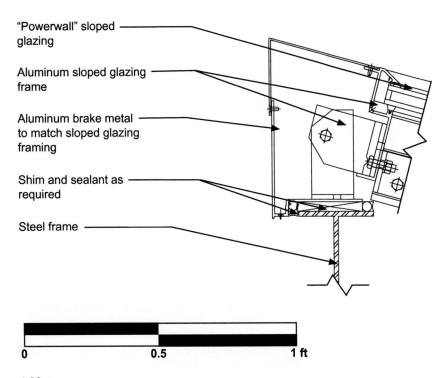

| 0 | 0.5 | 1 ft |

1.36
Section detail: high side at photovoltaic skylight

Structural column and base beyond

Concrete slab on fill

Control joint - Width to match decorative score joints

T.O. Perimeter Slab
0' - 0"

Continuous keyway

Chamfered edge, TYP

Line of vertical control joint beyond

Concrete base wall

Fill

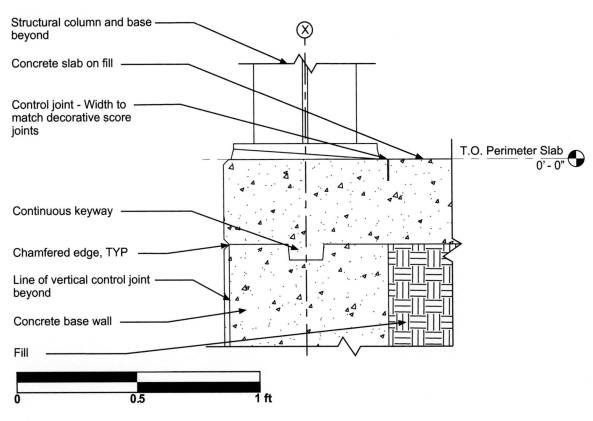

| 0 | 0.5 | 1 ft |

1.37
Section detail: perimeter wall

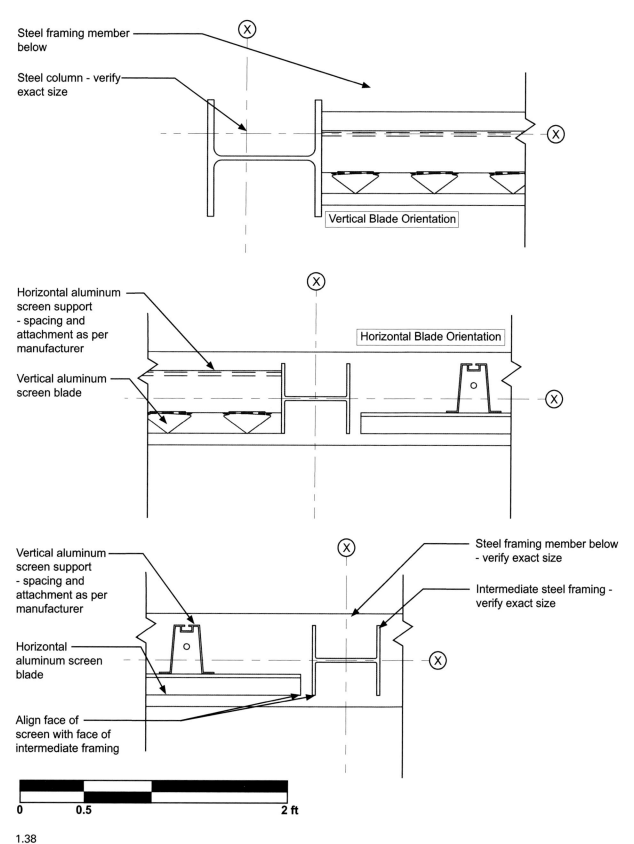

Steel framing member below

Steel column - verify exact size

Vertical Blade Orientation

Horizontal aluminum screen support - spacing and attachment as per manufacturer

Horizontal Blade Orientation

Vertical aluminum screen blade

Vertical aluminum screen support - spacing and attachment as per manufacturer

Steel framing member below - verify exact size

Intermediate steel framing - verify exact size

Horizontal aluminum screen blade

Align face of screen with face of intermediate framing

0   0.5   2 ft

1.38
Plan detail: grillwork

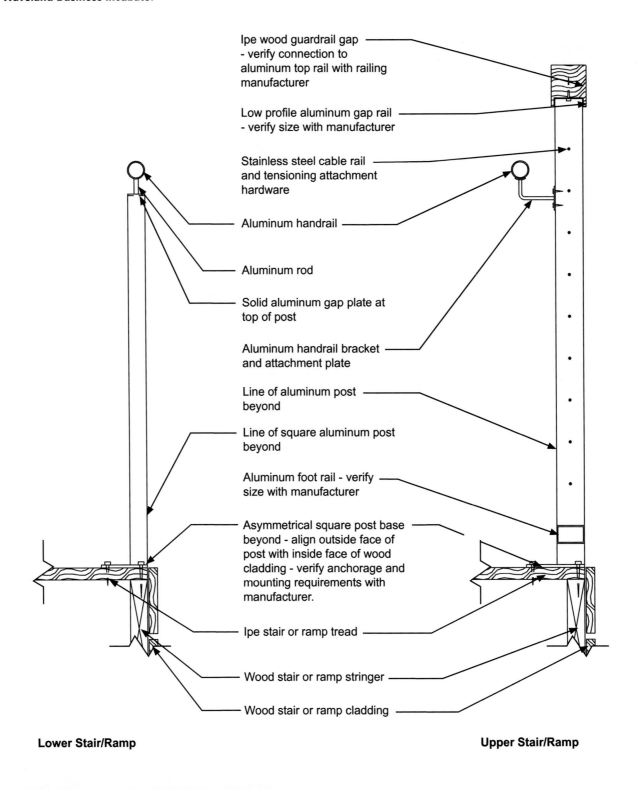

Ipe wood guardrail gap - verify connection to aluminum top rail with railing manufacturer

Low profile aluminum gap rail - verify size with manufacturer

Stainless steel cable rail and tensioning attachment hardware

Aluminum handrail

Aluminum rod

Solid aluminum gap plate at top of post

Aluminum handrail bracket and attachment plate

Line of aluminum post beyond

Line of square aluminum post beyond

Aluminum foot rail - verify size with manufacturer

Asymmetrical square post base beyond - align outside face of post with inside face of wood cladding - verify anchorage and mounting requirements with manufacturer.

Ipe stair or ramp tread

Wood stair or ramp stringer

Wood stair or ramp cladding

Lower Stair/Ramp

Upper Stair/Ramp

0   0.5   2 ft

1.39
Section detail: guardrails

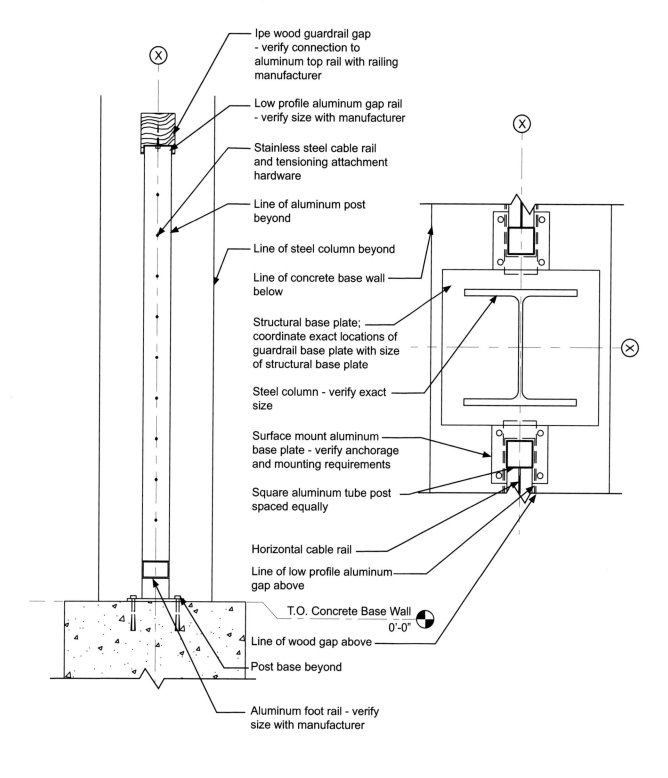

Ipe wood guardrail gap
- verify connection to
aluminum top rail with railing
manufacturer

Low profile aluminum gap rail
- verify size with manufacturer

Stainless steel cable rail
and tensioning attachment
hardware

Line of aluminum post
beyond

Line of steel column beyond

Line of concrete base wall
below

Structural base plate;
coordinate exact locations of
guardrail base plate with size
of structural base plate

Steel column - verify exact
size

Surface mount aluminum
base plate - verify anchorage
and mounting requirements

Square aluminum tube post
spaced equally

Horizontal cable rail

Line of low profile aluminum
gap above

T.O. Concrete Base Wall
0'-0"

Line of wood gap above

Post base beyond

Aluminum foot rail - verify
size with manufacturer

0	0.5		2 ft

1.40
Section detail: guardrail – upper deck

0	0.5		2 ft

1.41
Plan detail: railing/column

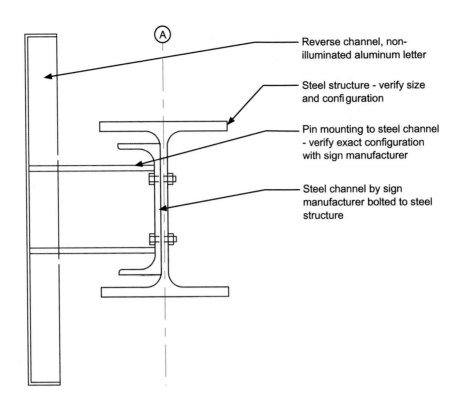

Reverse channel, non-illuminated aluminum letter

Steel structure - verify size and configuration

Pin mounting to steel channel - verify exact configuration with sign manufacturer

Steel channel by sign manufacturer bolted to steel structure

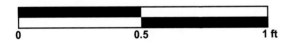

| 0 | 0.5 | 1 ft |

1.42
Section detail: building sign

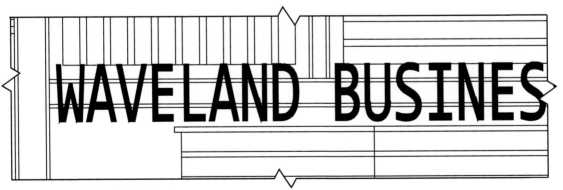

Font: Agency, .75 width factor
Space letters as required to fit as shown
Verify copy with architect and owner prior to fabrication

| 0 | 0.5 | 2 ft |

1.43
Elevation detail: building sign

2.1
Front entrance

Credit: Archimania and Hank Mardukas Photography

2: Hatiloo Theatre

Memphis, TN, Archimania

Architect's Design Intent and Reasoning Behind Material and Tectonic Choices

The first African-American repertory theatre in Memphis planned to relocate from their start-up space to an existing parking lot in an urban arts and entertainment district undergoing a resurgence – fulfilling a much-needed presence for an under-represented segment of the Memphis Arts Community within its most prominent district. The site is directly south of historic Overton Square and is surrounded by multiple performing arts venues. Hattiloo's new building is designed to promote their art by establishing a distinct presence on the corner of a primary artery of the district. The new building had a modest budget for a contemporary theatre, when compared to precedents and case studies. Given the requirement of maximum community impact on a tight budget, we formulated early strategies rooted in durability, combined with presenting clarity of form and establishing a public presence, with two core principles: (1) define components that were permanent and components that could be added over time based on continued fundraising and profit (this would allow the theatre to add lighting, etc., but not sacrifice building quality), and (2) keep it simple. The result is a building represented in two architecturally and programmatically distinct volumes – the performance volume, which features two black box theatres and support spaces, and an administration volume that extends its form into the public way.

The administrative component, conceived as a lighter and more porous volume, sits on the south side of the site and houses the entry lobby, ticketing, and administrative spaces, presenting a welcoming pedestrian scale along the southern edge of the secondary street, Monroe Avenue. This one-story volume is framed with light gauge metal framing and metal truss roof joists. The monolithic mass is clad in A606 weathering steel standing seam panels, used for the material's ability to form a rusty, self-protective finish through oxidization over time. This richly textured material contrasts its precisely crafted panels to add to the unique character of the entertainment district. The weathering steel also adds a distinct permanence to the building and reflects the gritty, grassroots nature of the small but rapidly growing theater program. The vertical surfaces are broken down into three horizontal bands of standing seam panels that provide both aesthetic and functional value. The graduating scale of the siding helps reduce the overall scale of the building and provides an opportunity for

2.2
Lobby view
Credit: Archimania and Hank Mardukas Photography

2.3
View of southwest corner
Credit: Archimania and Hank Mardukas Photography

2.4
View towards back entrance
Credit: Archimania and Hank Mardukas Photography

2.5
Back entrance
Credit: Archimania and Hank Mardukas Photography

2.6
Front entrance canopy
Credit: Archimania and Hank Mardukas Photography

2.7
View of weathering steel siding
Credit: Archimania and Hank Mardukas Photography

pattern where the metal seams shift horizontally between bands. These bands also provide datums for fenestration and other façade elements. Functionally, the metal trim pieces that separate bands serve as window head and sill trim, and valleys of the panels are detailed to visually grow into collection boxes that screen roof scuppers. The overall volume is conceptually and visually lifted at the street to shelter a public lobby and plaza. The interior and exterior are separated by a floor-to-ceiling storefront system of black anodized aluminum and insulated glazing. The top band of metal panels continues overhead to unify the public lobby with a 16′ cantilever. The soffit of this band is an exterior finish plaster system painted white to visually extend the white ceiling of the lobby interior. This volume meets the ground with a white plinth made out of concrete masonry units with a complementary plaster finish surrounded by a landscaping bed containing Mississippi River Reeds. This bed both softens the transition between building and ground as well as provides a trough to catch the rust drip off the weathering steel siding.

Programmatically dictated to be windowless boxes, the two theatres and dressing rooms occupy the volume at the northern edge of the site, abutting a neighboring parking lot. This form, notably taller and heavier than the adjacent administrative block, is structured with load-bearing concrete masonry unit walls and a thickened concrete roof on steel decking. These structural materials provide acoustic dampening due to their inherent mass, preventing sound from penetrating the building's skin. The reflective burnished block delivers contrast to the adjacent matte weathering steel and the impression of refinement and permanence to the hefty performance volume. The irregular massing is reflective of the required internal volume, yet they are both clad as a unified whole. The upper portion is wrapped in cementitious panels applied as a lapped rainscreen system. The fiber cement panels are applied to metal framing attached to the concrete masonry volume as a scalar element to add a macro-texture and provide detail to the taller mass. Dark accent panels are scattered within the field of white panels as vertical counterpoints to the horizontality of the rainscreen bands. The rainscreen loosely resembles the traditional tiled mansard roof prevalent to the surrounding context and provides a screen for metal conductor heads and downspouts. The HVAC units are on the lower section of the building, rather than typically placed above the taller spaces, in order to eliminate or minimize vibration and noise over the black box performance spaces.

The interior finishes and detailing provide a continuity between interior and exterior spaces, reinforces the two distinct volumes, and affords durability while creating an atmosphere of anticipation for the forthcoming show. From the street, the floor-to-ceiling glass offers transparency to the community as a welcoming presence, ever-changing in activity and energy. The smooth, white finish plaster system of the soffit is continued inside by a monolithic white gypsum board ceiling. This same ceiling is drastically transformed within the lobby as it transitions into a bold, faceted, red gypsum board ceiling. This ceiling conceptually flips the traditional "red carpet" as it extends to the rear parking lot entrance. In this circulation spine, lighting shifts from recessed cans to recessed linear fixtures where the lobby and corridor converge. The same exterior concrete masonry abuts the highly formal red ceiling, completing the shape of the performance volume. A light cove in the ceiling runs between these elements, further reinforcing the programmatic and visual distinction between the two forms where they meet. The floor is covered in a carpet that complements the red ceiling and warm concrete masonry. Beyond these public spaces, the theatres and back-of-house spaces are designed for efficiency and performance, making way for the art to take center stage.

Todd Walker, FAIA
Principal

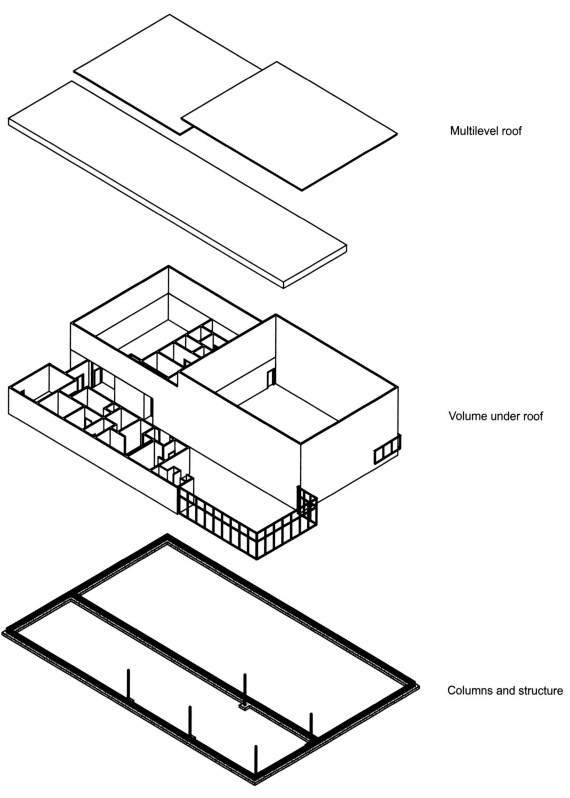

Multilevel roof

Volume under roof

Columns and structure

2.8
Major building components
(Not to scale.)

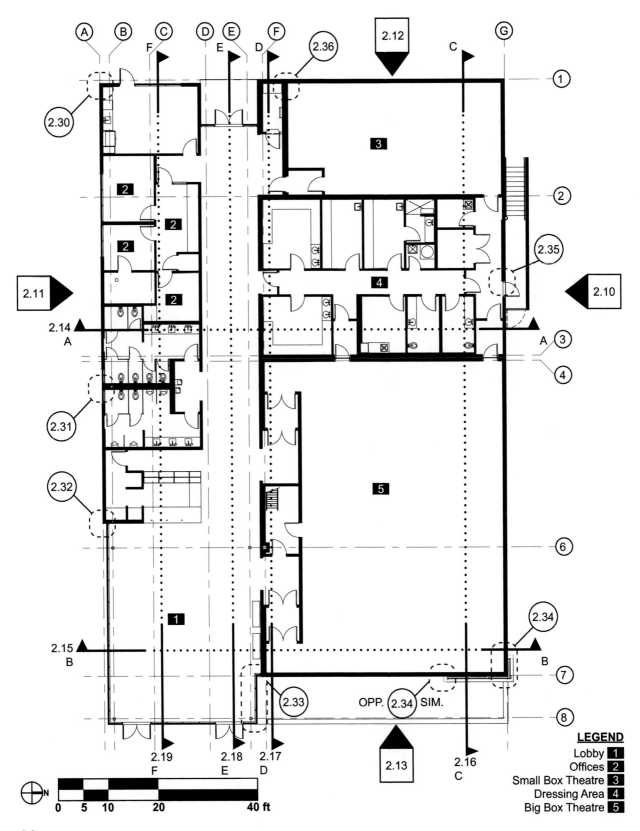

2.9
Floor plan

LEGEND
Lobby **1**
Offices **2**
Small Box Theatre **3**
Dressing Area **4**
Big Box Theatre **5**

0 5 10 20 40 ft

N

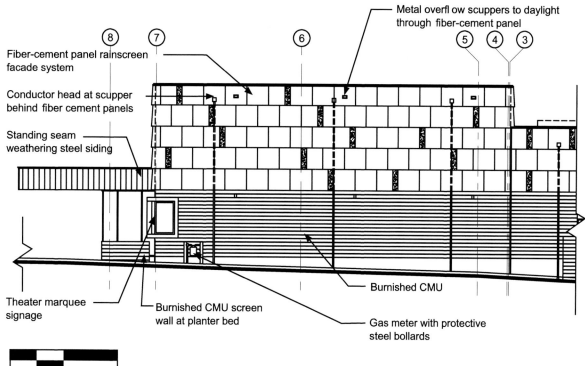

Metal overflow scuppers to daylight through fiber-cement panel

Fiber-cement panel rainscreen facade system

Conductor head at scupper behind fiber cement panels

Standing seam weathering steel siding

Burnished CMU

Theater marquee signage

Burnished CMU screen wall at planter bed

Gas meter with protective steel bollards

0   5   10   20 ft

2.10a
North elevation

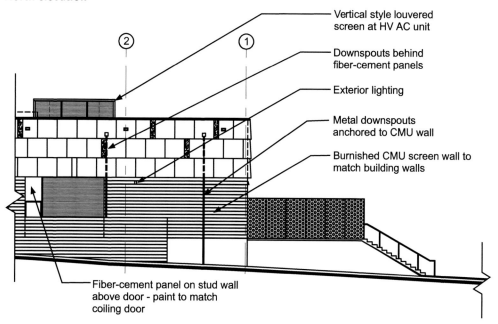

Vertical style louvered screen at HV AC unit

Downspouts behind fiber-cement panels

Exterior lighting

Metal downspouts anchored to CMU wall

Burnished CMU screen wall to match building walls

Fiber-cement panel on stud wall above door - paint to match coiling door

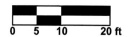

0   5   10   20 ft

2.10b
North elevation

Hatiloo Theatre

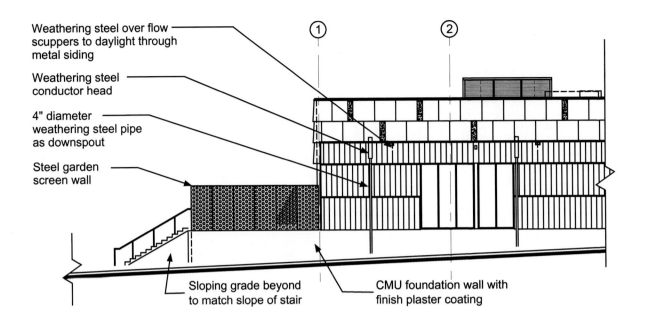

Weathering steel over flow scuppers to daylight through metal siding

Weathering steel conductor head

4" diameter weathering steel pipe as downspout

Steel garden screen wall

① ②

Sloping grade beyond to match slope of stair

CMU foundation wall with finish plaster coating

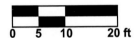

0 5 10 20 ft

2.11a
South elevation

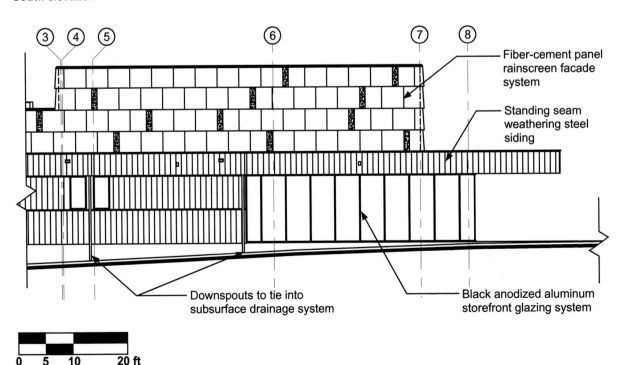

③ ④ ⑤ ⑥ ⑦ ⑧

Fiber-cement panel rainscreen facade system

Standing seam weathering steel siding

Downspouts to tie into subsurface drainage system

Black anodized aluminum storefront glazing system

0 5 10 20 ft

2.11b
South elevation

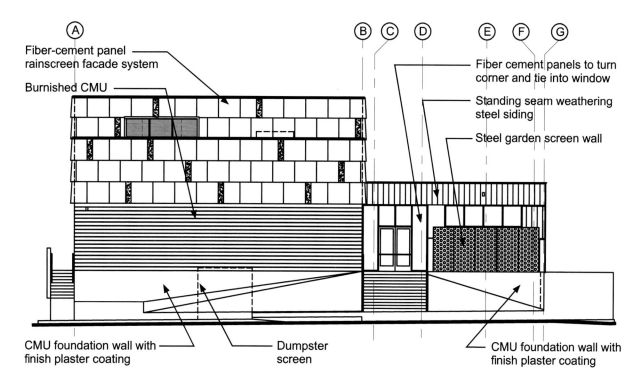

Fiber-cement panel rainscreen facade system

Burnished CMU

Fiber cement panels to turn corner and tie into window

Standing seam weathering steel siding

Steel garden screen wall

CMU foundation wall with finish plaster coating

Dumpster screen

CMU foundation wall with finish plaster coating

0   5   10   20 ft

2.12
West elevation

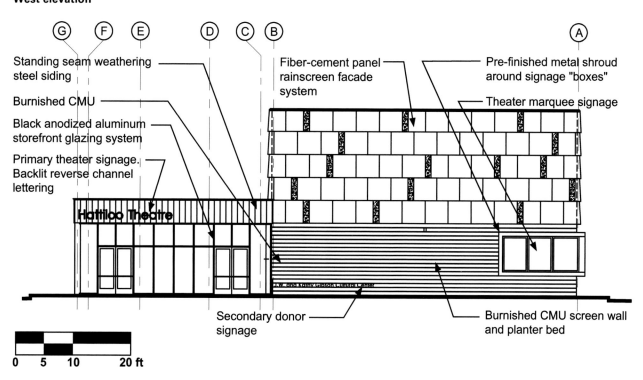

Standing seam weathering steel siding

Burnished CMU

Black anodized aluminum storefront glazing system

Primary theater signage. Backlit reverse channel lettering

Fiber-cement panel rainscreen facade system

Pre-finished metal shroud around signage "boxes"

Theater marquee signage

Hatiloo Theatre

J.W. and Kathy Gibson Cultural Center

Secondary donor signage

Burnished CMU screen wall and planter bed

0   5   10   20 ft

2.13
East elevation

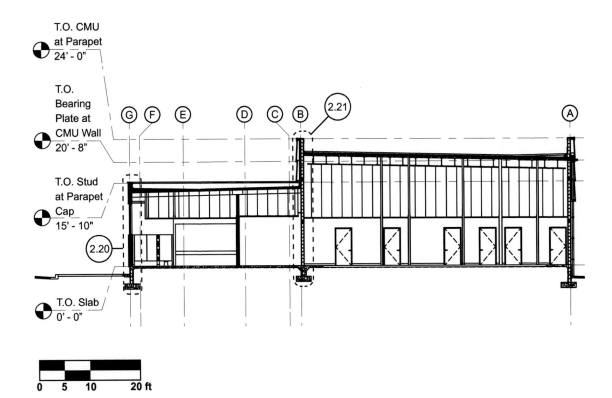

T.O. CMU
at Parapet
24' - 0"

T.O.
Bearing
Plate at
CMU Wall
20' - 8"

T.O. Stud
at Parapet
Cap
15' - 10"

T.O. Slab
0' - 0"

0 5 10   20 ft

2.14
North/south building section A-A

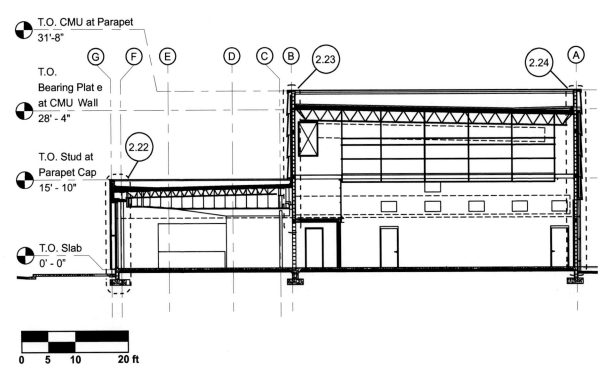

T.O. CMU at Parapet
31'-8"

T.O.
Bearing Plat e
at CMU Wall
28' - 4"

T.O. Stud at
Parapet Cap
15' - 10"

T.O. Slab
0' - 0"

0 5 10   20 ft

2.15
North/south building section B-B

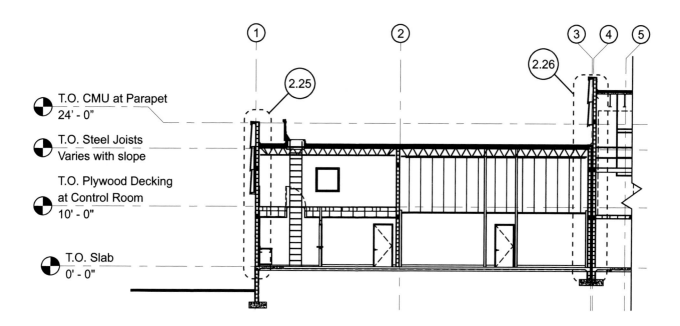

T.O. CMU at Parapet
24' - 0"

T.O. Steel Joists
Varies with slope

T.O. Plywood Decking
at Control Room
10' - 0"

T.O. Slab
0' - 0"

0   5   10   20 ft

2.16a
East/west building section C-C

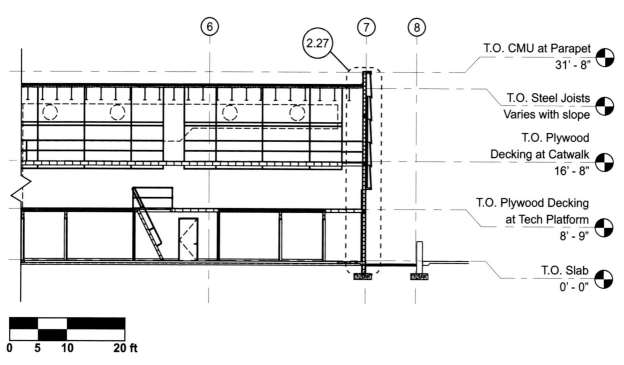

T.O. CMU at Parapet
31' - 8"

T.O. Steel Joists
Varies with slope

T.O. Plywood
Decking at Catwalk
16' - 8"

T.O. Plywood Decking
at Tech Platform
8' - 9"

T.O. Slab
0' - 0"

0   5   10   20 ft

2.16b
East/west building section C-C

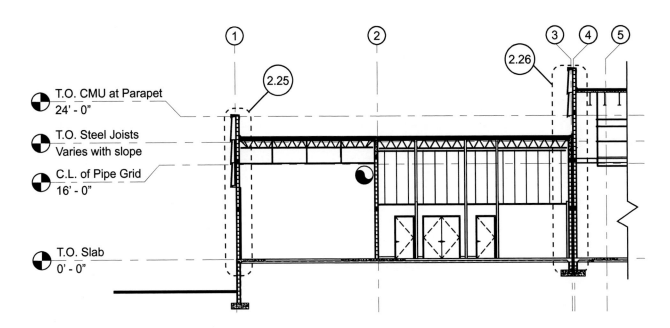

T.O. CMU at Parapet
24' - 0"

T.O. Steel Joists
Varies with slope

C.L. of Pipe Grid
16' - 0"

T.O. Slab
0' - 0"

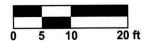

0 5 10   20 ft

2.17a
East/west building section D-D

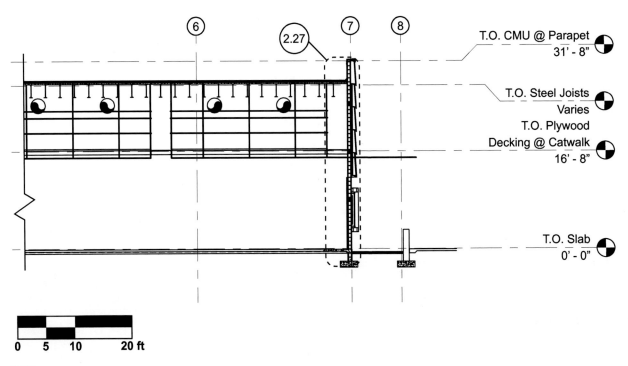

T.O. CMU @ Parapet
31' - 8"

T.O. Steel Joists
Varies

T.O. Plywood
Decking @ Catwalk
16' - 8"

T.O. Slab
0' - 0"

0 5 10   20 ft

2.17b
East/west building section D-D

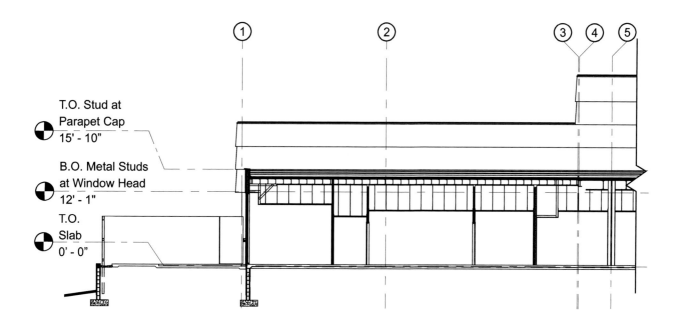

T.O. Stud at
Parapet Cap
15' - 10"

B.O. Metal Studs
at Window Head
12' - 1"

T.O.
Slab
0' - 0"

0   5   10   20 ft

2.18a
East/west building section E-E

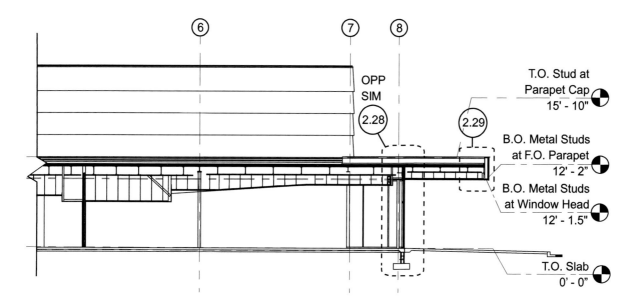

OPP
SIM

2.28

2.29

T.O. Stud at
Parapet Cap
15' - 10"

B.O. Metal Studs
at F.O. Parapet
12' - 2"

B.O. Metal Studs
at Window Head
12' - 1.5"

T.O. Slab
0' - 0"

0   5   10   20 ft

2.18b
East/west building section E-E

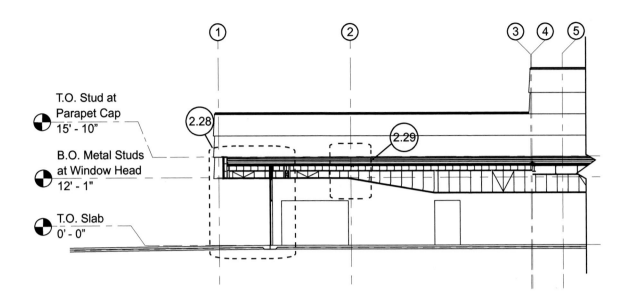

① ② ③ ④ ⑤

2.28

2.29

T.O. Stud at
Parapet Cap
15' - 10"

B.O. Metal Studs
at Window Head
12' - 1"

T.O. Slab
0' - 0"

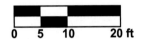

0   5   10   20 ft

2.19a
East/west building section F-F

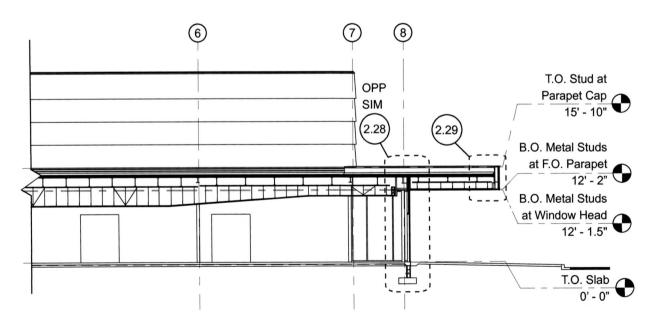

⑥ ⑦ ⑧

OPP
SIM

2.28

2.29

T.O. Stud at
Parapet Cap
15' - 10"

B.O. Metal Studs
at F.O. Parapet
12' - 2"

B.O. Metal Studs
at Window Head
12' - 1.5"

T.O. Slab
0' - 0"

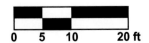

0   5   10   20 ft

2.19b
East/west building section F-F

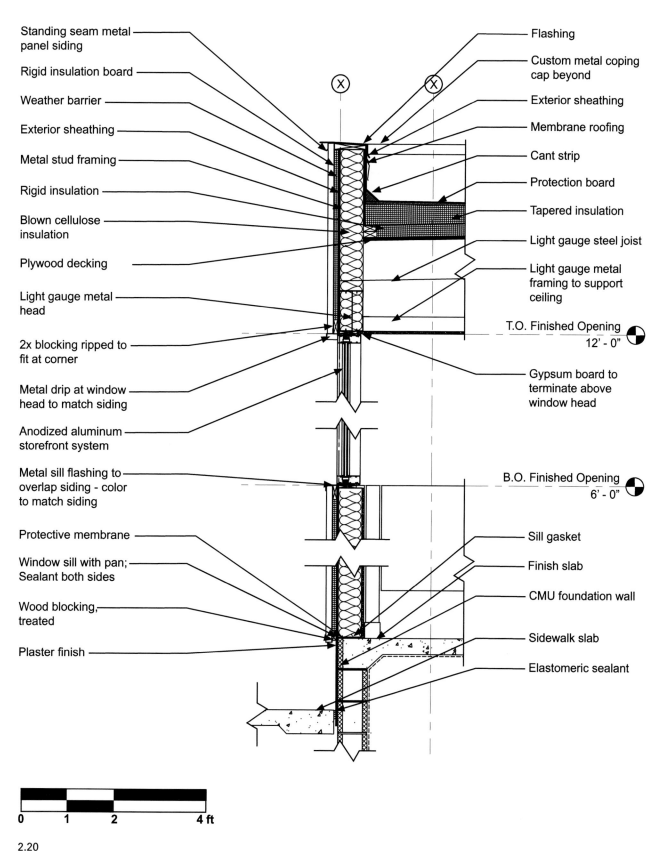

Standing seam metal panel siding

Rigid insulation board

Weather barrier

Exterior sheathing

Metal stud framing

Rigid insulation

Blown cellulose insulation

Plywood decking

Light gauge metal head

2x blocking ripped to fit at corner

Metal drip at window head to match siding

Anodized aluminum storefront system

Metal sill flashing to overlap siding - color to match siding

Protective membrane

Window sill with pan; Sealant both sides

Wood blocking, treated

Plaster finish

Flashing

Custom metal coping cap beyond

Exterior sheathing

Membrane roofing

Cant strip

Protection board

Tapered insulation

Light gauge steel joist

Light gauge metal framing to support ceiling

T.O. Finished Opening
12' - 0"

Gypsum board to terminate above window head

B.O. Finished Opening
6' - 0"

Sill gasket

Finish slab

CMU foundation wall

Sidewalk slab

Elastomeric sealant

0   1   2   4 ft

2.20
Wall section: north/south building section A-A

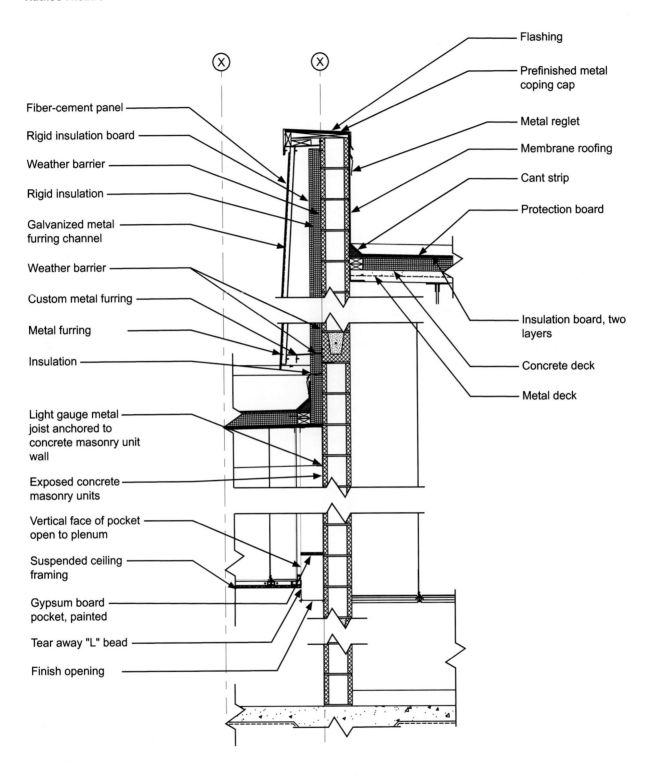

Flashing

Prefinished metal coping cap

Metal reglet

Membrane roofing

Cant strip

Protection board

Insulation board, two layers

Concrete deck

Metal deck

Fiber-cement panel

Rigid insulation board

Weather barrier

Rigid insulation

Galvanized metal furring channel

Weather barrier

Custom metal furring

Metal furring

Insulation

Light gauge metal joist anchored to concrete masonry unit wall

Exposed concrete masonry units

Vertical face of pocket open to plenum

Suspended ceiling framing

Gypsum board pocket, painted

Tear away "L" bead

Finish opening

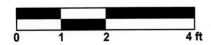

0   1   2   4 ft

2.21
Wall section: north/south building section A-A

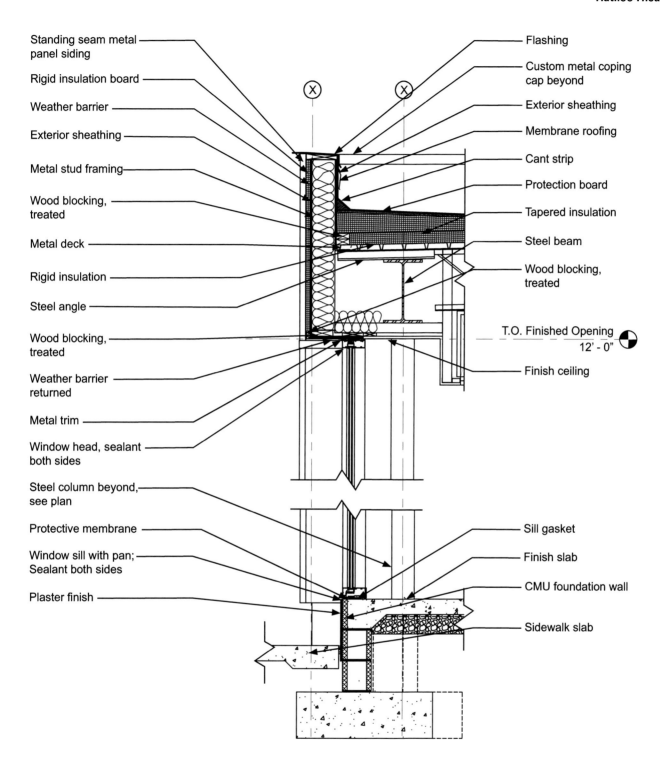

Standing seam metal panel siding

Rigid insulation board

Weather barrier

Exterior sheathing

Metal stud framing

Wood blocking, treated

Metal deck

Rigid insulation

Steel angle

Wood blocking, treated

Weather barrier returned

Metal trim

Window head, sealant both sides

Steel column beyond, see plan

Protective membrane

Window sill with pan; Sealant both sides

Plaster finish

Flashing

Custom metal coping cap beyond

Exterior sheathing

Membrane roofing

Cant strip

Protection board

Tapered insulation

Steel beam

Wood blocking, treated

T.O. Finished Opening
12' - 0"

Finish ceiling

Sill gasket

Finish slab

CMU foundation wall

Sidewalk slab

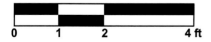

0   1   2   4 ft

2.22
Wall section: north/south building section B-B

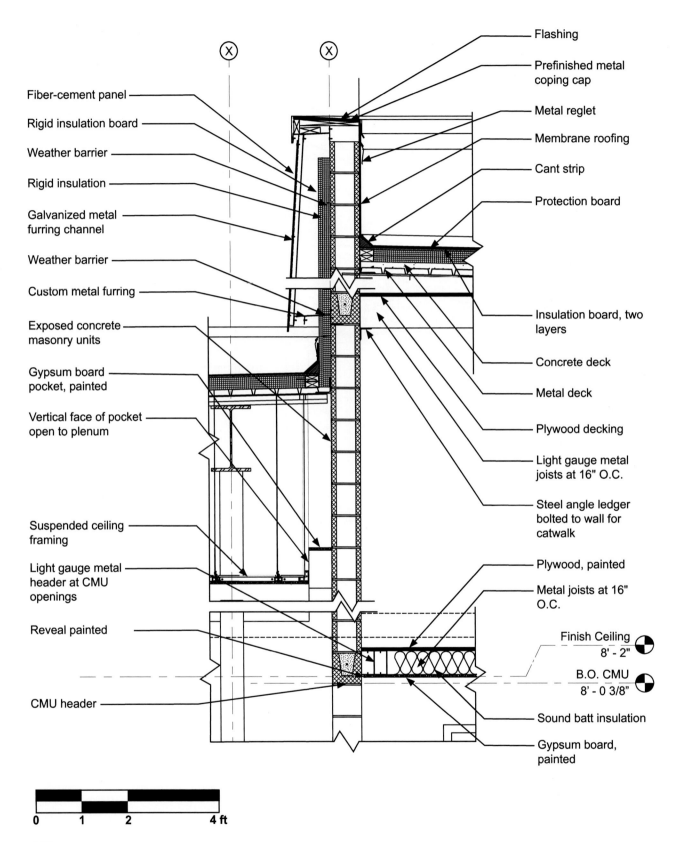

Fiber-cement panel

Rigid insulation board

Weather barrier

Rigid insulation

Galvanized metal furring channel

Weather barrier

Custom metal furring

Exposed concrete masonry units

Gypsum board pocket, painted

Vertical face of pocket open to plenum

Suspended ceiling framing

Light gauge metal header at CMU openings

Reveal painted

CMU header

Flashing

Prefinished metal coping cap

Metal reglet

Membrane roofing

Cant strip

Protection board

Insulation board, two layers

Concrete deck

Metal deck

Plywood decking

Light gauge metal joists at 16" O.C.

Steel angle ledger bolted to wall for catwalk

Plywood, painted

Metal joists at 16" O.C.

Finish Ceiling
8' - 2"

B.O. CMU
8' - 0 3/8"

Sound batt insulation

Gypsum board, painted

0   1   2   4 ft

2.23
Wall section: north/south building section B-B

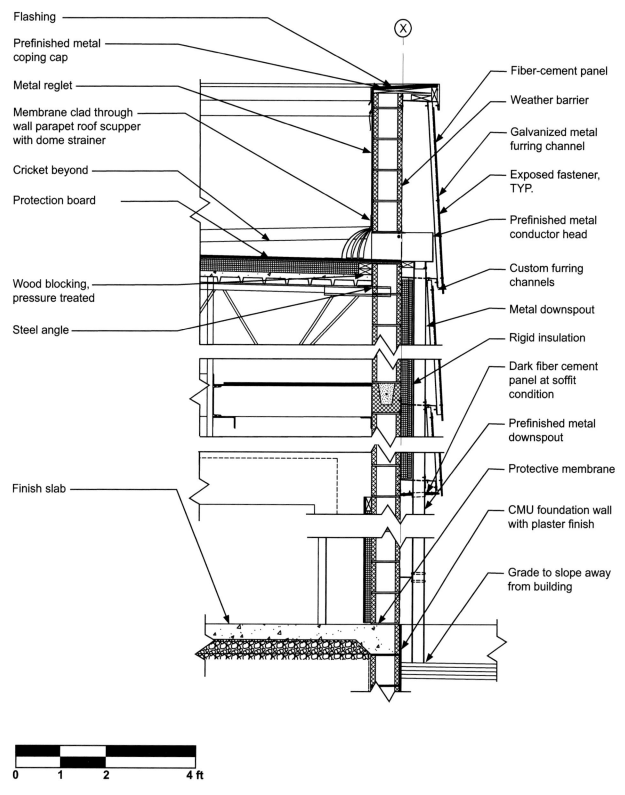

Flashing

Prefinished metal coping cap

Metal reglet

Membrane clad through wall parapet roof scupper with dome strainer

Cricket beyond

Protection board

Wood blocking, pressure treated

Steel angle

Finish slab

Fiber-cement panel

Weather barrier

Galvanized metal furring channel

Exposed fastener, TYP.

Prefinished metal conductor head

Custom furring channels

Metal downspout

Rigid insulation

Dark fiber cement panel at soffit condition

Prefinished metal downspout

Protective membrane

CMU foundation wall with plaster finish

Grade to slope away from building

X

0   1   2   4 ft

2.24
Wall section: north/south building section B-B

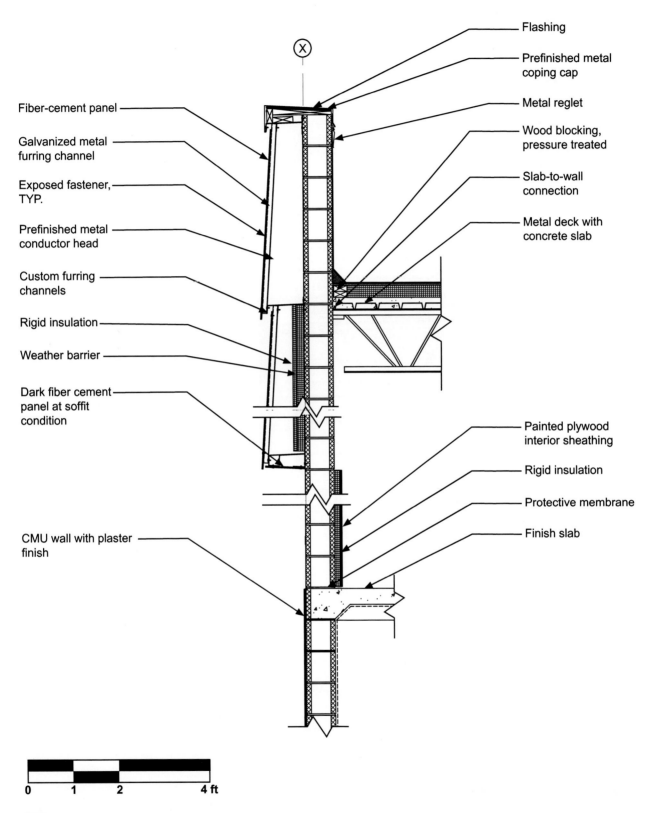

Flashing

Prefinished metal coping cap

Metal reglet

Wood blocking, pressure treated

Slab-to-wall connection

Metal deck with concrete slab

Fiber-cement panel

Galvanized metal furring channel

Exposed fastener, TYP.

Prefinished metal conductor head

Custom furring channels

Rigid insulation

Weather barrier

Dark fiber cement panel at soffit condition

Painted plywood interior sheathing

Rigid insulation

Protective membrane

Finish slab

CMU wall with plaster finish

0 1 2 4 ft

2.25
Wall section: east/west building section C-C and D-D

Flashing

Prefinished metal
coping cap

Single-ply roofing at
face of CMU wall -
overlap vertical leg of
expansion joint

Expansion joint

Sloped cant strip
to accommodate
expansion joint

Slab-to-wall
connection per
structural

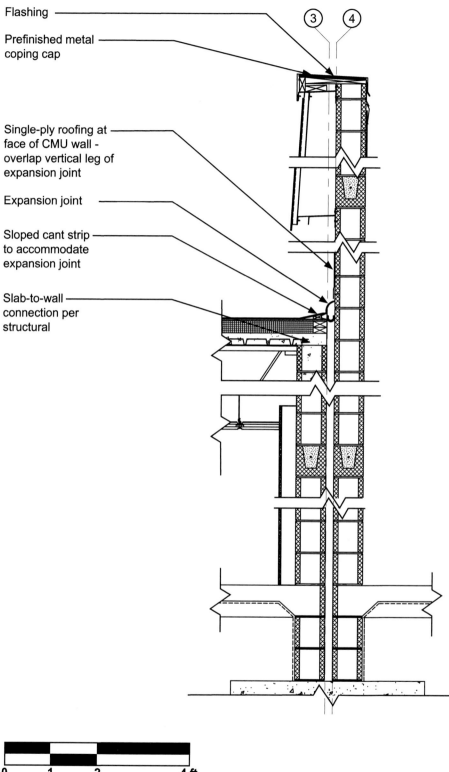

0   1   2   4 ft

2.26
Wall section: east/west building section C-C and D-D

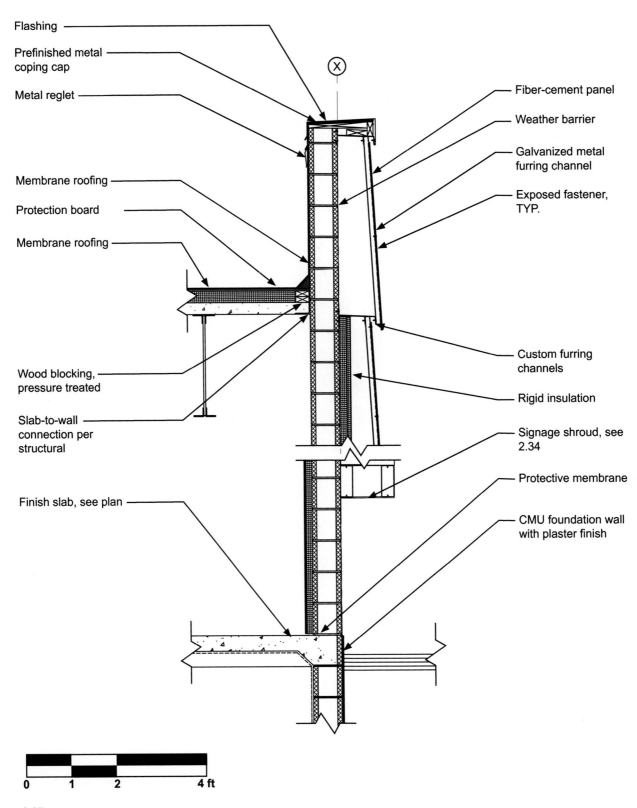

Flashing

Prefinished metal coping cap

Metal reglet

Membrane roofing

Protection board

Membrane roofing

Wood blocking, pressure treated

Slab-to-wall connection per structural

Finish slab, see plan

Fiber-cement panel

Weather barrier

Galvanized metal furring channel

Exposed fastener, TYP.

Custom furring channels

Rigid insulation

Signage shroud, see 2.34

Protective membrane

CMU foundation wall with plaster finish

X

0 1 2 4 ft

2.27
Wall section: east/west building section C-C and D-D

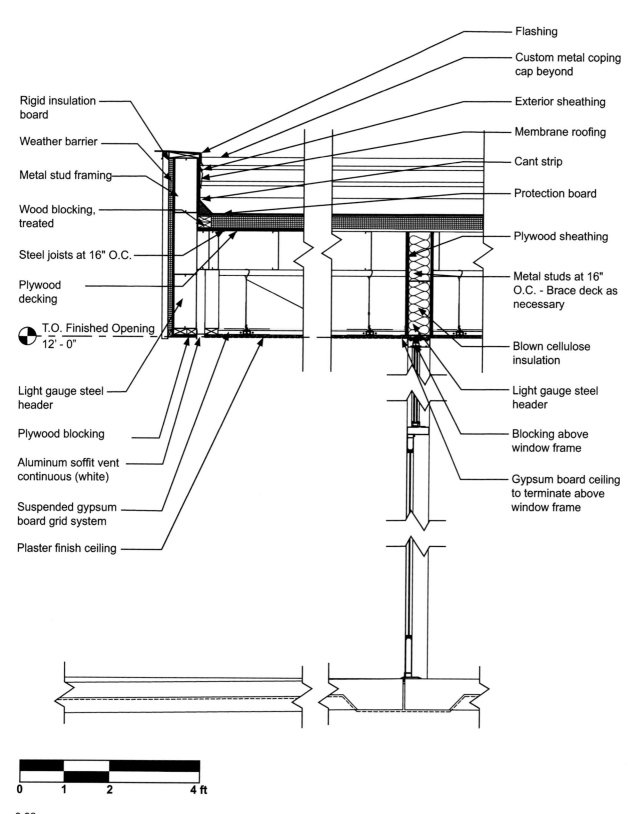

Flashing

Custom metal coping cap beyond

Exterior sheathing

Membrane roofing

Cant strip

Protection board

Plywood sheathing

Metal studs at 16" O.C. - Brace deck as necessary

Blown cellulose insulation

Light gauge steel header

Blocking above window frame

Gypsum board ceiling to terminate above window frame

Rigid insulation board

Weather barrier

Metal stud framing

Wood blocking, treated

Steel joists at 16" O.C.

Plywood decking

T.O. Finished Opening 12' - 0"

Light gauge steel header

Plywood blocking

Aluminum soffit vent continuous (white)

Suspended gypsum board grid system

Plaster finish ceiling

0 1 2 4 ft

2.28
Wall section: east/west building section E-E and F-F

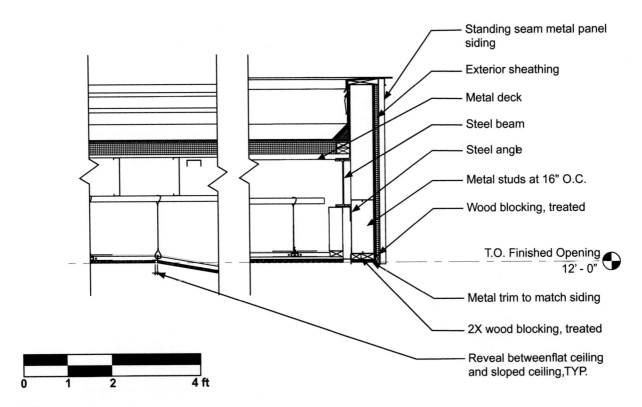

Standing seam metal panel siding

Exterior sheathing

Metal deck

Steel beam

Steel angle

Metal studs at 16" O.C.

Wood blocking, treated

T.O. Finished Opening
12' - 0"

Metal trim to match siding

2X wood blocking, treated

Reveal between flat ceiling and sloped ceiling, TYP.

0 1 2   4 ft

2.29
Wall section: east/west building section E-E and F-F

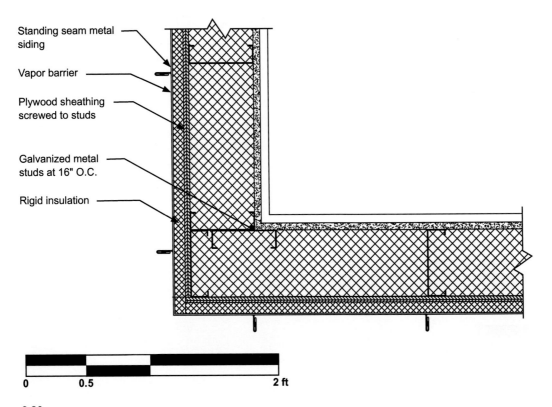

Standing seam metal siding

Vapor barrier

Plywood sheathing screwed to studs

Galvanized metal studs at 16" O.C.

Rigid insulation

0   0.5   2 ft

2.30
Plan detail: southwest corner of building

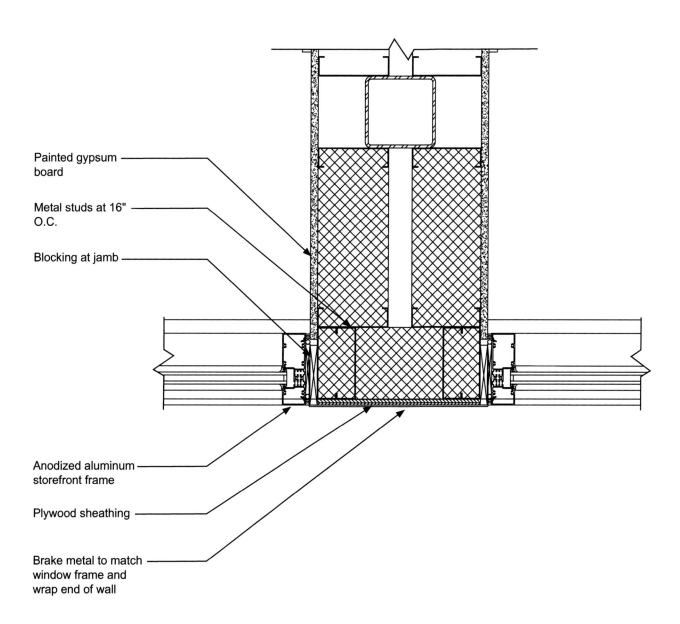

Painted gypsum
board

Metal studs at 16"
O.C.

Blocking at jamb

Anodized aluminum
storefront frame

Plywood sheathing

Brake metal to match
window frame and
wrap end of wall

0   0.5   2 ft

2.31
Plan detail: public restroom plumbing wall

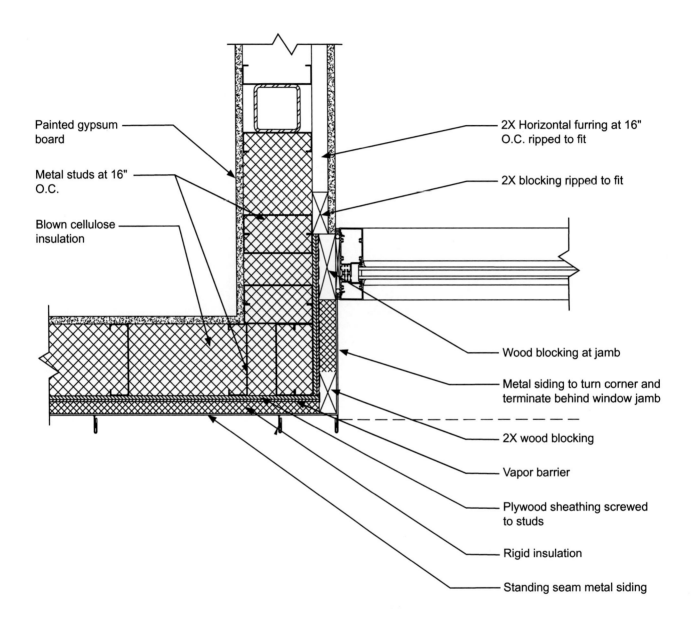

Painted gypsum board

Metal studs at 16" O.C.

Blown cellulose insulation

2X Horizontal furring at 16" O.C. ripped to fit

2X blocking ripped to fit

Wood blocking at jamb

Metal siding to turn corner and terminate behind window jamb

2X wood blocking

Vapor barrier

Plywood sheathing screwed to studs

Rigid insulation

Standing seam metal siding

0   0.5   2 ft

2.32
Plan detail: intersection of weathering steel and storefront

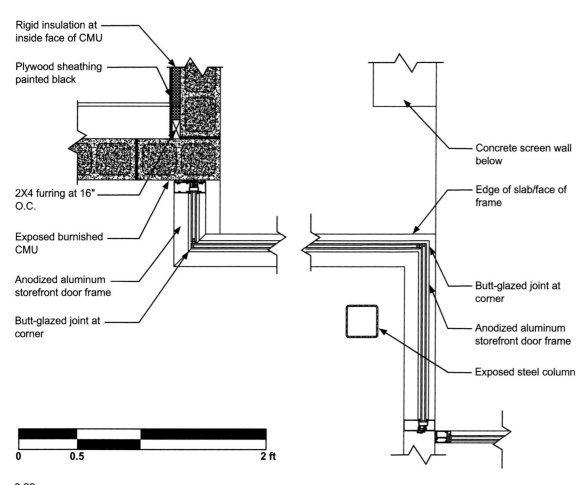

Rigid insulation at inside face of CMU

Plywood sheathing painted black

2X4 furring at 16" O.C.

Exposed burnished CMU

Anodized aluminum storefront door frame

Butt-glazed joint at corner

Concrete screen wall below

Edge of slab/face of frame

Butt-glazed joint at corner

Anodized aluminum storefront door frame

Exposed steel column

0   0.5   2 ft

2.33
Plan detail: lobby storefront

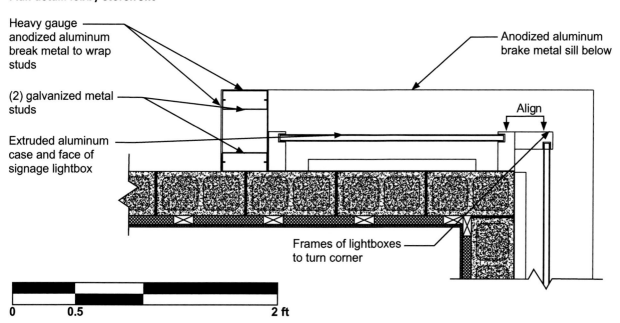

Heavy gauge anodized aluminum break metal to wrap studs

(2) galvanized metal studs

Extruded aluminum case and face of signage lightbox

Anodized aluminum brake metal sill below

Align

Frames of lightboxes to turn corner

0   0.5   2 ft

2.34
Plan detail: theatre signage

Hatiloo Theatre

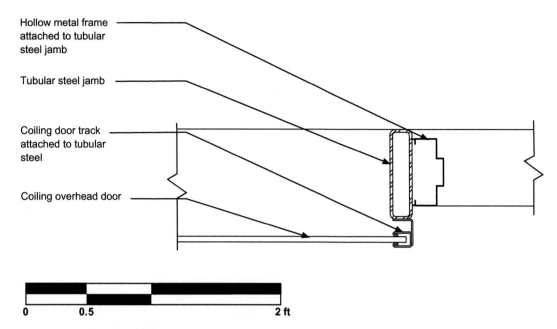

Hollow metal frame attached to tubular steel jamb

Tubular steel jamb

Coiling door track attached to tubular steel

Coiling overhead door

0   0.5   2 ft

2.35
Plan detail: exit door by overhead door

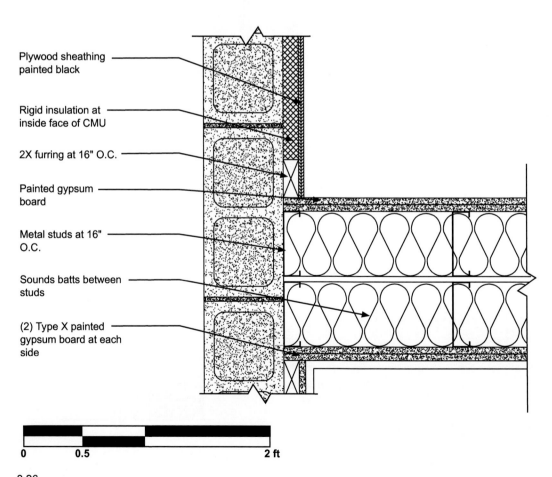

Plywood sheathing painted black

Rigid insulation at inside face of CMU

2X furring at 16" O.C.

Painted gypsum board

Metal studs at 16" O.C.

Sounds batts between studs

(2) Type X painted gypsum board at each side

0   0.5   2 ft

2.36
Plan detail: acoustic wall at small box theatre

72

3.1
View of northeast corner

Credit: Francis Dzikowski / OTTO

3: Maritime and Seafood Industry Museum

Biloxi, MS, H3 Hardy Collaboration Architecture

Architect's Design Intent and Reasoning Behind Material and Tectonic Choices

On August 29, 2005, Hurricane Katrina made landfall in Biloxi, Mississippi, bringing with it a 30' 0" tidal surge. The Maritime and Seafood Industry Museum (MSIM) was destroyed, along with much of its collection. Determined to continue its mission to preserve and exhibit the Gulf Coast's maritime heritage, the museum's board worked tirelessly for a decade to rebuild its collection and build a new home.

With the decision to rebuild the Museum at its original Point Cadet site in east Biloxi came the challenge of situating the building on its property outside of the newly defined Velocity Zone. Allowed to sit in the Coastal A Floodplain, the building was elevated to meet FEMA's flood proofing requirements.[1] The site constraints influenced the building's massing, while its elevation requirements provided the inspiration for the pier-like stair and porch and the under-building bonus space now used for summer camp and living exhibits.

Situated in the Biloxi Waterfront Park, the Museum has become the new icon of Point Cadet, the traditional home of Biloxi's seafood families. One approach to the site, from the 95' 0" main span height of the Ocean Springs Bridge, offers an unobstructed view of the building and the main gallery that houses the *Nydia*, an 1896 Biloxi built sloop that was donated to the Museum in 2009. The design emphasizes the location and transparency of the main gallery viewed from the bridge and the beachfront thoroughfare of Highway 90. While the design relies heavily on the appeal of the eastern façade as the building's primary focus, the remaining façades contribute to the movement of the building in a three-dimensional experience from all approaches. The slight tilt of the gallery wing's roof provides dynamic movement to the building's composition.

The design of the Maritime and Seafood Industry Museum is conceived as a two-part composition. The administrative wing is a closed block, containing the behind-the-scenes and supportive functions of the Museum while the gallery wing, an open and transparent volume, reveals the contents of Museum's collection. Descending the Ocean Springs Bridge, you are presented with the view of the sloop *Nydia*, perceived as "a ship in a bottle." Exhibited behind a curtain wall, the sloop will beckon visitors to take a closer look. At night, the lighted gallery volume housing the *Nydia* is a beacon, drawing attention to the museum.

The open and closed concept of the building's exterior components is evident once inside the building. At the lobby, the closed spaces of the administrative wing are

Maritime and Seafood Industry Museum

3.2
View of main entrance on east side
Credit: Francis Dzikowski / OTTO

3.3
View of southeast corner
Credit: Francis Dzikowski / OTTO

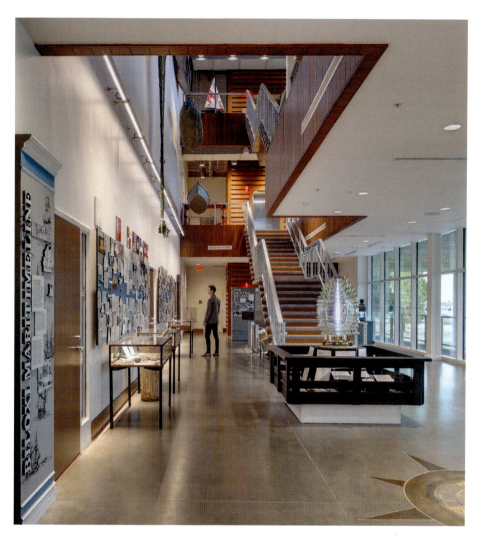

3.4
View from first floor lobby
Credit: Francis Dzikowski / OTTO

contained behind walls, while the open spaces of the gallery wing flow seamlessly one after the other. There are two major multi-story spaces within the Museum. The primary gallery space, 40′ 0″ in height, is designed to house the *Nydia*'s 30′ 0″ plus high mast, sloops, cat boats and other masted boats with sails up. The secondary multi-story space occurs at the Museum's interior stair. The triple height feature wall, adjacent to the interior stair, provides the Museum the opportunity to display large-scale artifacts such as fishing nets, multiple buoys or large-scale art pieces. In addition, this wall is envisioned as a screen for projected images and rotating video displays, with views from each level. The gallery spaces, not only aesthetically, but also functionally, achieve a balance between open areas for the boats and closed areas for more delicate materials. The main gallery space is sized to house tall sailing vessels at the

3.5
View towards first floor lobby
Credit: Francis Dzikowski / OTTO

building's northern end, while the contained gallery vault and additional windowless gallery spaces at the south end of the museum house the sensitive artifacts shielded from the sunlight.

The building materials, massing and composition pay tribute to the old Point Cadet neighborhood, while providing residents and tourists an exemplary structure to house important historic and cultural artifacts and a place for continual exploration and reflection on Biloxi's maritime history. The design utilizes a palette of materials that recall the neighborhood of Point Cadet. The administrative wing is clad in a white, pre-cast concrete panel system meant to evoke memories of the lap siding used in the factory cottages that once dominated the neighborhood. The solar screens, located on the south and east faces of the main gallery curtain wall are a reference to the roof structures of these cottages traditionally constructed from corrugated tin. Constructed from aluminum and kept in their natural color, these solar fins will provide shade and control glare in the gallery areas.

3.6
View of second floor gallery
Credit: Francis Dzikowski / OTTO

3.7
View down into second floor gallery
Credit: Francis Dzikowski / OTTO

Maritime and Seafood Industry Museum

The spatial program for the museum was limited by FEMA reconstruction regulations, making the new museum of 19,580 SF smaller in size than its pre-Katrina facility. The new building contains galleries, a video theater, library, gift shop, workshop/ storage room, meeting rooms, and administrative offices. With their artifacts and exhibits decimated by the Hurricane, H3 worked with the Museum and curator to envision how to best exhibit recovered artifacts and how best to plan for unknown and generally large scale wooden boat donations. Through a desire to exhibit boats with their mast and sails raised, the spatial program had to consider the volume of the space, not just the footprint of each artifact. Storage and workshop spaces were compromised to ensure that the maximum square footage was allocated to exhibits.

H3 followed the FEMA technical bulletins to reinforce the building to resist hurricane force winds and the force of oncoming water. The museum is elevated off the ground plane to a level one foot above the site's base flood elevation level. The ground floor has no occupiable space, though the void space beneath the museum is used for the Sea-n-Sail camp and living exhibits. The porches are breakaway structures, meant to detach from the structure and float away in floodwaters. At the Museum site, silty sand and soft clay properties of the soils required that a system of 16" diameter auger cast pile foundations be utilized to 40' 0" below the surface to support the building, but also lead to the decision of using 36" diameter cast in place concrete column for the building's main supports. The round shape of the columns direct floodwaters around the column and remove the possibility of square edges being chipped by floating debris. The building is anchored to the ground by the massive poured in place fire stairs that counter balance lateral forces and required a FEMA-approved flood vent at their base that balance water pressure against this stair tower. Meanwhile the break-away stair structures and wood detailing at grade are made of easily replaceable materials and required only wood piles for their structural support. With a 6" frame, the curtain wall structure has a substantial cross section and is reinforced with both horizontal and diagonal cross bracings. The curtain wall utilizes multiple layers of heat-strengthened laminated glass and has a PVB inner layer to resist 140 mph winds.

We considered an alternate exterior wall system, consisting of light gauge metal framing, multiple layers of sheathing, and standard lap siding, which met FEMA impact testing requirements, in lieu of the pre-cast concrete panels. The precast concrete panel system offered strength, durability and ease of maintenance and installation, while also providing a material of permanence, suitable for a building with a large civic presence. The ability of precast concrete, to be molded with an appropriately scaled lap siding, visible from the building's various approaches, ultimately led to the decision to use precast concrete. By following the FEMA technical bulletins, the building should sustain minimal damage from future hurricanes.

In many communities, local heritage is being replaced by a homogenized American culture. What defined the Mississippi Gulf Coast in the early 1900s was the seafood industry and its immigrant families that came to work in the factories. The Museum not only preserves this important aspect of Mississippi's history, but its collections are a significant educational tool. School visits make up a significant number of the Museum's visitors. The new building supports the Museum's mission by not only providing a container for its artifacts, but also through design reflecting the factory neighborhood that once surrounded it.

Viewed as a catalyst for the redevelopment of the Point Cadet neighborhood of Biloxi, the new Museum has revived the site as a cultural destination and event space for the City of Biloxi as a counterpoint to the adjacent casinos. In its first year of operation, the Museum welcomed 30,000 visitors, entertained 400 children during the summer's six-week long Sea-n-Sail camp, and hosted over 100 business and social events, ranging from the Mississippi Episcopal Diocese Annual Conference to the Building Officials of Mississippi Annual Reception.

The under-platform space was developed with the Sea-n-Sail camp in mind, taking advantage of the covered area and constant breeze generated by the Gulf of Mexico. The back porch feature allows the campers access to the meeting rooms and toilet facilities without entering the museum gallery spaces. The meeting rooms are located on the Museum's first floor, so that after-hours events can be hosted without access to other areas of the museum. The design accommodates meeting space for civic groups and provides a revenue generating opportunity for the Museum by having the meeting rooms located so that they can be easily accessed. The museum expanded upon this idea and co-located their kitchen adjacent to the meeting rooms, where catered events are frequent.

The museum is operated with a staff of only six full-time employees. The design assists the staff through its use of open floor plates that are both self- directing through the gallery spaces and easy to monitor for security surveillance.

As a city building, an important objective of the Museum is to have a minimal power bill. During the design of the Museum, H3 developed two detailed energy models to determine the best solid/void composition to eliminate heat gain, while still providing the large expanse of windows that reveal the sloop *Nydia*. Energy consumption is kept to a minimum even during the intense summer season by designing the south and west façades as solid and specifying a highly efficient glass panel system.

The new building provides a fitting, visible new home from which the Maritime and Seafood Industry Museum can continue to preserve the history of the industry, neighborhood and the city. It serves as a symbol of resilience as the city continues to rebuild after Hurricane Katrina and provide a new place for the community to come together and honor its heritage, year-round.

Daria F. Pizzetta, FAIA
Principal

Note

1   https://www.fema.gov/media-library/collections/4

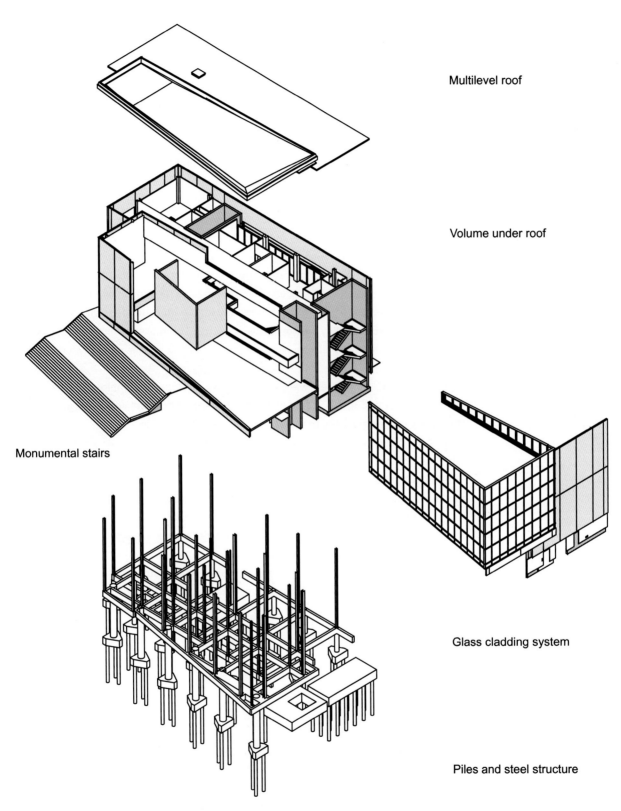

Multilevel roof

Volume under roof

Monumental stairs

Glass cladding system

Piles and steel structure

3.8
Major building components
(Not to scale.)

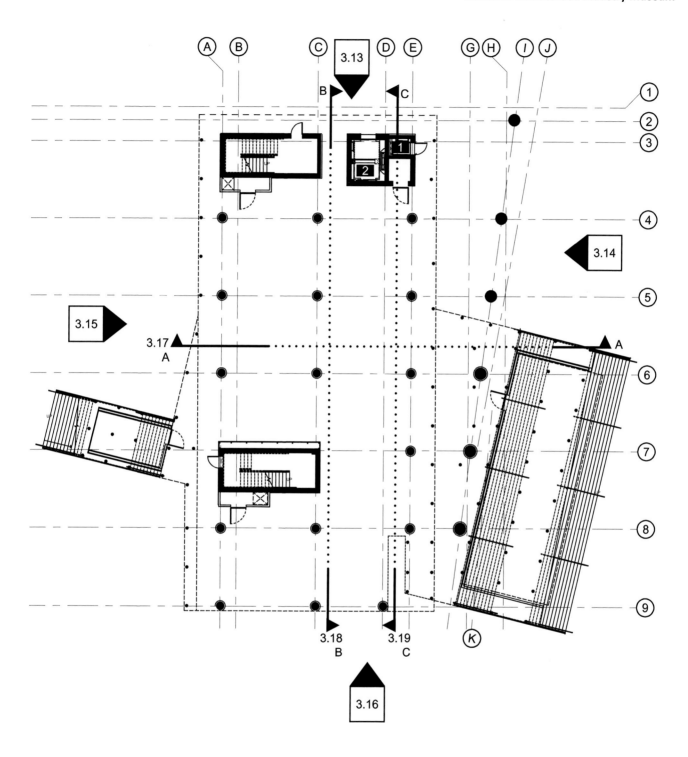

3.13
3.14
3.15
3.17
3.18
B
3.19
C
3.16

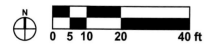

N
0 5 10   20   40 ft

LEGEND
ADA Elevator **1**
Service & Passenger Elevator **2**

3.9
Ground floor plan

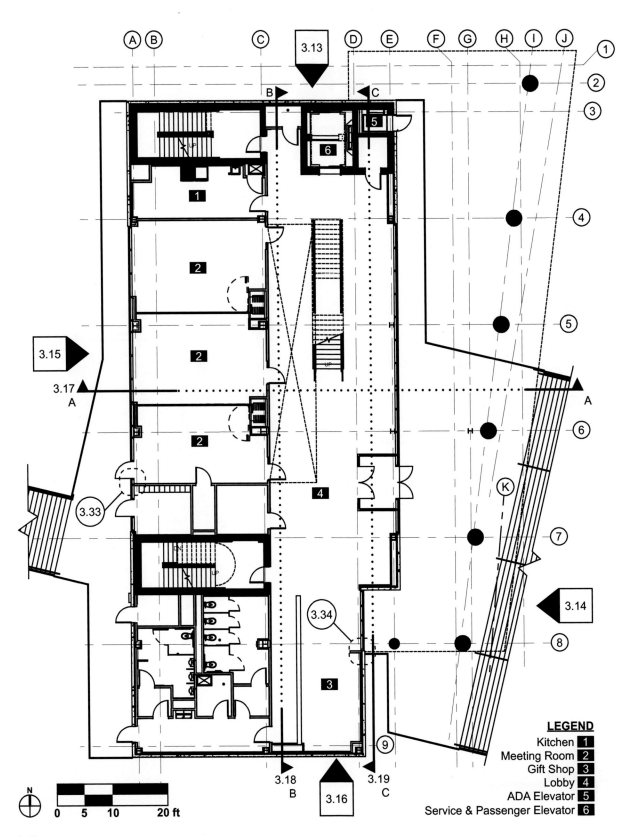

LEGEND

Kitchen	**1**
Meeting Room	**2**
Gift Shop	**3**
Lobby	**4**
ADA Elevator	**5**
Service & Passenger Elevator	**6**

N

0 5 10   20 ft

3.10
First floor plan

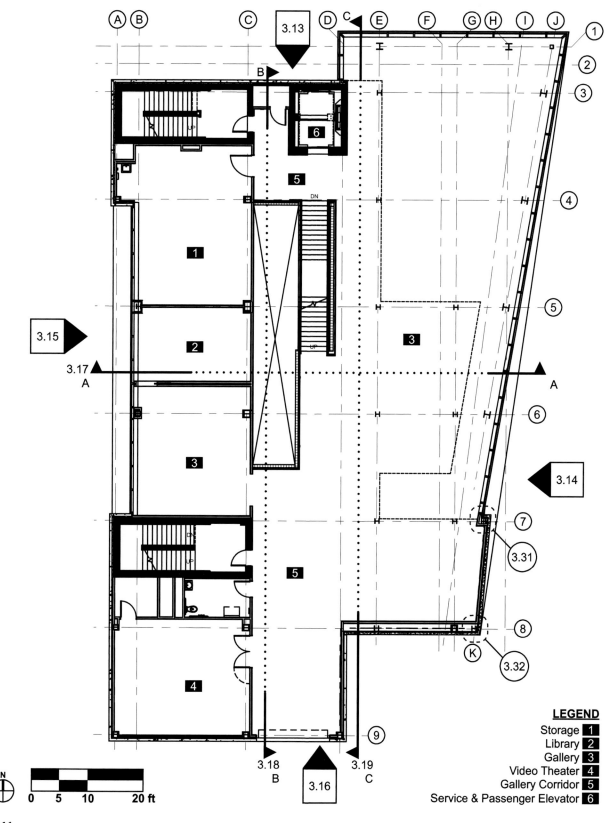

3.11
Second floor plan

LEGEND
Storage **1**
Library **2**
Gallery **3**
Video Theater **4**
Gallery Corridor **5**
Service & Passenger Elevator **6**

N
0 5 10 20 ft

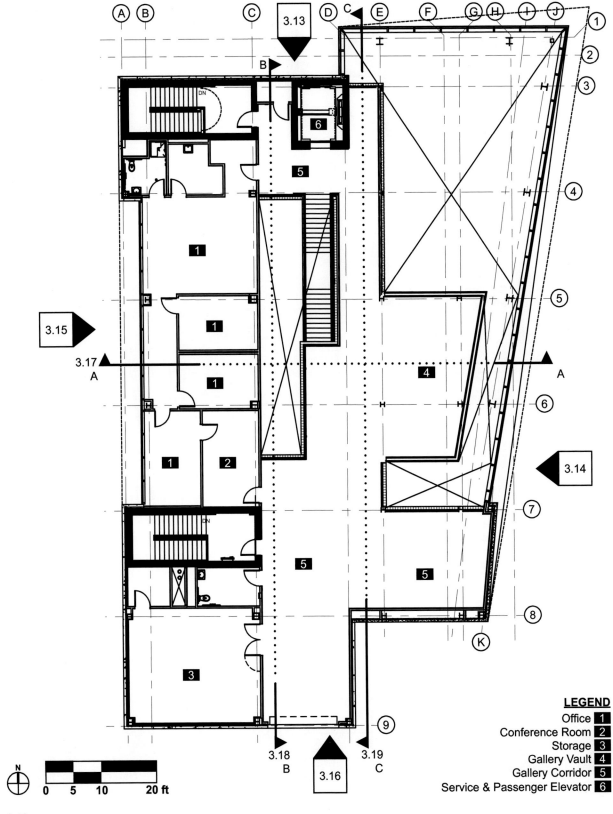

3.13

3.15

3.17
A

3.14

3.18
B

3.16

3.19
C

9

N
0 5 10   20 ft

LEGEND
Office **1**
Conference Room **2**
Storage **3**
Gallery Vault **4**
Gallery Corridor **5**
Service & Passenger Elevator **6**

3.12
Third floor plan

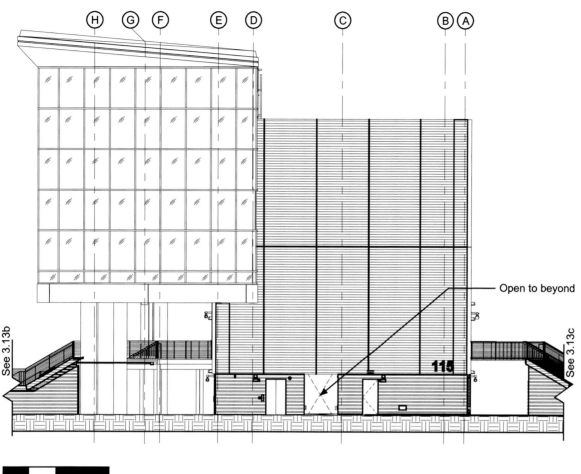

(H) (G) (F) (E) (D) (C) (B) (A)

Open to beyond

See 3.13b

See 3.13c

115

0 5 10 20 ft

3.13a
North elevation

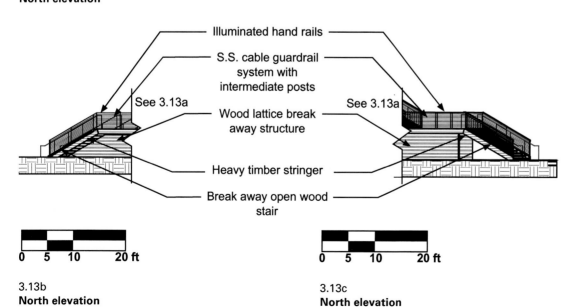

Illuminated hand rails

S.S. cable guardrail system with intermediate posts

See 3.13a

See 3.13a

Wood lattice break away structure

Heavy timber stringer

Break away open wood stair

0 5 10 20 ft

3.13b
North elevation

0 5 10 20 ft

3.13c
North elevation

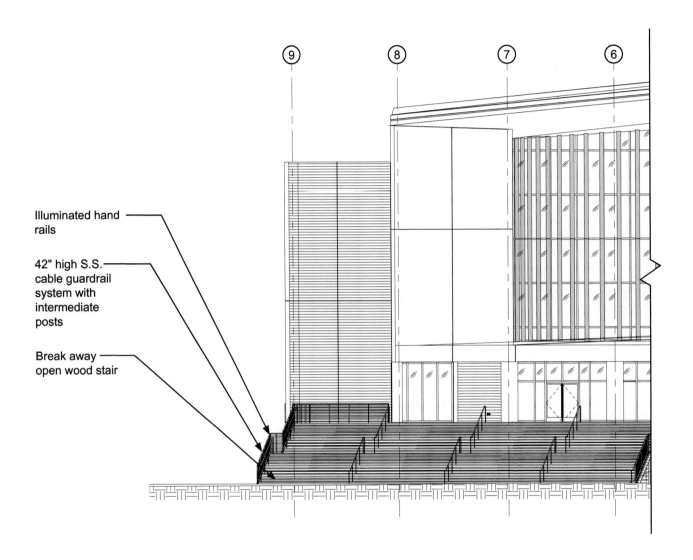

Illuminated hand rails

42" high S.S. cable guardrail system with intermediate posts

Break away open wood stair

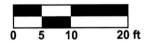

0   5   10   20 ft

3.14a
East elevation

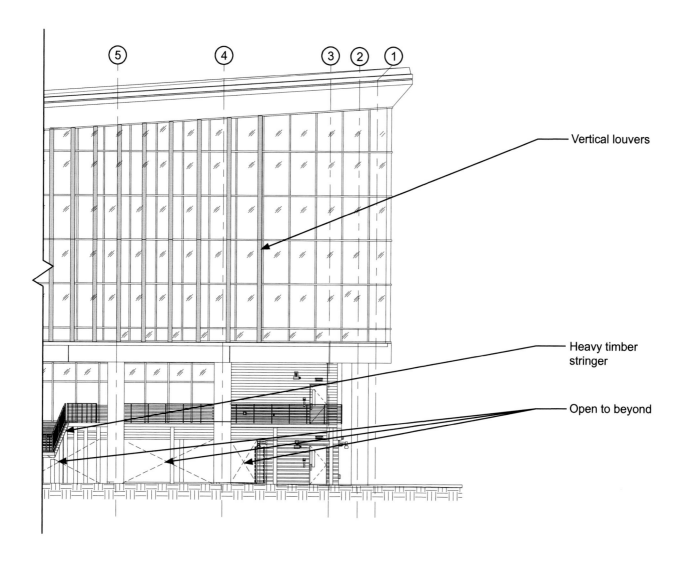

Vertical louvers

Heavy timber stringer

Open to beyond

0   5   10   20 ft

3.14b
East elevation

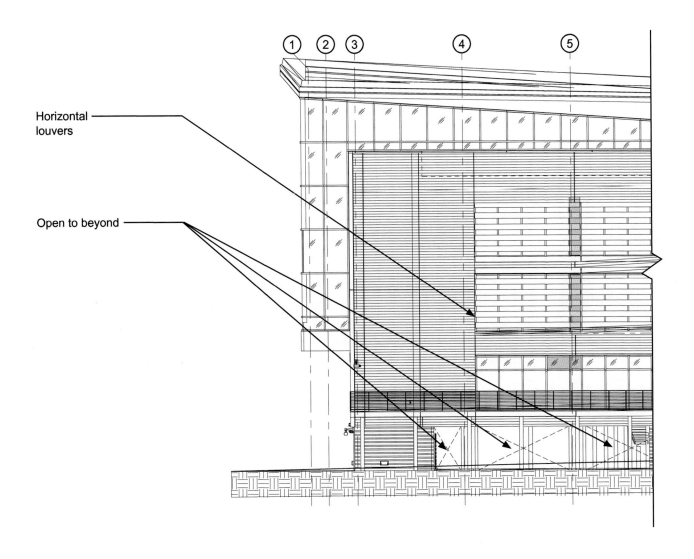

Horizontal louvers

Open to beyond

0   5   10   20 ft

3.15a
West elevation

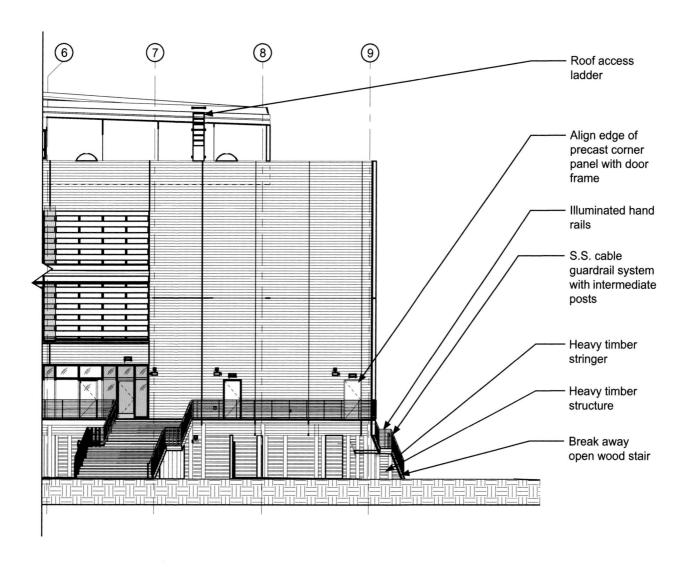

Roof access ladder

Align edge of precast corner panel with door frame

Illuminated hand rails

S.S. cable guardrail system with intermediate posts

Heavy timber stringer

Heavy timber structure

Break away open wood stair

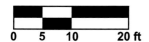

0   5   10   20 ft

3.15b
West elevation

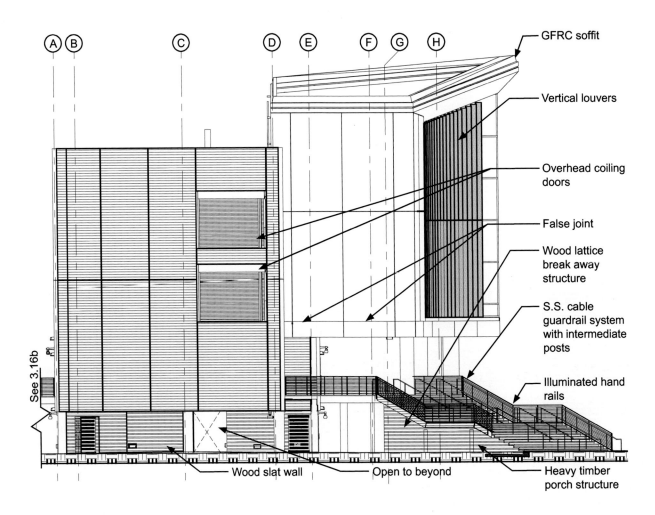

GFRC soffit

Vertical louvers

Overhead coiling doors

False joint

Wood lattice break away structure

S.S. cable guardrail system with intermediate posts

Illuminated hand rails

Heavy timber porch structure

See 3.16b

Wood slat wall

Open to beyond

0   5   10   20 ft

3.16a
South elevation

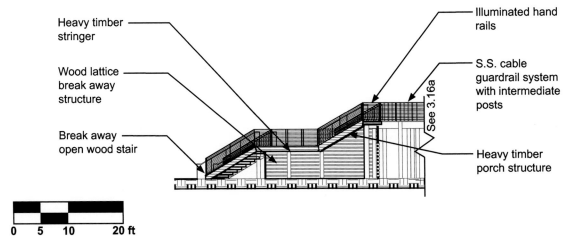

Heavy timber stringer

Wood lattice break away structure

Break away open wood stair

Illuminated hand rails

S.S. cable guardrail system with intermediate posts

See 3.16a

Heavy timber porch structure

0   5   10   20 ft

3.16b
South elevation

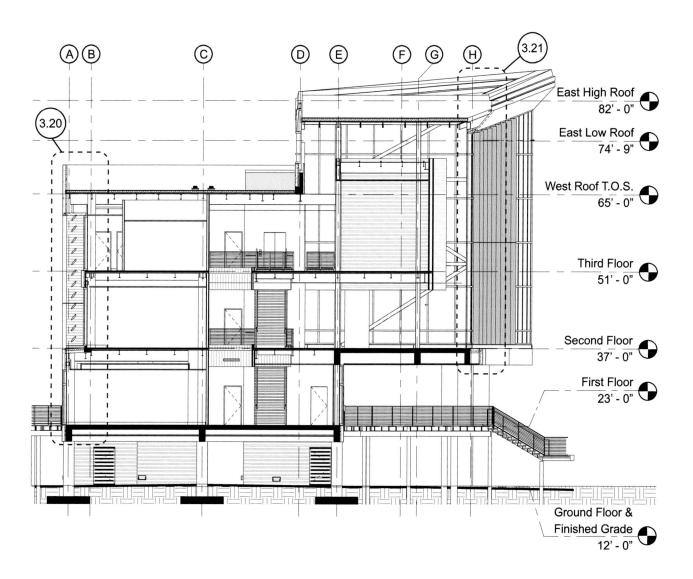

A B   C   D E   F G   H   3.21

3.20

East High Roof
82' - 0"

East Low Roof
74' - 9"

West Roof T.O.S.
65' - 0"

Third Floor
51' - 0"

Second Floor
37' - 0"

First Floor
23' - 0"

Ground Floor &
Finished Grade
12' - 0"

0   5   10   20 ft

3.17
East/west building section A-A

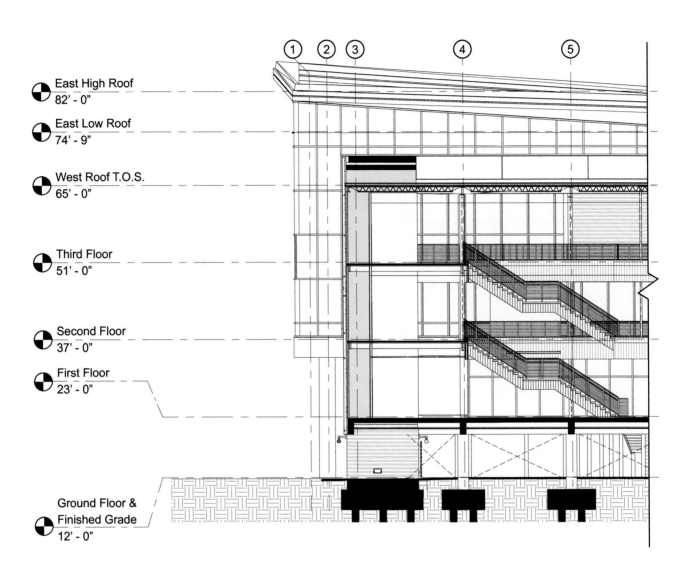

East High Roof
82' - 0"

East Low Roof
74' - 9"

West Roof T.O.S.
65' - 0"

Third Floor
51' - 0"

Second Floor
37' - 0"

First Floor
23' - 0"

Ground Floor &
Finished Grade
12' - 0"

0   5   10   20 ft

3.18a
North/south building section at lobby B-B

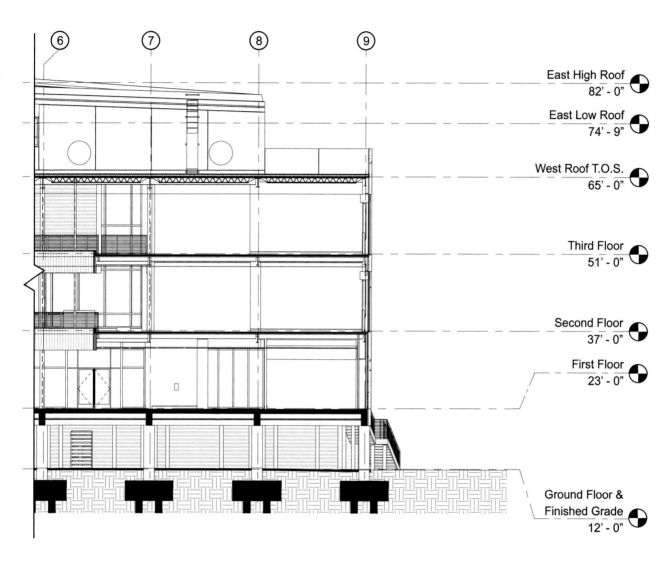

East High Roof
82' - 0"

East Low Roof
74' - 9"

West Roof T.O.S.
65' - 0"

Third Floor
51' - 0"

Second Floor
37' - 0"

First Floor
23' - 0"

Ground Floor &
Finished Grade
12' - 0"

0   5   10   20 ft

3.18b
North/south building section at lobby B-B

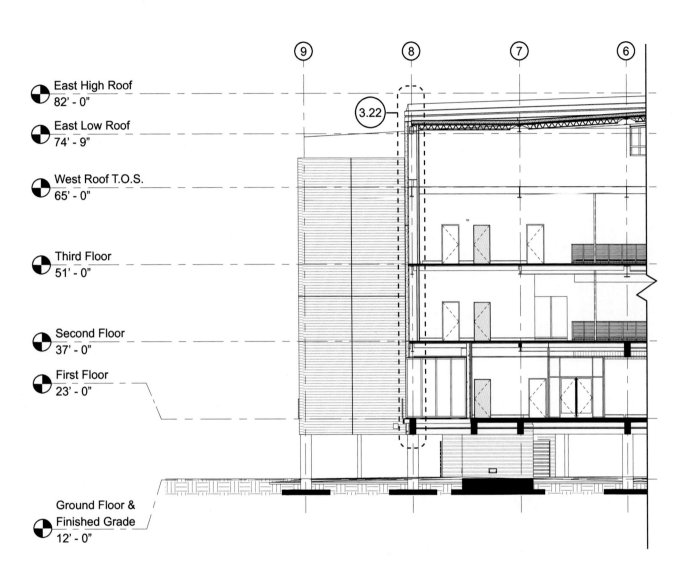

East High Roof
82' - 0"

East Low Roof
74' - 9"

West Roof T.O.S.
65' - 0"

Third Floor
51' - 0"

Second Floor
37' - 0"

First Floor
23' - 0"

Ground Floor &
Finished Grade
12' - 0"

0   5   10   20 ft

3.19a
North/south building section C-C

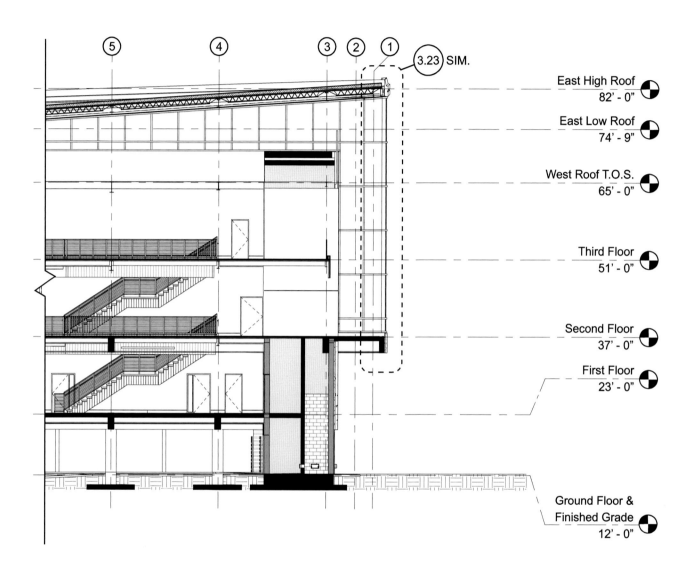

East High Roof
82' - 0"

East Low Roof
74' - 9"

West Roof T.O.S.
65' - 0"

Third Floor
51' - 0"

Second Floor
37' - 0"

First Floor
23' - 0"

Ground Floor &
Finished Grade
12' - 0"

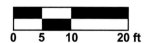

0   5   10   20 ft

3.19b
North/south building section C-C

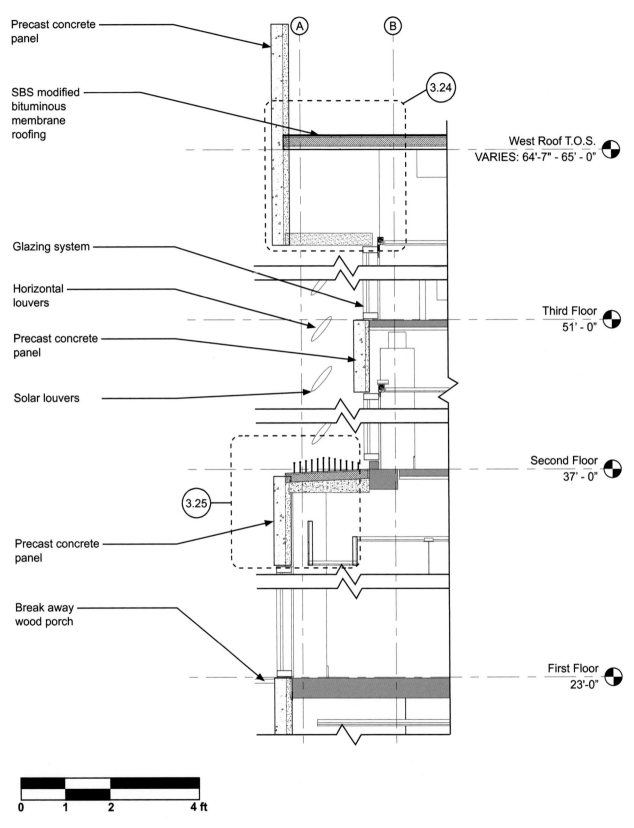

Precast concrete panel

SBS modified bituminous membrane roofing

(A) (B)

3.24

West Roof T.O.S.
VARIES: 64'-7" - 65' - 0"

Glazing system

Horizontal louvers

Third Floor
51' - 0"

Precast concrete panel

Solar louvers

Second Floor
37' - 0"

3.25

Precast concrete panel

Break away wood porch

First Floor
23'-0"

0   1   2   4 ft

3.20
Wall section: west at storefront

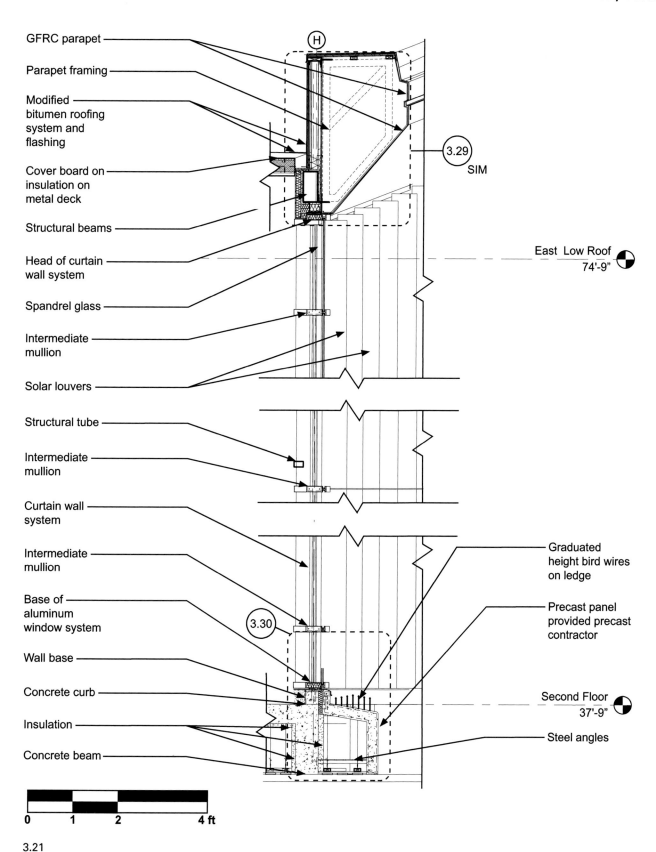

GFRC parapet

Parapet framing

Modified bitumen roofing system and flashing

Cover board on insulation on metal deck

Structural beams

Head of curtain wall system

Spandrel glass

Intermediate mullion

Solar louvers

Structural tube

Intermediate mullion

Curtain wall system

Intermediate mullion

Base of aluminum window system

Wall base

Concrete curb

Insulation

Concrete beam

H

3.29
SIM

East Low Roof
74'-9"

3.30

Graduated height bird wires on ledge

Precast panel provided precast contractor

Second Floor
37'-9"

Steel angles

0 1 2 4 ft

3.21
Wall section: east curtain wall

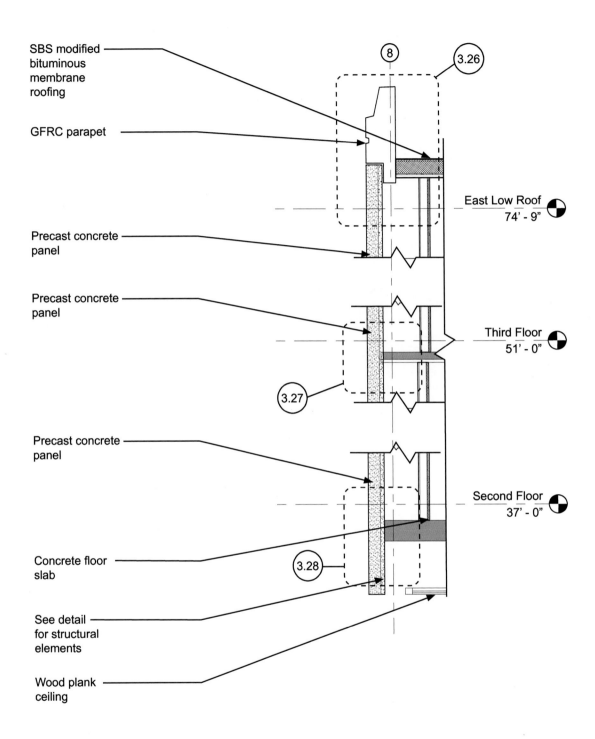

SBS modified
bituminous
membrane
roofing

GFRC parapet

Precast concrete
panel

Precast concrete
panel

Precast concrete
panel

Concrete floor
slab

See detail
for structural
elements

Wood plank
ceiling

East Low Roof
74' - 9"

Third Floor
51' - 0"

Second Floor
37' - 0"

3.22
Wall section: south precast at east gallery

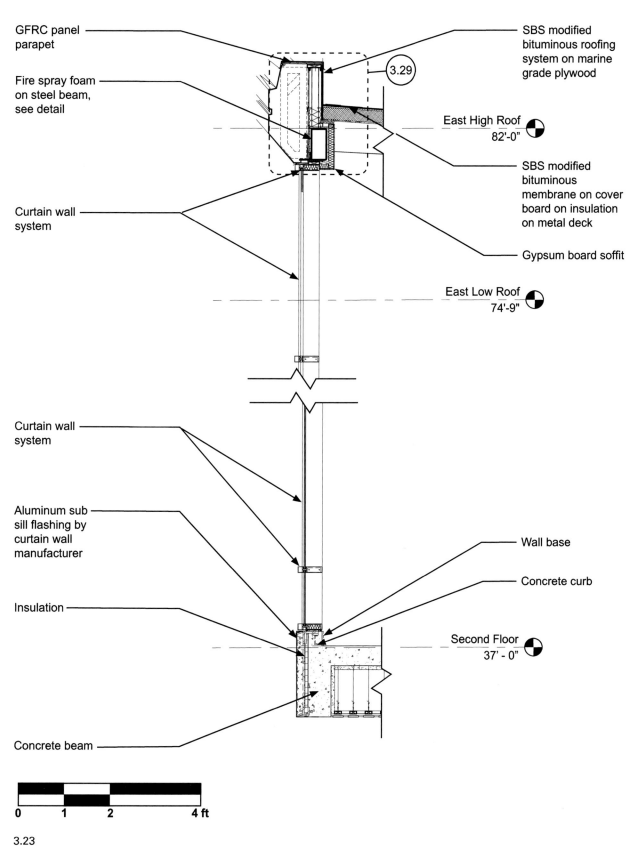

GFRC panel parapet

Fire spray foam on steel beam, see detail

Curtain wall system

SBS modified bituminous roofing system on marine grade plywood

3.29

East High Roof
82'-0"

SBS modified bituminous membrane on cover board on insulation on metal deck

Gypsum board soffit

East Low Roof
74'-9"

Curtain wall system

Aluminum sub sill flashing by curtain wall manufacturer

Insulation

Wall base

Concrete curb

Second Floor
37' - 0"

Concrete beam

0   1   2   4 ft

3.23
Wall section: north curtain wall

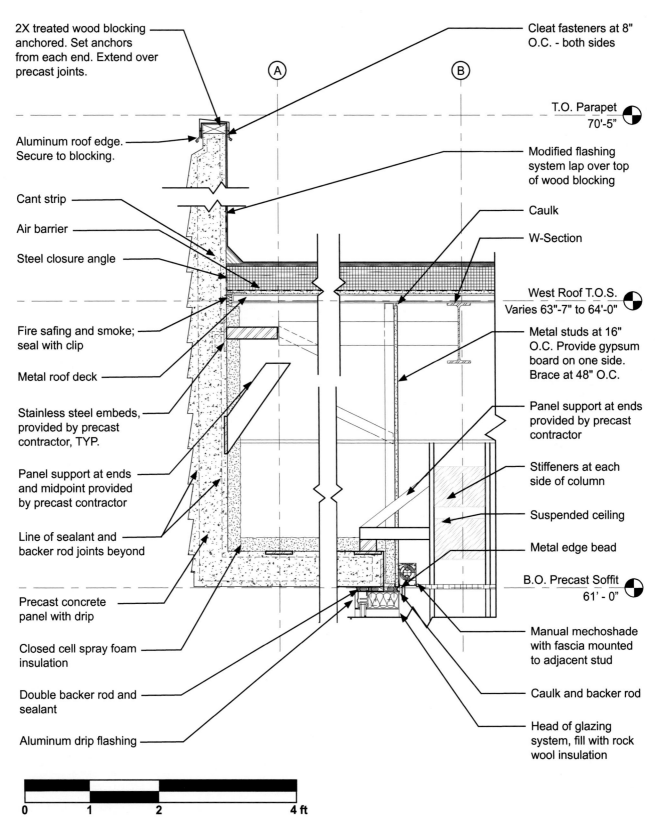

2X treated wood blocking anchored. Set anchors from each end. Extend over precast joints.

Aluminum roof edge. Secure to blocking.

Cant strip

Air barrier

Steel closure angle

Fire safing and smoke; seal with clip

Metal roof deck

Stainless steel embeds, provided by precast contractor, TYP.

Panel support at ends and midpoint provided by precast contractor

Line of sealant and backer rod joints beyond

Precast concrete panel with drip

Closed cell spray foam insulation

Double backer rod and sealant

Aluminum drip flashing

Cleat fasteners at 8" O.C. - both sides

Ⓐ   Ⓑ

T.O. Parapet
70'-5"

Modified flashing system lap over top of wood blocking

Caulk

W-Section

West Roof T.O.S.
Varies 63"-7" to 64'-0"

Metal studs at 16" O.C. Provide gypsum board on one side. Brace at 48" O.C.

Panel support at ends provided by precast contractor

Stiffeners at each side of column

Suspended ceiling

Metal edge bead

B.O. Precast Soffit
61' - 0"

Manual mechoshade with fascia mounted to adjacent stud

Caulk and backer rod

Head of glazing system, fill with rock wool insulation

0   1   2   4 ft

3.24
Section detail: west storefront head

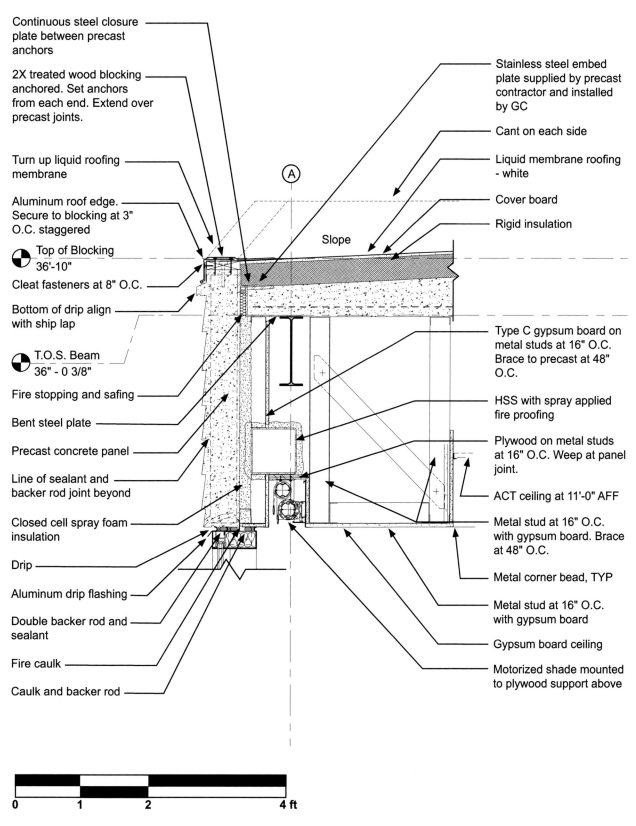

Continuous steel closure plate between precast anchors

2X treated wood blocking anchored. Set anchors from each end. Extend over precast joints.

Turn up liquid roofing membrane

Aluminum roof edge. Secure to blocking at 3" O.C. staggered

Top of Blocking
36'-10"

Cleat fasteners at 8" O.C.

Bottom of drip align with ship lap

T.O.S. Beam
36" - 0 3/8"

Fire stopping and safing

Bent steel plate

Precast concrete panel

Line of sealant and backer rod joint beyond

Closed cell spray foam insulation

Drip

Aluminum drip flashing

Double backer rod and sealant

Fire caulk

Caulk and backer rod

Stainless steel embed plate supplied by precast contractor and installed by GC

Cant on each side

Liquid membrane roofing - white

Cover board

Rigid insulation

Slope

A

Type C gypsum board on metal studs at 16" O.C. Brace to precast at 48" O.C.

HSS with spray applied fire proofing

Plywood on metal studs at 16" O.C. Weep at panel joint.

ACT ceiling at 11'-0" AFF

Metal stud at 16" O.C. with gypsum board. Brace at 48" O.C.

Metal corner bead, TYP

Metal stud at 16" O.C. with gypsum board

Gypsum board ceiling

Motorized shade mounted to plywood support above

0   1   2   4 ft

3.25
Section detail: precast/storefront west

Maritime and Seafood Industry Museum

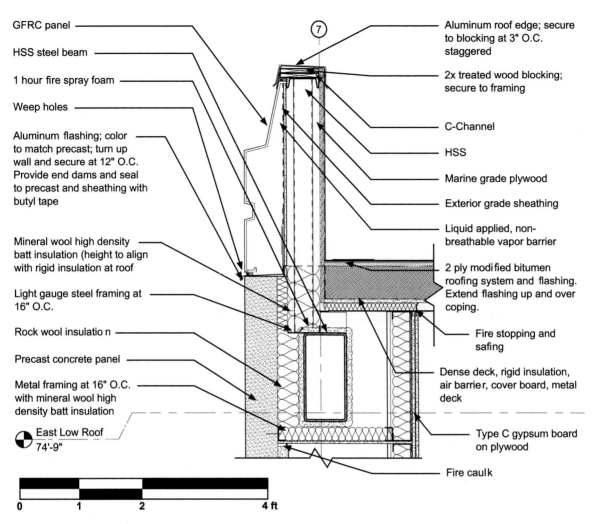

GFRC panel

HSS steel beam

1 hour fire spray foam

Weep holes

Aluminum flashing; color to match precast; turn up wall and secure at 12" O.C. Provide end dams and seal to precast and sheathing with butyl tape

Mineral wool high density batt insulation (height to align with rigid insulation at roof

Light gauge steel framing at 16" O.C.

Rock wool insulatio n

Precast concrete panel

Metal framing at 16" O.C. with mineral wool high density batt insulation

East Low Roof
74'-9"

Aluminum roof edge; secure to blocking at 3" O.C. staggered

2x treated wood blocking; secure to framing

C-Channel

HSS

Marine grade plywood

Exterior grade sheathing

Liquid applied, non-breathable vapor barrier

2 ply modified bitumen roofing system and flashing. Extend flashing up and over coping.

Fire stopping and safing

Dense deck, rigid insulation, air barrier, cover board, metal deck

Type C gypsum board on plywood

Fire caulk

0 1 2 4 ft

3.26
Section detail: south curtain wall head

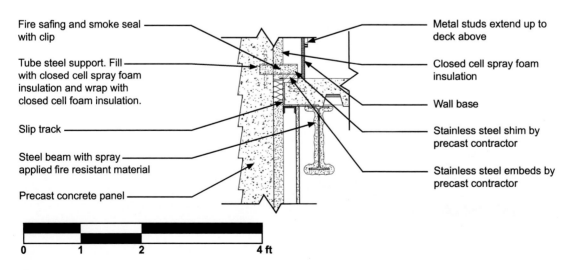

Fire safing and smoke seal with clip

Tube steel support. Fill with closed cell spray foam insulation and wrap with closed cell foam insulation.

Slip track

Steel beam with spray applied fire resistant material

Precast concrete panel

Metal studs extend up to deck above

Closed cell spray foam insulation

Wall base

Stainless steel shim by precast contractor

Stainless steel embeds by precast contractor

0 1 2 4 ft

3.27
Section detail: composite floor

104

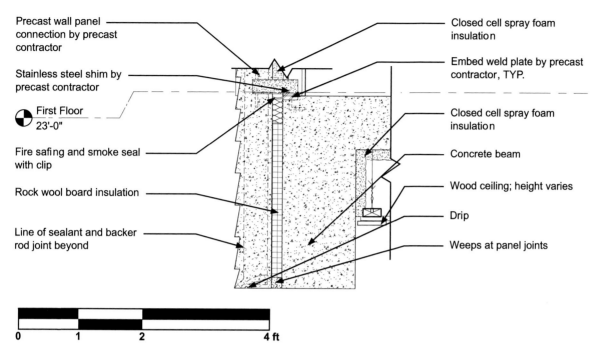

Precast wall panel connection by precast contractor

Stainless steel shim by precast contractor

First Floor
23'-0"

Fire safing and smoke seal with clip

Rock wool board insulation

Line of sealant and backer rod joint beyond

Closed cell spray foam insulation

Embed weld plate by precast contractor, TYP.

Closed cell spray foam insulation

Concrete beam

Wood ceiling; height varies

Drip

Weeps at panel joints

0   1   2   4 ft

3.28
Section detail: precast at concrete beam

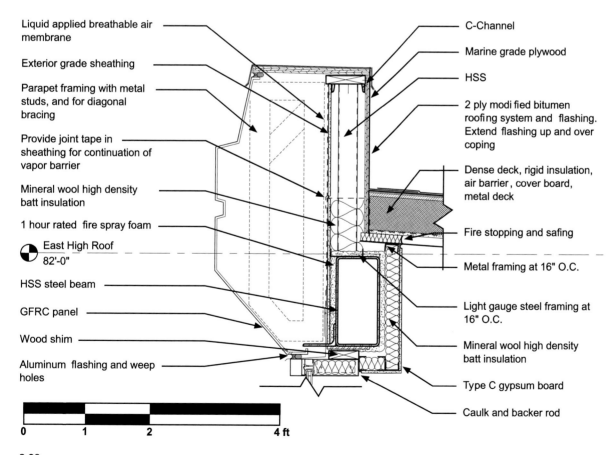

Liquid applied breathable air membrane

Exterior grade sheathing

Parapet framing with metal studs, and for diagonal bracing

Provide joint tape in sheathing for continuation of vapor barrier

Mineral wool high density batt insulation

1 hour rated fire spray foam

East High Roof
82'-0"

HSS steel beam

GFRC panel

Wood shim

Aluminum flashing and weep holes

C-Channel

Marine grade plywood

HSS

2 ply modified bitumen roofing system and flashing. Extend flashing up and over coping

Dense deck, rigid insulation, air barrier, cover board, metal deck

Fire stopping and safing

Metal framing at 16" O.C.

Light gauge steel framing at 16" O.C.

Mineral wool high density batt insulation

Type C gypsum board

Caulk and backer rod

0   1   2   4 ft

3.29
Section detail: north curtain wall head

105

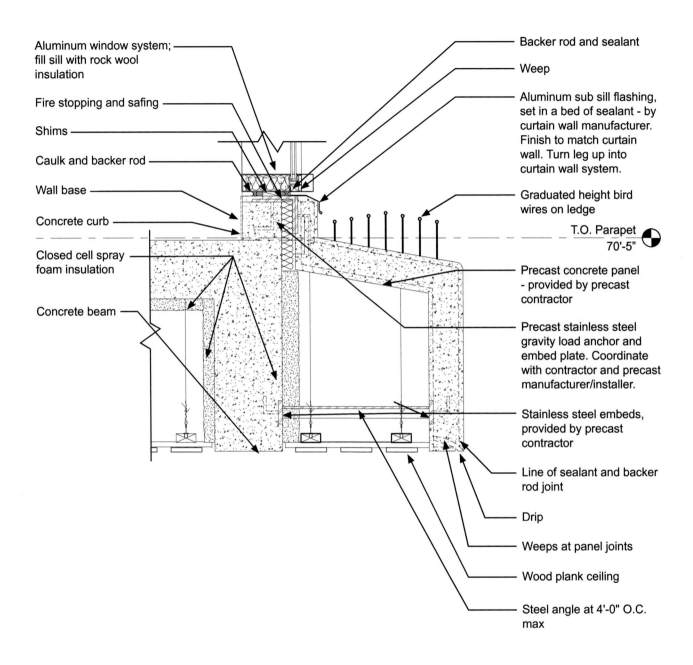

Aluminum window system; fill sill with rock wool insulation

Fire stopping and safing

Shims

Caulk and backer rod

Wall base

Concrete curb

Closed cell spray foam insulation

Concrete beam

Backer rod and sealant

Weep

Aluminum sub sill flashing, set in a bed of sealant - by curtain wall manufacturer. Finish to match curtain wall. Turn leg up into curtain wall system.

Graduated height bird wires on ledge

T.O. Parapet
70'-5"

Precast concrete panel - provided by precast contractor

Precast stainless steel gravity load anchor and embed plate. Coordinate with contractor and precast manufacturer/installer.

Stainless steel embeds, provided by precast contractor

Line of sealant and backer rod joint

Drip

Weeps at panel joints

Wood plank ceiling

Steel angle at 4'-0" O.C. max

0   1   2   4 ft

3.30
Section detail: east curtain wall base

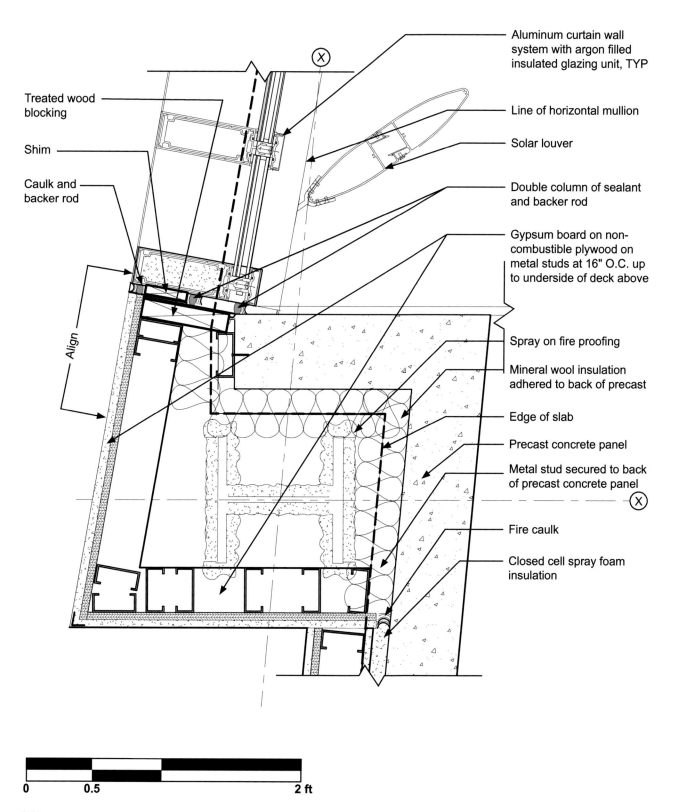

Aluminum curtain wall system with argon filled insulated glazing unit, TYP

Treated wood blocking

Line of horizontal mullion

Shim

Solar louver

Caulk and backer rod

Double column of sealant and backer rod

Gypsum board on non-combustible plywood on metal studs at 16" O.C. up to underside of deck above

Align

Spray on fire proofing

Mineral wool insulation adhered to back of precast

Edge of slab

Precast concrete panel

Metal stud secured to back of precast concrete panel

Fire caulk

Closed cell spray foam insulation

X

0   0.5   2 ft

3.31
Plan detail: curtain wall at precast

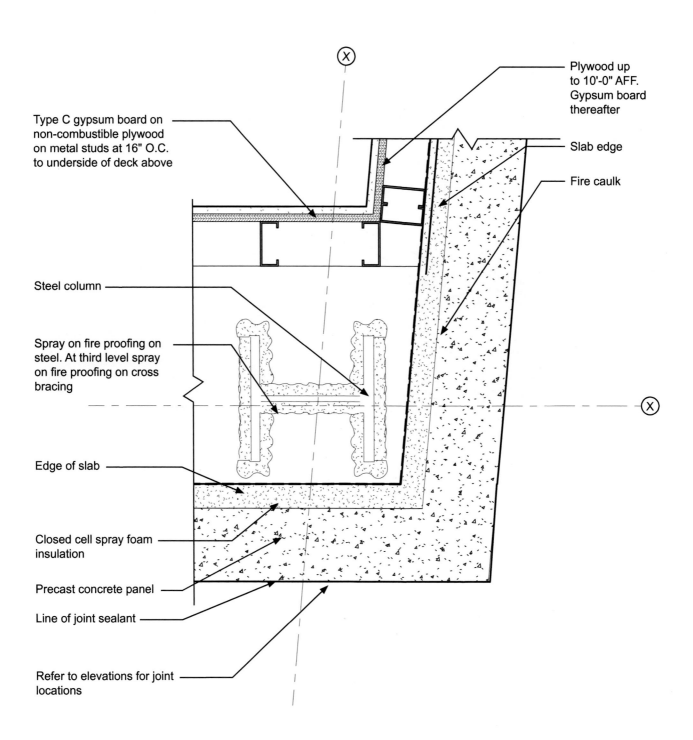

Plywood up to 10'-0" AFF. Gypsum board thereafter

Type C gypsum board on non-combustible plywood on metal studs at 16" O.C. to underside of deck above

Slab edge

Fire caulk

Steel column

Spray on fire proofing on steel. At third level spray on fire proofing on cross bracing

Edge of slab

Closed cell spray foam insulation

Precast concrete panel

Line of joint sealant

Refer to elevations for joint locations

0   0.5   2 ft

3.32
Plan detail: steel enclosure

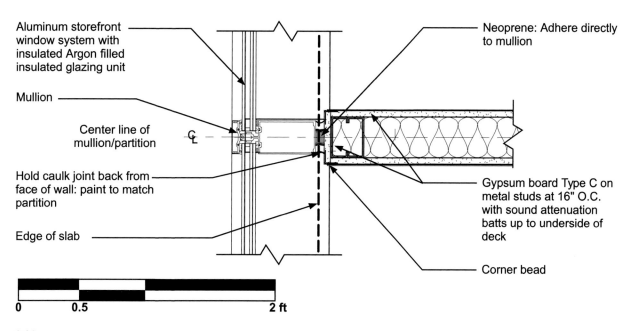

Aluminum storefront window system with insulated Argon filled insulated glazing unit

Mullion

Center line of mullion/partition

Hold caulk joint back from face of wall: paint to match partition

Edge of slab

Neoprene: Adhere directly to mullion

Gypsum board Type C on metal studs at 16" O.C. with sound attenuation batts up to underside of deck

Corner bead

0   0.5   2 ft

3.33
Plan detail: first floor mullion detail

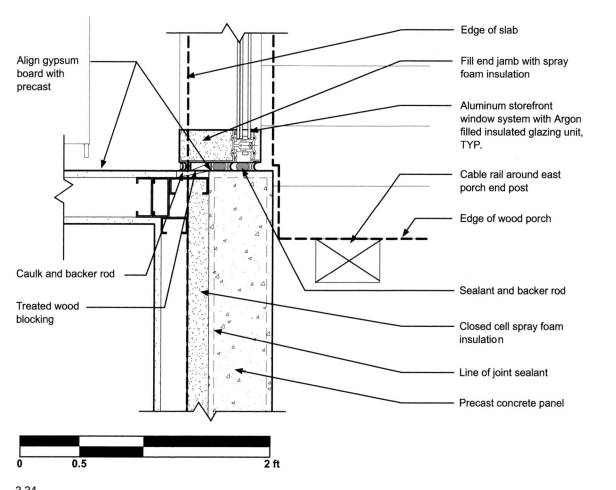

Align gypsum board with precast

Caulk and backer rod

Treated wood blocking

Edge of slab

Fill end jamb with spray foam insulation

Aluminum storefront window system with Argon filled insulated glazing unit, TYP.

Cable rail around east porch end post

Edge of wood porch

Sealant and backer rod

Closed cell spray foam insulation

Line of joint sealant

Precast concrete panel

0   0.5   2 ft

3.34
Plan detail: first floor gift shop 2

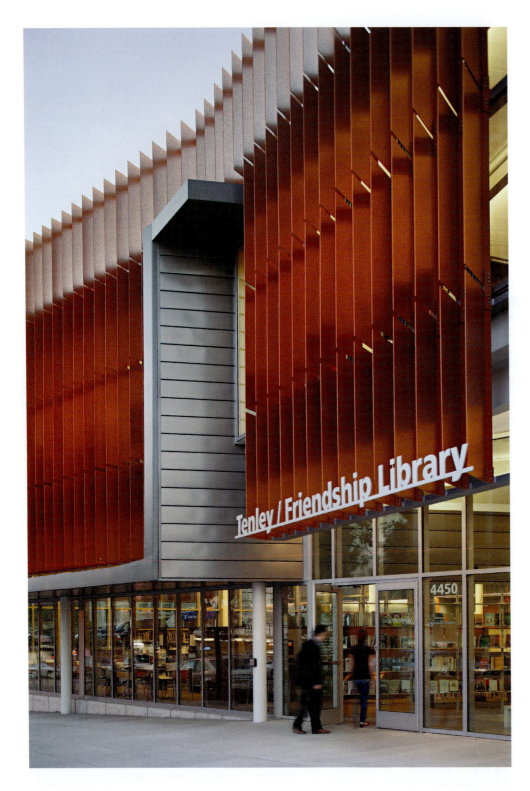

4.1
View of main entrance on east façade

Credit: Mark Herboth

4: Tenley-Friendship Library

Washington, DC, The Freelon Group (now part of Perkins + Will)

Architect's Design Intent and Reasoning Behind Material and Tectonic Choices

The Tenley-Friendship Libraries serves two distinct communities located in the northwest area of Washington DC – Tenleytown and Friendship Heights. Both communities are among the wealthiest in DC. They have historically been well served with good roads and public transportation and they are both currently served by the Washington Metropolitan Area Transit Authority's (WMATA) light rail Red Line. In 1890, the Washington streetcar service came to this area, running along Wisconsin Avenue (from Georgetown into Montgomery County, Maryland) until the service was abandoned in 1960.

Friendship Heights is a residential neighborhood and a commercial area that lies partly in Washington and partly in southern Montgomery County. In addition to single family and multi-family residences, Friendship Heights has a substantial shopping area surrounding the intersection of Wisconsin and Western Avenues.

Tenleytown is Washington DC's second oldest village, after Georgetown, and part of the sizable tract called "Friendship," named in recognition of the relationship between the two grantees to this land. The name Tenleytown for this particular part of Friendship goes back to 1790 when it was called Tennally's Town after John Tennally, owner of the local tavern at the intersection of River Road and what is now Wisconsin Avenue. The village slowly grew around this intersection and it became "Tenleytown" in the nineteenth century.

The context of the area is a rich mixture of historical and eclectic buildings comprising nostalgic places such as Fort Reno and the twentieth century landmark Sears Roebuck. As a part of the evolution of the community, the intent of the new library is to recognize and reinforce the character of the new contemporary urban fabric evolving in the community while respecting the traditional roots and history of Tenleytown.

Of particular interest and influence on the new design is the fusion of the historic town grid and the modern-day orthogonal street grid. The site for the new library sits at the intersection of these two grid systems at the corner of Wisconsin Avenue and Albemarle Street. The streets create a series of irregular or "polygonal" shaped sites in the area, one of which is the library site. These lines define the edges of the polygonal library form. Extrapolation of the grids further defines the geometry and interior spaces of the library massing. Some of the angles are also derived from the L'Enfant grid of DC, thus respecting the historical planning influences of the capital city master plan.

4.2
View of main east façade
Credit: Mark Herboth

4.3
View of northeast corner at twilight
Credit: Mark Herboth

4.4
View of north façade at twilight

Credit: Mark Herboth

4.5
View from second floor lobby looking north

Credit: Mark Herboth

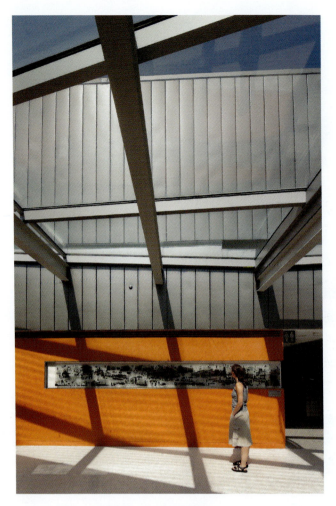

4.6
View of second floor atrium looking west
Credit: Mark Herboth

The site was also previously developed and by reusing this site in an urban area it was an excellent way to minimize encroachment on previously unused land and sustainably develop the project. Green space areas created on the site provide a site-balance of natural elements (including a rock garden, shrubs, trees, and vinery) against the building and hardscape, and hosts native and adaptive plants that require no irrigation to maintain. Transportation to the site is easier due to several bus stations and a WMATA light rail station located nearby. Also, the site offers the same number of parking spaces as the previous library, promoting the use of ride sharing, bicycles, walking, and public transportation.

Tenley-Friendship Library has historically been one of the busiest branches in the District of Columbia Public Library (DCPL) system, ranking third and averaging 6,373 circulations per month in fiscal year 2004, the last full year before closing. The new

4.7
View from first floor lobby looking north
Credit: Mark Herboth

interim library, with about 5,000 SF, averaged about 6,000 circulations per month in fiscal year 2007 even with its "soft opening" in January 2007. Indeed, during the last half of the fiscal year (March through September), the interim averaged over 7,700 items per month, a 21% increase over the former, much larger branch. The new, 21,500 SF library with a larger collection and more services is expected to greatly exceed the past circulation.

Inspiration for the library form is derived from an "open book" metaphor. The exterior skin of the building on the west side of the plan, in a theoretical sense, wraps the building like the hard back cover of a book. This "cover" abstractly acts as a protector of knowledge with its opaque skin. In contrast, the east elevation of the building is designed as a more transparent façade, as if it were a clear book cover, allowing views through the

4.8
View of second floor reading room looking south
Credit: Mark Herboth

skin. This façade welcomes pedestrians walking and traveling along Wisconsin Avenue and Albemarle Street. Conceived as pages of the book this façade is designed with copper fins reinforcing openness and transparency to the street.

The openness and transparency allows the reading rooms and stack areas to take advantage of natural day lighting for the interior spaces. The fins will allow the light to be diffused and controlled relative to glare.

As a plan parti, the major circulation runs down the center of the building dividing the plan into two "halves." This circulation spine also acts as a portal for funneling natural light into the center of the building, by way of a full skylight running its length, and a floor-to-ceiling curtain-wall system on both the North and South façades. The western half of the building houses the more program-specific and private functions, including staff workrooms, conferencing spaces, multi-purpose room, and general gross building functions (vertical circulation, restrooms, janitorial, etc.). In contrast, the eastern half is more fluidly public; primarily reserved for open stack areas, with seated reading spaces, and some private study rooms. The eastern half also receives the public through the major entry lobby positioned at northeast corner, off the intersection of Wisconsin Avenue and Albemarle Street.

The approximately 21,500 GSF program for the Library resolves itself into a two-story building with a partial third floor for mechanical equipment, a roof terrace and a green/garden roof. The new facility provides adult studies and computers, children's services, conference rooms, project work rooms, a young adults division, and office and work space for administration. The "active and fast" elements of the program are located on the first floor of the library while "slower and quite" areas of the program are located on the second floor.

The western façade of the library is designed as a party wall facing the Janney Elementary School. This windowless wall minimizes western heat gain to the building interior and allows for future adjacent development. The south elevation maintains a 20' 0" overhang from the second floor which allows for five covered parking spaces and sun shading of the first floor reading room areas. Service access to the building is also provided along this façade. The north and east façades along Albemarle Street and Wisconsin Avenue respectively, are the primary public faces of the project. One enters at the corner, beneath a slight overhang which houses the young adults program on the second floor, and is drawn inside along a two-sided transparent display wall into a two-story atrium space facing Albemarle Street. This lobby contains the elevator and a public monumental stair for the library which directs visitors upwards towards the second floor. The enclosed elements of the program such as the workroom, book drop, and meeting rooms are situated to the west side of the plan while allowing the eastern half to be maintained as open, high ceiling stack and seating areas.

The primary materials for the Library are glass curtain wall, perforated copper metal panel and architecturally treated concrete. The structural system is a combination of poured-in-place concrete and steel framing. The building exterior has several sustainable design elements. First, is the TPO white roofing that reflects sunlight to manage solar heat gain, which allows the HVAC system not to have to work as hard in the summer months. A green roof includes native and adaptive plantings that provide a natural insulation system for the roof. This minimizes solar heat gain and decreases the power load on the HVAC system that keeps the building cool during summer months. Solar hot water collectors are also placed on the roof to absorb solar heat energy to provide heated water to the building's lavatories. Natural lighting is emphasized through a center skylight to bring natural lighting deep into the bookstacks and main reading space, with exterior glazing to connect patrons with the outside and allow natural daylight to enter the space, ultimately helping to decrease the power load for electrical lighting. Another material used to decrease the heating and power load are perforated vertical sunshades that cover portions of the glass façade to help block unwanted heat gain and glare from the sun.

Additionally, sustainable building materials were used throughout the building. Recycled materials for the building's construction were used wherever possible, including content in the steel, glass, and concrete. Regional materials that were utilized for the building's construction were within a 500-mile radius of the site, and were given highest priority in order to minimize pollution caused by excessive transportation efforts. Interior materials like certified wood that comes from environmentally responsible companies, and materials with low VOCs (volatile organic compounds) that are typically found in common construction adhesives, sealants, paints, carpets, and composite wood, and are known to be odorous, irritating, and harmful to occupants were kept at low levels to prioritize better indoor air quality.

Ultimately the project will provide a destination that is a welcoming gathering place satisfying the need for prompt, convenient access to publications, information, and learning opportunities.

Zena Howard, AIA, LEED AP
Principal

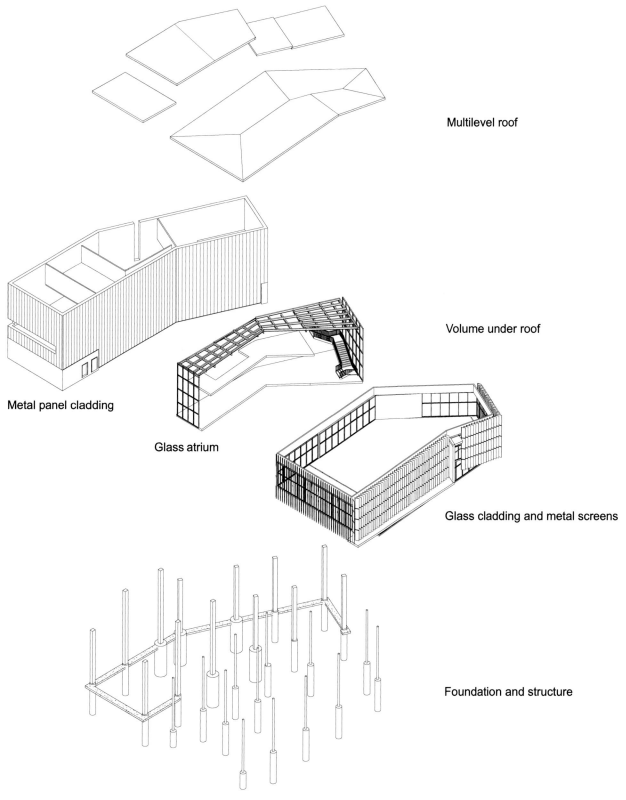

Multilevel roof

Volume under roof

Metal panel cladding

Glass atrium

Glass cladding and metal screens

Foundation and structure

4.9
Major building components
(Not to scale.)

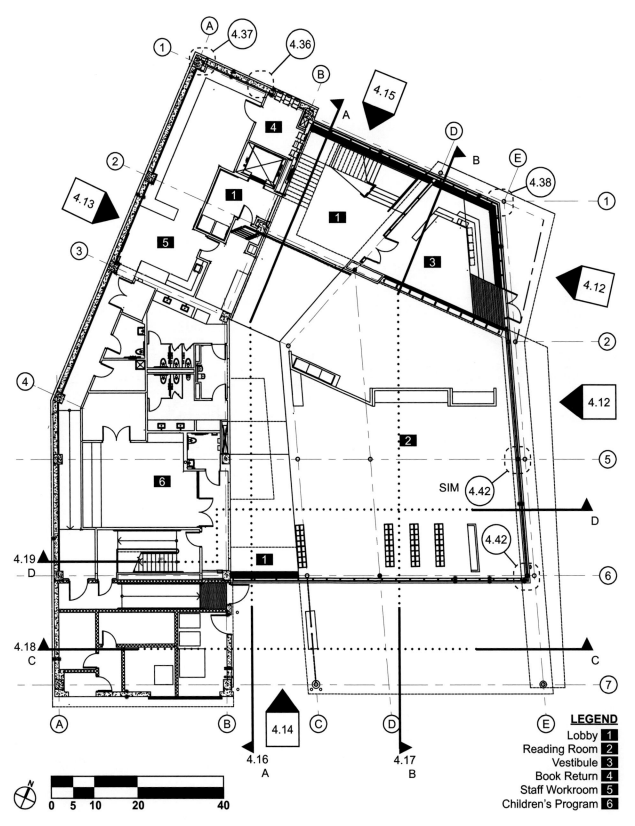

4.10
First floor plan

N
0 5 10   20   40

LEGEND
Lobby **1**
Reading Room **2**
Vestibule **3**
Book Return **4**
Staff Workroom **5**
Children's Program **6**

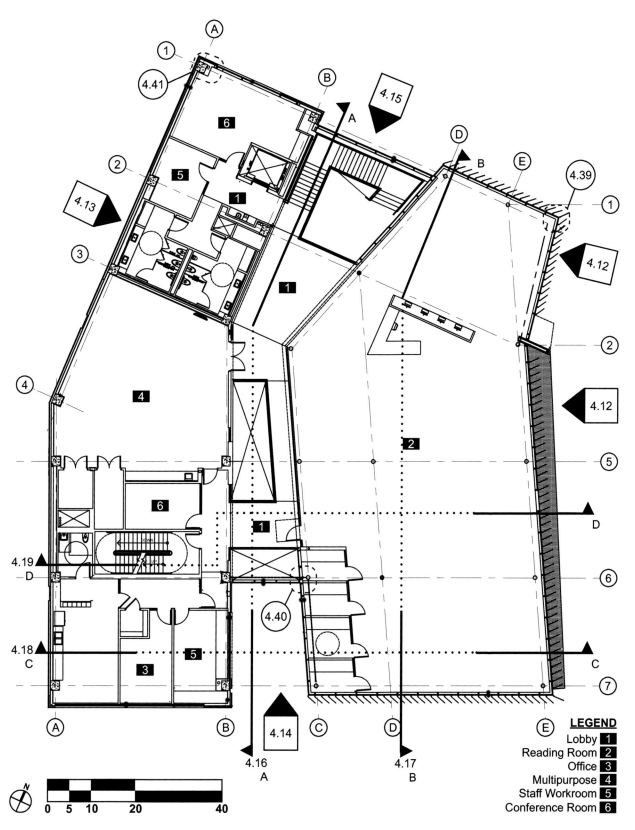

4.11
Second floor plan

LEGEND
Lobby 1
Reading Room 2
Office 3
Multipurpose 4
Staff Workroom 5
Conference Room 6

N
0 5 10 20 40

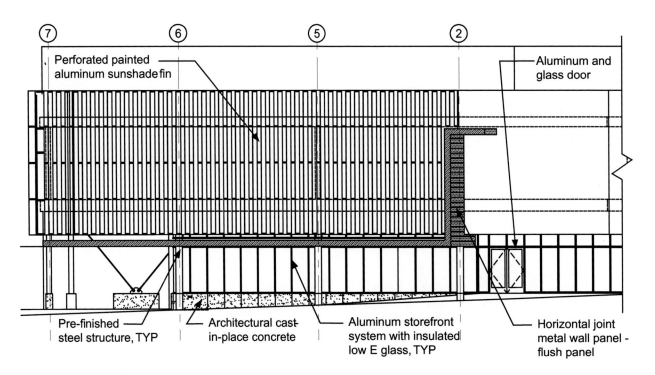

Perforated painted aluminum sunshade fin

Aluminum and glass door

Pre-finished steel structure, TYP

Architectural cast-in-place concrete

Aluminum storefront system with insulated low E glass, TYP

Horizontal joint metal wall panel - flush panel

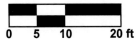
0   5   10   20 ft

4.12a
East entry elevation

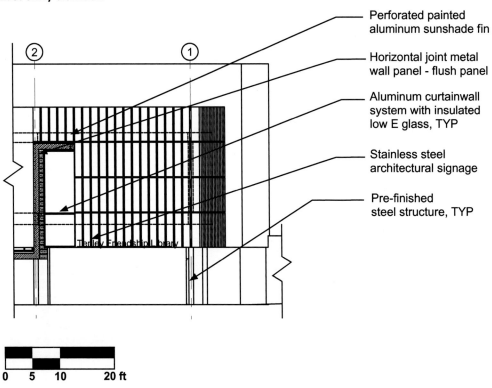

Perforated painted aluminum sunshade fin

Horizontal joint metal wall panel - flush panel

Aluminum curtainwall system with insulated low E glass, TYP

Stainless steel architectural signage

Pre-finished steel structure, TYP

Tenley-Friendship Library

0   5   10   20 ft

4.12b
East entry elevation

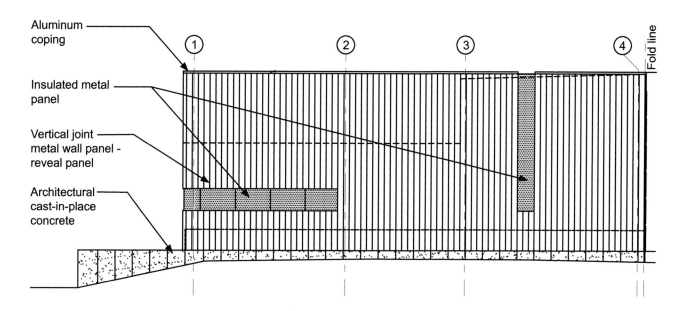

Aluminum coping

Insulated metal panel

Vertical joint metal wall panel - reveal panel

Architectural cast-in-place concrete

1   2   3   4

Fold line

0   5   10   20 ft

4.13a
West elevation (north)

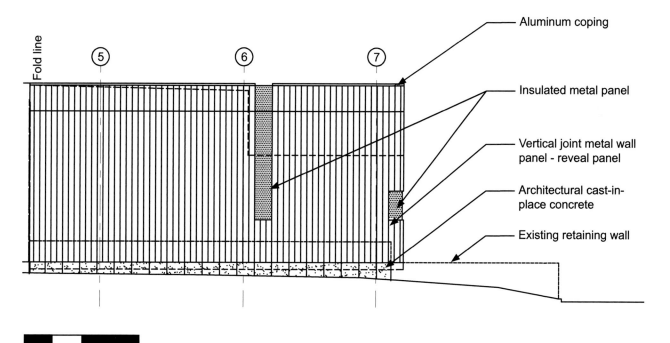

Fold line

5   6   7

Aluminum coping

Insulated metal panel

Vertical joint metal wall panel - reveal panel

Architectural cast-in-place concrete

Existing retaining wall

0   5   10   20 ft

4.13b
West elevation (south)

Tenley-Friendship Library

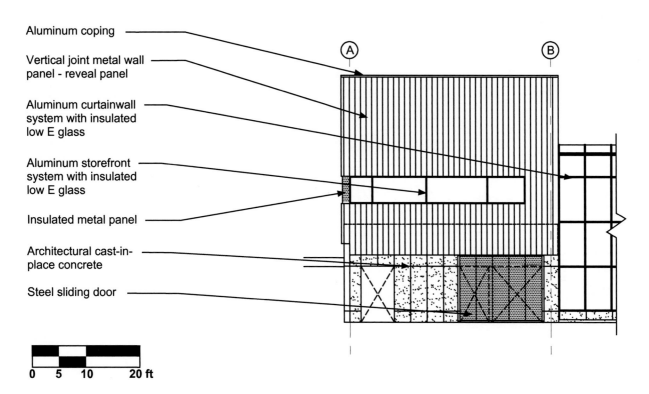

Aluminum coping

Vertical joint metal wall panel - reveal panel

Aluminum curtainwall system with insulated low E glass

Aluminum storefront system with insulated low E glass

Insulated metal panel

Architectural cast-in-place concrete

Steel sliding door

0 5 10 20 ft

4.14a
South elevation

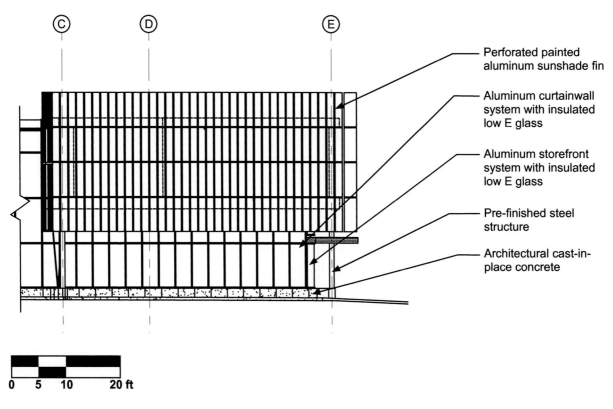

Perforated painted aluminum sunshade fin

Aluminum curtainwall system with insulated low E glass

Aluminum storefront system with insulated low E glass

Pre-finished steel structure

Architectural cast-in-place concrete

0 5 10 20 ft

4.14b
South elevation

124

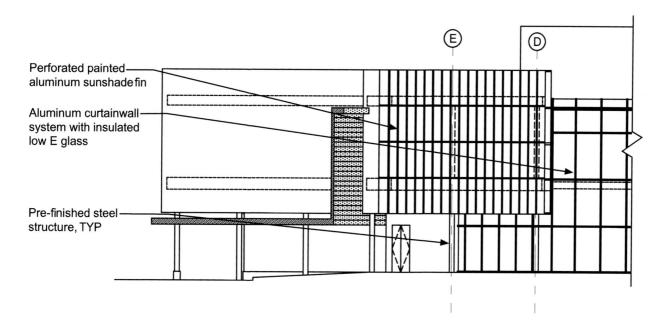

Perforated painted aluminum sunshade fin

Aluminum curtainwall system with insulated low E glass

Pre-finished steel structure, TYP

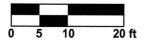
0   5   10   20 ft

4.15a
North elevation

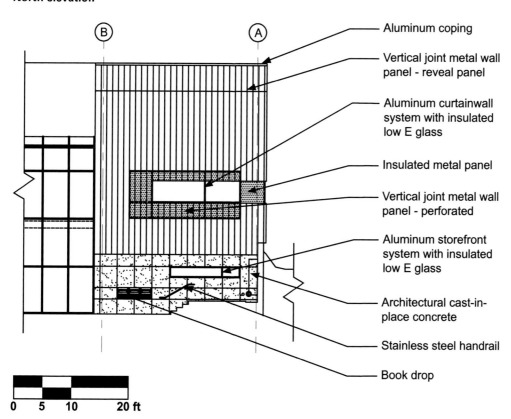

Aluminum coping

Vertical joint metal wall panel - reveal panel

Aluminum curtainwall system with insulated low E glass

Insulated metal panel

Vertical joint metal wall panel - perforated

Aluminum storefront system with insulated low E glass

Architectural cast-in-place concrete

Stainless steel handrail

Book drop

0   5   10   20 ft

4.15b
North elevation

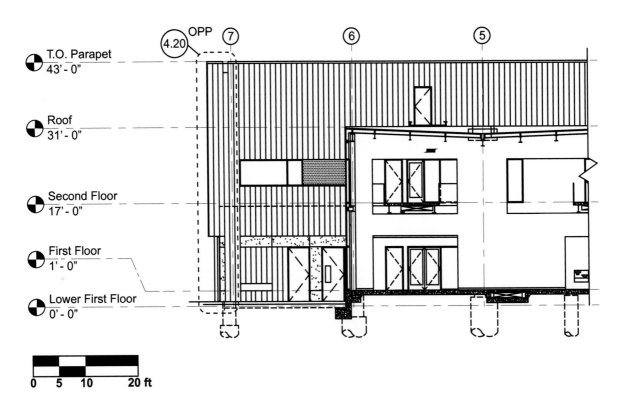

T.O. Parapet
43' - 0"

Roof
31' - 0"

Second Floor
17' - 0"

First Floor
1' - 0"

Lower First Floor
0' - 0"

0   5   10   20 ft

4.16a
South/north building section A-A

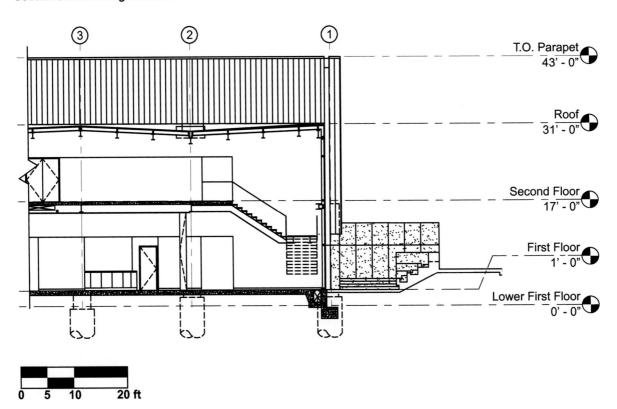

T.O. Parapet
43' - 0"

Roof
31' - 0"

Second Floor
17' - 0"

First Floor
1' - 0"

Lower First Floor
0' - 0"

0   5   10   20 ft

4.16b
South/north building section A-A

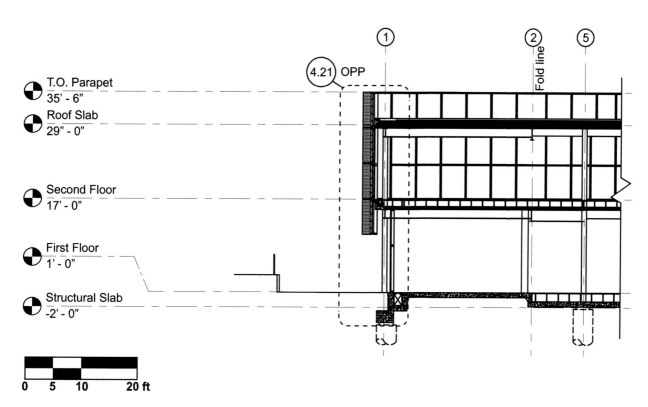

T.O. Parapet
35' - 6"

Roof Slab
29" - 0"

Second Floor
17' - 0"

First Floor
1' - 0"

Structural Slab
-2' - 0"

0 5 10 20 ft

4.17a
North/south building section B-B

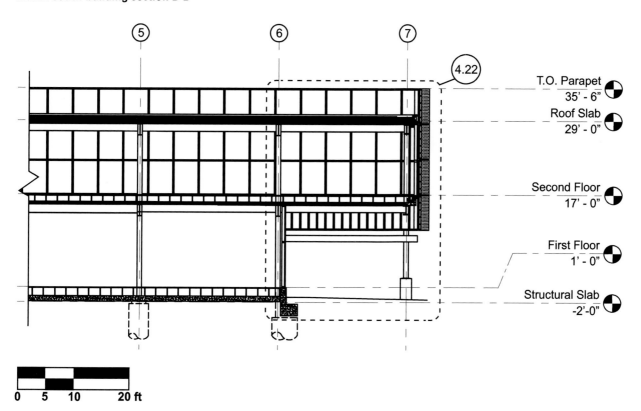

T.O. Parapet
35' - 6"

Roof Slab
29' - 0"

Second Floor
17' - 0"

First Floor
1' - 0"

Structural Slab
-2'-0"

0 5 10 20 ft

4.17b
North/south building section B-B

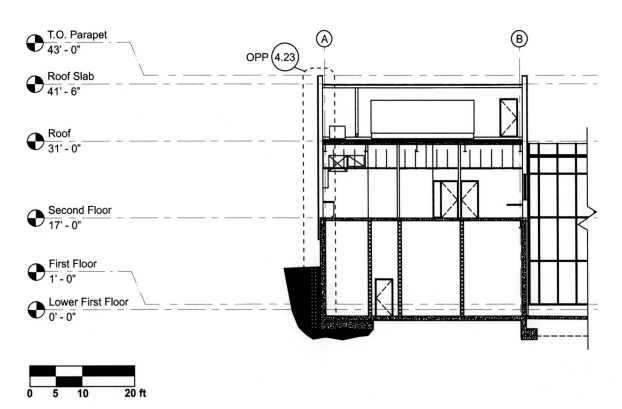

T.O. Parapet
43' - 0"

Roof Slab
41' - 6"

Roof
31' - 0"

Second Floor
17' - 0"

First Floor
1' - 0"

Lower First Floor
0' - 0"

OPP (4.23)

Ⓐ   Ⓑ

0   5   10   20 ft

4.18a
West/east building section C-C

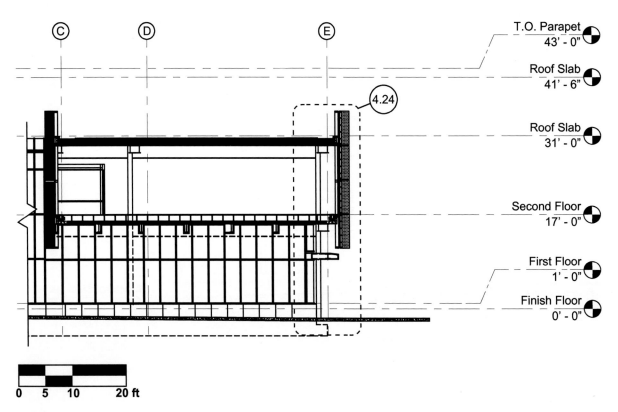

Ⓒ   Ⓓ   Ⓔ

(4.24)

T.O. Parapet
43' - 0"

Roof Slab
41' - 6"

Roof Slab
31' - 0"

Second Floor
17' - 0"

First Floor
1' - 0"

Finish Floor
0' - 0"

0   5   10   20 ft

4.18b
West/east building section C-C

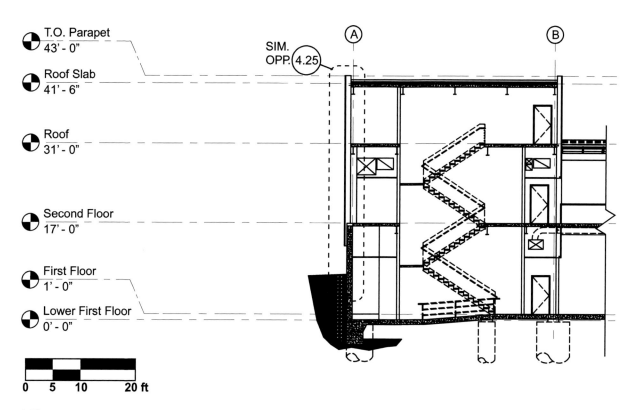

T.O. Parapet
43' - 0"

Roof Slab
41' - 6"

Roof
31' - 0"

Second Floor
17' - 0"

First Floor
1' - 0"

Lower First Floor
0' - 0"

SIM.
OPP. 4.25

Ⓐ   Ⓑ

0   5   10   20 ft

4.19a
West/east building section D-D

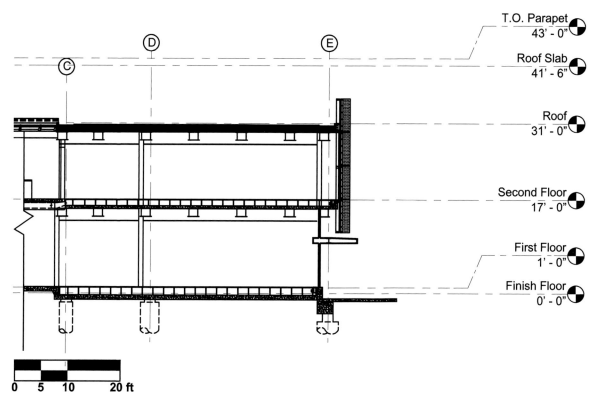

Ⓒ   Ⓓ   Ⓔ

T.O. Parapet
43' - 0"

Roof Slab
41' - 6"

Roof
31' - 0"

Second Floor
17' - 0"

First Floor
1' - 0"

Finish Floor
0' - 0"

0   5   10   20 ft

4.19b
West/east building section D-D

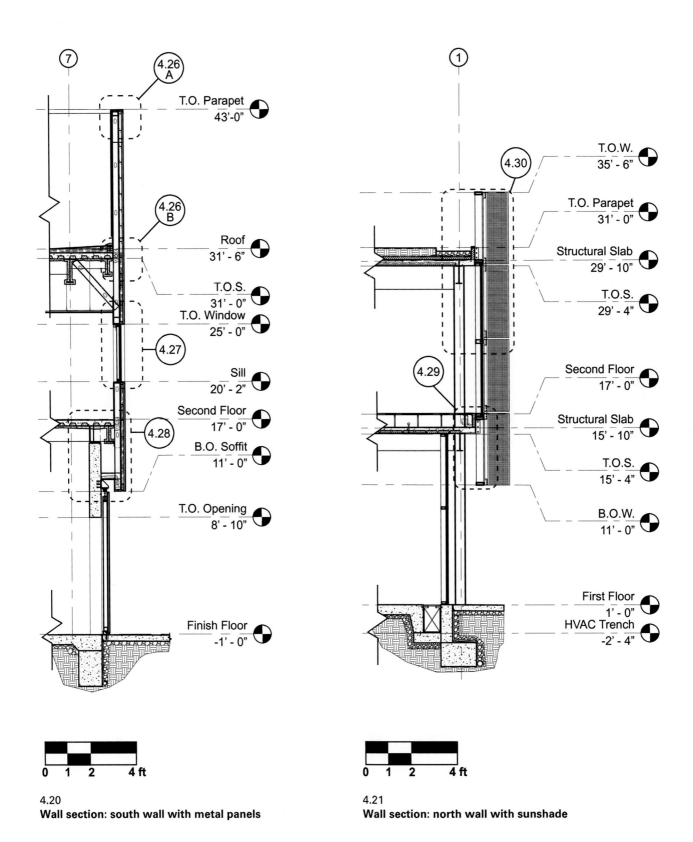

7

4.26
A

T.O. Parapet
43'-0"

4.26
B

Roof
31' - 6"

T.O.S.
31' - 0"

T.O. Window
25' - 0"

4.27

Sill
20' - 2"

Second Floor
17' - 0"

4.28

B.O. Soffit
11' - 0"

T.O. Opening
8' - 10"

Finish Floor
-1' - 0"

1

4.30

T.O.W.
35' - 6"

T.O. Parapet
31' - 0"

Structural Slab
29' - 10"

T.O.S.
29' - 4"

4.29

Second Floor
17' - 0"

Structural Slab
15' - 10"

T.O.S.
15' - 4"

B.O.W.
11' - 0"

First Floor
1' - 0"

HVAC Trench
-2' - 4"

0   1   2   4 ft

0   1   2   4 ft

4.20
Wall section: south wall with metal panels

4.21
Wall section: north wall with sunshade

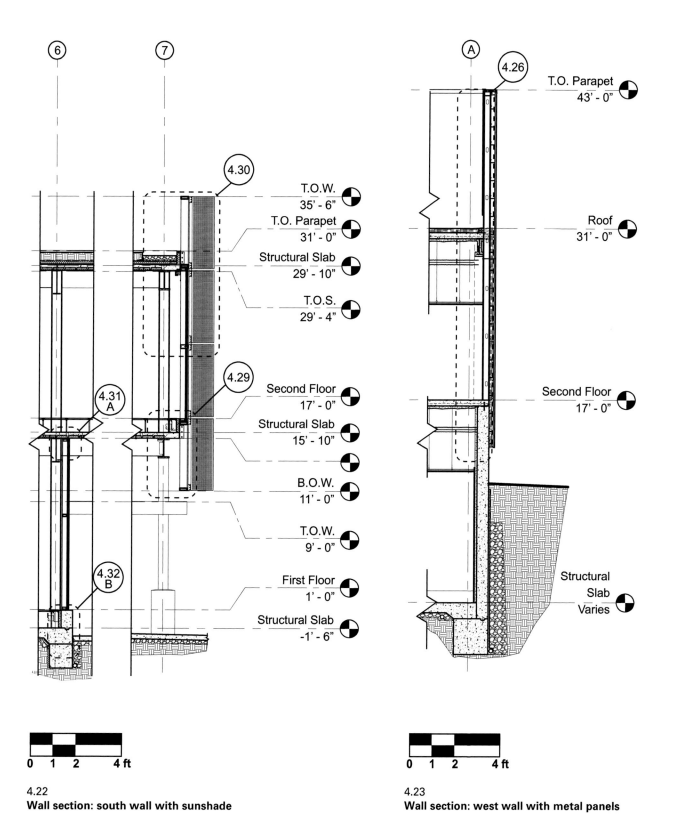

6 7

4.30

T.O.W.
35' - 6"

T.O. Parapet
31' - 0"

Structural Slab
29' - 10"

T.O.S.
29' - 4"

4.31
A

4.29

Second Floor
17' - 0"

Structural Slab
15' - 10"

B.O.W.
11' - 0"

T.O.W.
9' - 0"

4.32
B

First Floor
1' - 0"

Structural Slab
-1' - 6"

0 1 2   4 ft

4.22
Wall section: south wall with sunshade

A

4.26

T.O. Parapet
43' - 0"

Roof
31' - 0"

Second Floor
17' - 0"

Structural
Slab
Varies

0 1 2   4 ft

4.23
Wall section: west wall with metal panels

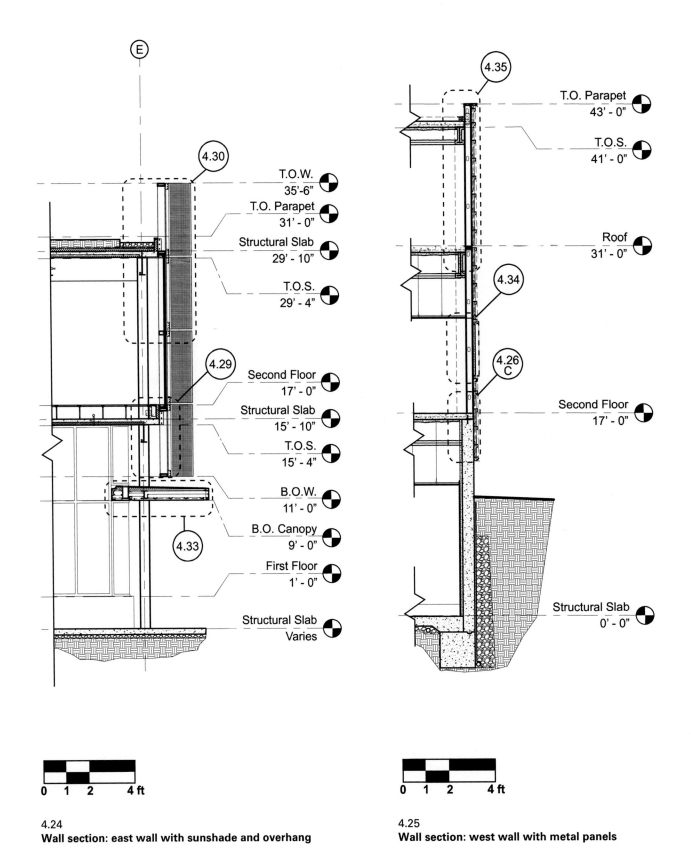

4.24
Wall section: east wall with sunshade and overhang

4.25
Wall section: west wall with metal panels

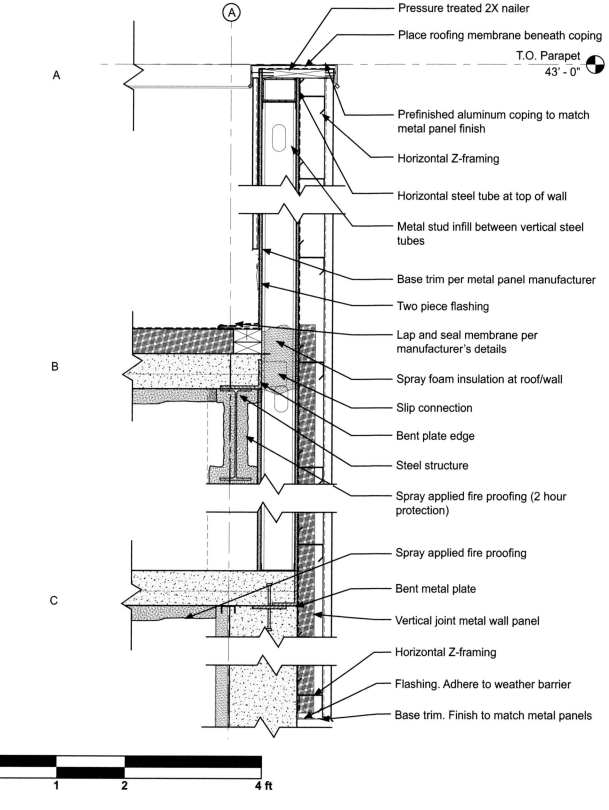

Pressure treated 2X nailer

Place roofing membrane beneath coping

T.O. Parapet
43' - 0"

Prefinished aluminum coping to match metal panel finish

Horizontal Z-framing

Horizontal steel tube at top of wall

Metal stud infill between vertical steel tubes

Base trim per metal panel manufacturer

Two piece flashing

Lap and seal membrane per manufacturer's details

Spray foam insulation at roof/wall

Slip connection

Bent plate edge

Steel structure

Spray applied fire proofing (2 hour protection)

Spray applied fire proofing

Bent metal plate

Vertical joint metal wall panel

Horizontal Z-framing

Flashing. Adhere to weather barrier

Base trim. Finish to match metal panels

A

B

C

0   1   2   4 ft

4.26
Section detail: tall parapet at metal wall panel

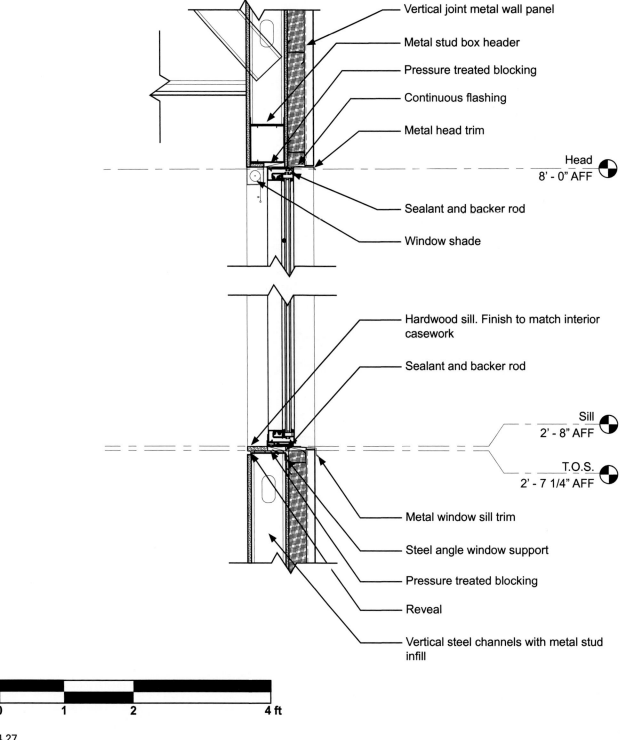

Vertical joint metal wall panel

Metal stud box header

Pressure treated blocking

Continuous flashing

Metal head trim

Head
8' - 0" AFF

Sealant and backer rod

Window shade

Hardwood sill. Finish to match interior casework

Sealant and backer rod

Sill
2' - 8" AFF

T.O.S.
2' - 7 1/4" AFF

Metal window sill trim

Steel angle window support

Pressure treated blocking

Reveal

Vertical steel channels with metal stud infill

0 1 2 4 ft

4.27
Section detail: window at metal wall panel

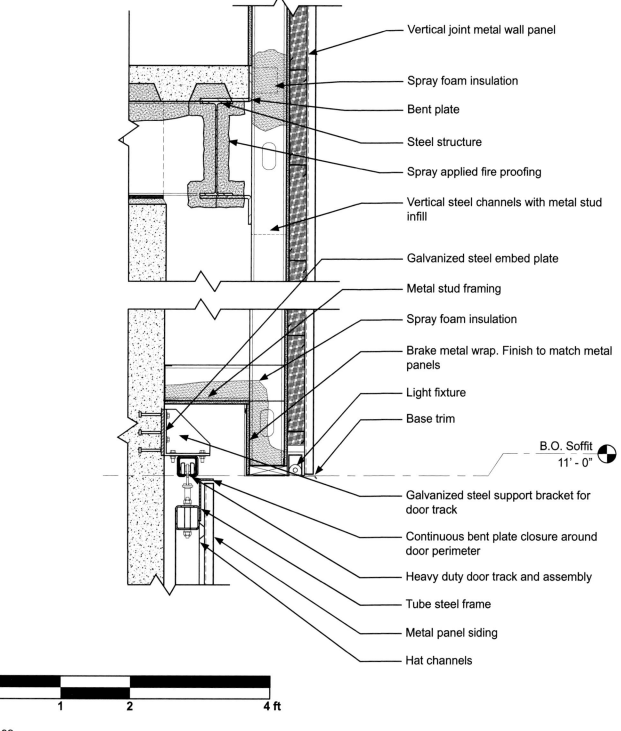

Vertical joint metal wall panel

Spray foam insulation

Bent plate

Steel structure

Spray applied fire proofing

Vertical steel channels with metal stud infill

Galvanized steel embed plate

Metal stud framing

Spray foam insulation

Brake metal wrap. Finish to match metal panels

Light fixture

Base trim

B.O. Soffit
11' - 0"

Galvanized steel support bracket for door track

Continuous bent plate closure around door perimeter

Heavy duty door track and assembly

Tube steel frame

Metal panel siding

Hat channels

0   1   2   4 ft

4.28
Section detail: track door at metal wall panel

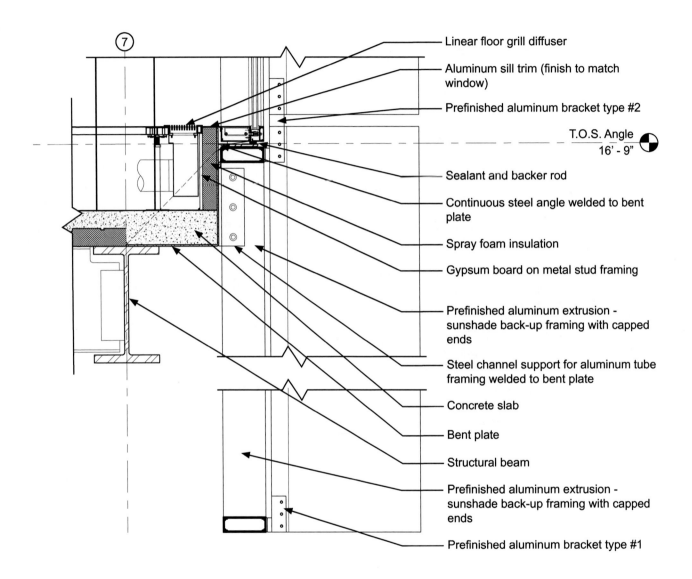

Linear floor grill diffuser

Aluminum sill trim (finish to match window)

Prefinished aluminum bracket type #2

T.O.S. Angle
16' - 9"

Sealant and backer rod

Continuous steel angle welded to bent plate

Spray foam insulation

Gypsum board on metal stud framing

Prefinished aluminum extrusion - sunshade back-up framing with capped ends

Steel channel support for aluminum tube framing welded to bent plate

Concrete slab

Bent plate

Structural beam

Prefinished aluminum extrusion - sunshade back-up framing with capped ends

Prefinished aluminum bracket type #1

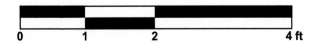

0   1   2   4 ft

4.29
Section detail: sunshade base structure

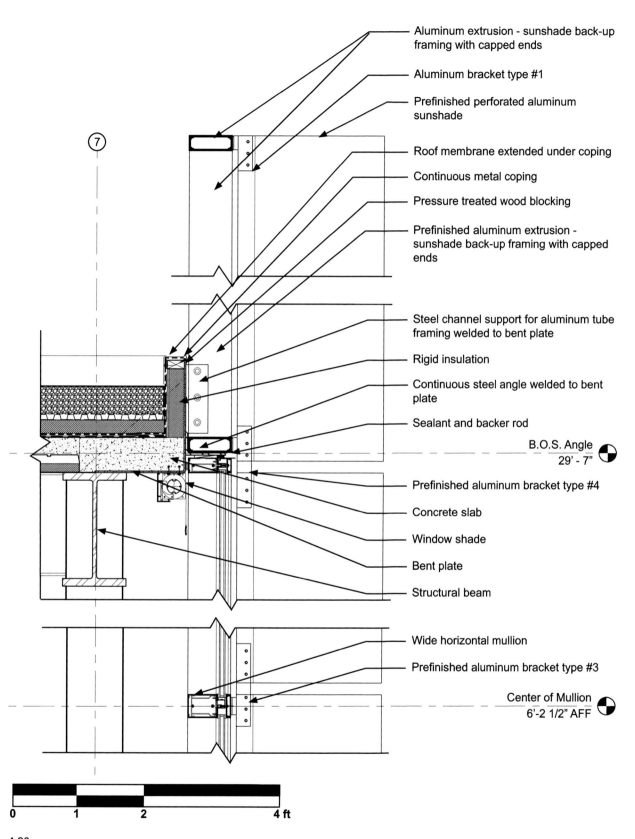

⑦

Aluminum extrusion - sunshade back-up framing with capped ends

Aluminum bracket type #1

Prefinished perforated aluminum sunshade

Roof membrane extended under coping

Continuous metal coping

Pressure treated wood blocking

Prefinished aluminum extrusion - sunshade back-up framing with capped ends

Steel channel support for aluminum tube framing welded to bent plate

Rigid insulation

Continuous steel angle welded to bent plate

Sealant and backer rod

B.O.S. Angle
29' - 7"

Prefinished aluminum bracket type #4

Concrete slab

Window shade

Bent plate

Structural beam

Wide horizontal mullion

Prefinished aluminum bracket type #3

Center of Mullion
6'-2 1/2" AFF

0   1   2   4 ft

4.30
Section detail: sunshade soffit structure

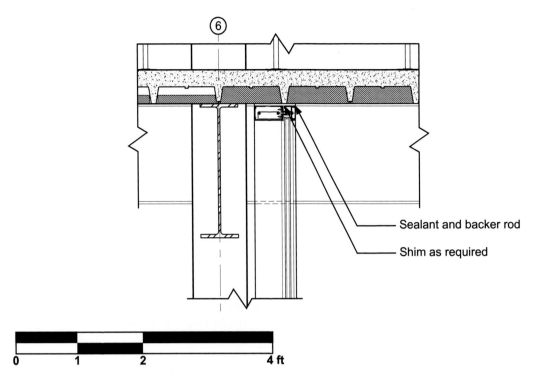

— Sealant and backer rod

— Shim as required

0 1 2 4 ft

4.31
Section detail: head at exterior glazing

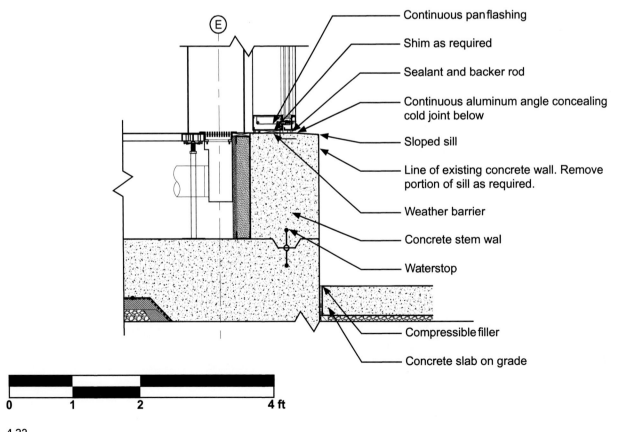

— Continuous pan flashing

— Shim as required

— Sealant and backer rod

— Continuous aluminum angle concealing cold joint below

— Sloped sill

— Line of existing concrete wall. Remove portion of sill as required.

— Weather barrier

— Concrete stem wal

— Waterstop

— Compressible filler

— Concrete slab on grade

0 1 2 4 ft

4.32
Section detail: sill at exterior glazing

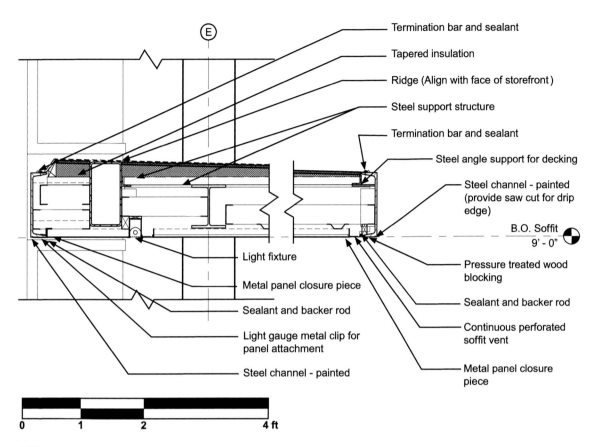

Termination bar and sealant

Tapered insulation

Ridge (Align with face of storefront)

Steel support structure

Termination bar and sealant

Steel angle support for decking

Steel channel - painted (provide saw cut for drip edge)

B.O. Soffit
9' - 0"

Pressure treated wood blocking

Sealant and backer rod

Continuous perforated soffit vent

Metal panel closure piece

Light fixture

Metal panel closure piece

Sealant and backer rod

Light gauge metal clip for panel attachment

Steel channel - painted

0   1   2   4 ft

4.33
Section detail: east wall overhang

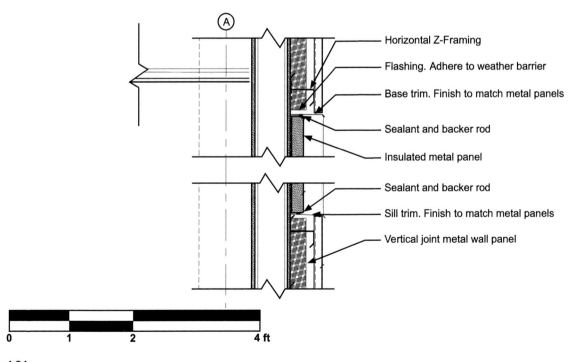

Horizontal Z-Framing

Flashing. Adhere to weather barrier

Base trim. Finish to match metal panels

Sealant and backer rod

Insulated metal panel

Sealant and backer rod

Sill trim. Finish to match metal panels

Vertical joint metal wall panel

0   1   2   4 ft

4.34
Section detail: insulated wall panel connection

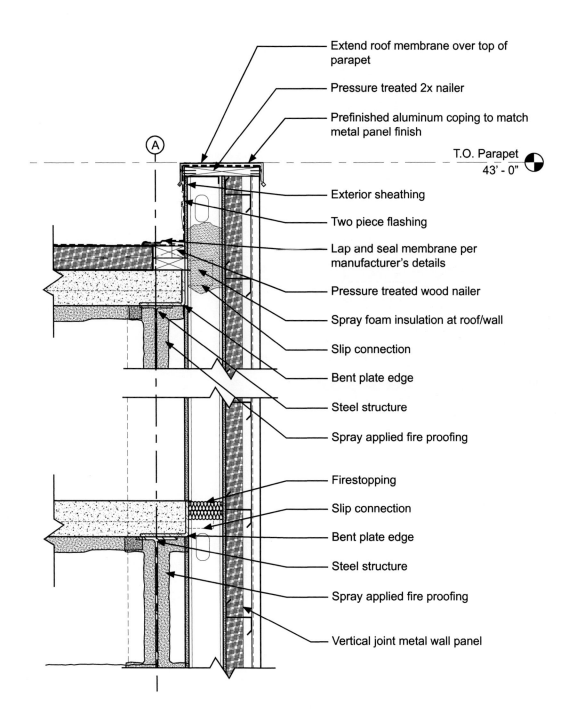

Extend roof membrane over top of parapet

Pressure treated 2x nailer

Prefinished aluminum coping to match metal panel finish

T.O. Parapet
43' - 0"

Exterior sheathing

Two piece flashing

Lap and seal membrane per manufacturer's details

Pressure treated wood nailer

Spray foam insulation at roof/wall

Slip connection

Bent plate edge

Steel structure

Spray applied fire proofing

Firestopping

Slip connection

Bent plate edge

Steel structure

Spray applied fire proofing

Vertical joint metal wall panel

Ⓐ

| 0 | 1 | 2 | | 4 ft |

4.35
Section detail: short parapet at metal wall panel

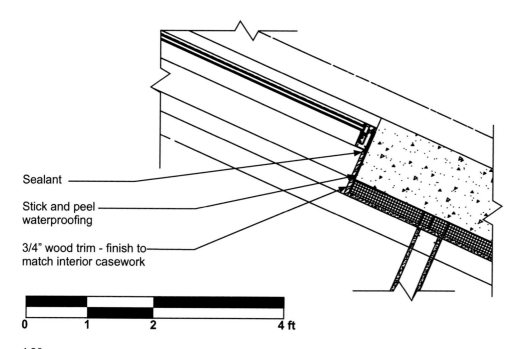

Sealant

Stick and peel
waterproofing

3/4" wood trim - finish to
match interior casework

0   1   2   4 ft

4.36
Plan detail: window jamb at clerestory in staff workroom

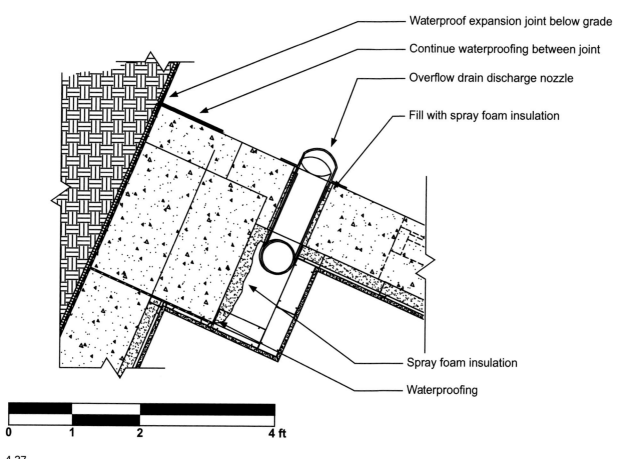

Waterproof expansion joint below grade

Continue waterproofing between joint

Overflow drain discharge nozzle

Fill with spray foam insulation

Spray foam insulation

Waterproofing

0   1   2   4 ft

4.37
Plan detail: overflow drain at column 1-A

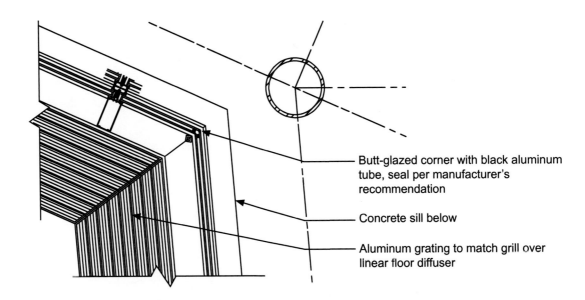

4.38
Plan detail: glazing at first floor northeast corner

Butt-glazed corner with black aluminum tube, seal per manufacturer's recommendation

Concrete sill below

Aluminum grating to match grill over linear floor diffuser

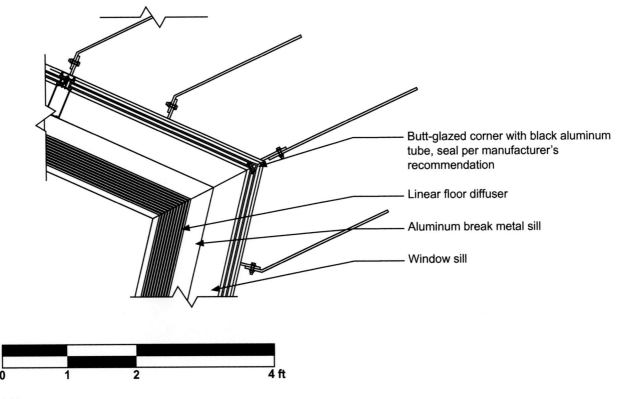

Butt-glazed corner with black aluminum tube, seal per manufacturer's recommendation

Linear floor diffuser

Aluminum break metal sill

Window sill

4.39
Plan detail: sunshades and glazing at second floor northeast corner

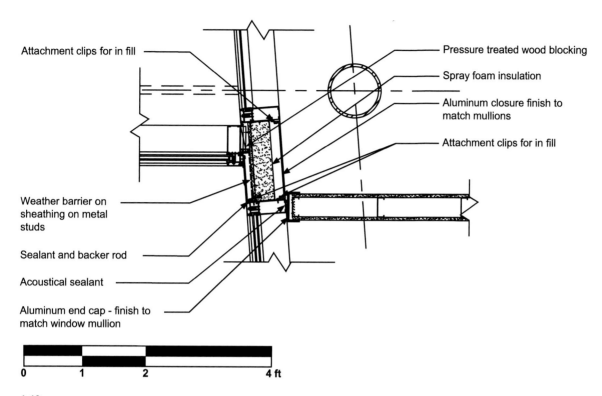

Attachment clips for in fill

Pressure treated wood blocking

Spray foam insulation

Aluminum closure finish to match mullions

Attachment clips for in fill

Weather barrier on sheathing on metal studs

Sealant and backer rod

Acoustical sealant

Aluminum end cap - finish to match window mullion

0   1   2   4 ft

4.40
Plan detail: wall intersection at column 6-C

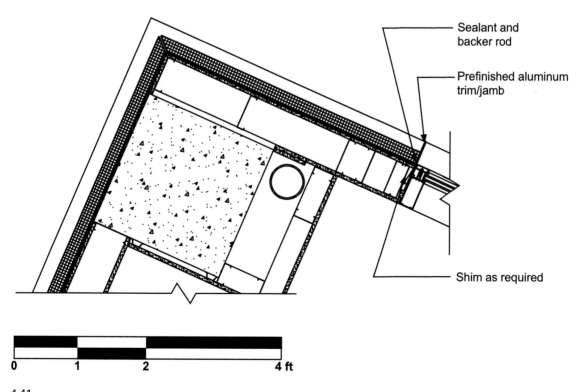

Sealant and backer rod

Prefinished aluminum trim/jamb

Shim as required

0   1   2   4 ft

4.41
Plan detail: window jamb at column 1-A

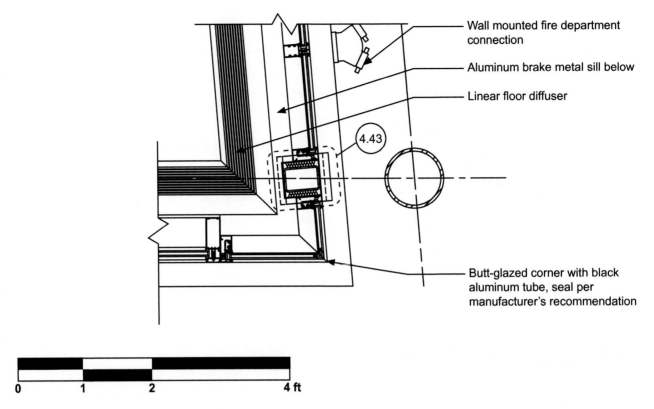

Wall mounted fire department connection

Aluminum brake metal sill below

Linear floor diffuser

Butt-glazed corner with black aluminum tube, seal per manufacturer's recommendation

4.42
Plan detail: glazing at first floor southeast corner

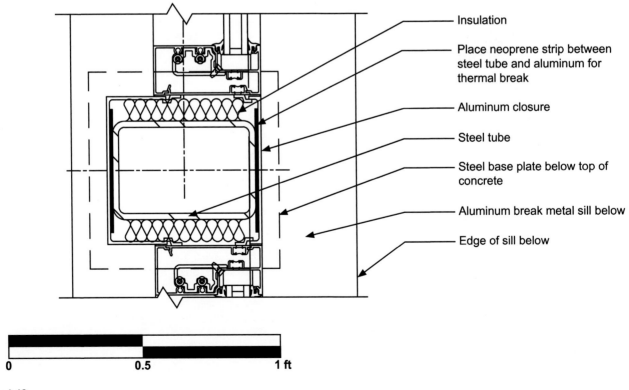

Insulation

Place neoprene strip between steel tube and aluminum for thermal break

Aluminum closure

Steel tube

Steel base plate below top of concrete

Aluminum break metal sill below

Edge of sill below

4.43
Plan detail: enlarged glazing structure at first floor southeast corner

5.1
View of east façade looking north

Credit: Lake Flato, Orcutt Winslow, and Bill Timmerman

5: Arizona State University Health Services Building

Tempe, AZ, Lake | Flato Architects in association with Orcutt | Winslow

Architect's Design Intent and Reasoning Behind Material and Tectonic Choices

The 39,600 SF Arizona State University Health Services Building (ASU HSB) is an adaptive reuse project that transformed the existing sterile health clinic into a clearly organized, efficient, and welcoming facility. The design imbues the new facility with a sense of health and wellness that leverages Tempe's natural environment and contributes to a more cohesive pedestrian-oriented campus. The renovated facility, new wing, and entry pavilion energizes the surrounding campus by engaging the historic Palm Walk – the campus' main pedestrian spine.

This project entailed the demolition of approximately 15,000 SF of a single-story facility; the renovation of 14,000 SF of an existing two-story structure containing administrative support, labs, wellness programs; and the addition of a new 21,330 SF two-story wing containing campus health clinics. In terms of both energy and campus engagement, the design transformed the existing, underperforming health clinic into an engaging and vibrant wellness center that is one of the best energy performers on campus as evidenced by ASU's Campus Metabolism, an interactive web-tool tracking real-time resource use. The building's energy performance is 49% below ASHRAE 90.1-2007, exceeding the current target of the 2030 Challenge. ASU HSB is certified LEED Platinum.

During the initial sustainability charrette, the design team, owner, user groups, student representatives, and consultants established the goal of meeting the 2012 target for the 2030 Challenge. Through an integrated process, a series of incremental efforts contribute to the building's 49% energy reduction below ASHRAE 90.1-2007 – including the elimination of thermal bridging, increased thermal barriers, high-efficiency mechanical systems, strategically located and high-performance glazing, and effective daylighting. The result is performance that exceeds the current target of the 2030 Challenge.

ASU HSB also reflects a "big picture" approach to sustainable design through strategic incorporation of campus context and biophilia. First, the design team reconsidered the university's planning concept and recommended an alternative scheme that reduced the building's program by 12% and footprint by 20%, preserving 5,000 SF of green space for wellness programming. Second, by employing regional material selection, access to daylight, and the use of programmed landscaped space, the

5.2
View of east façade at dusk

Credit: Lake Flato, Orcutt Winslow, and Bill Timmerman

5.3
View of east façade looking south

Credit: Lake Flato, Orcutt Winslow, and Bill Timmerman

5.4
East façade main entrance

Credit: Lake Flato, Orcutt Winslow, and Bill Timmerman

5.5
East façade lobby trellis

Credit: Lake Flato, Orcutt Winslow, and Bill Timmerman

5.6
Screen detail at west and south façades
Credit: Lake Flato, Orcutt Winslow, and Bill Timmerman

design reinforces the relationship between occupants and the natural environment. The project's biophilic design significantly contributes to the owner's primary goal of deinstitutionalizing the facility and fostering a sense of health and wellness within a welcoming environment in order to change the student and faculty perception of a "health clinic" and encourage the adoption of "healthy lifestyles."

The new entry pavilion is located along the intersection of a pedestrian bridge, the Palm Walk, residential core, and the main city street on campus with several bus stops and light rail nearby. As a result, the site has become a campus portal where commuters transition from bus, car, light rail, and bicycle at the pedestrian core. The site is reinforced with secure bike and skateboard racks, serving over 17% of the facility's occupants.

5.7
Interior lobby

Credit: Lake Flato, Orcutt
Winslow, and Bill Timmerman

5.8
Interior stair

Credit: Lake Flato, Orcutt
Winslow, and Bill Timmerman

5.9
View of reception at main entrance
Credit: Lake Flato, Orcutt Winslow, and Bill Timmerman

The design replaces 10,000 SF of turf grass with native landscaping that strengthens the Palm Walk and provides small landscaped courts serving as reflective spaces and outdoor waiting areas. The landscaping creates a sense of privacy for both the interior and exterior clinic waiting areas. The design team was able to convince ASU to rethink their initial proposed concept in order to preserve 5,000 SF of open green space for wellness programs. 80% of occupants use public transit, cycling or walking as means of transportation.

The built facility represents a significant departure from the university's original approach to the building's phasing and expansion. At the project's inception, the university proposed maintaining the entire existing facility and adding a new two-story 9,000 SF addition to the north end of the site upon existing open green space. Through a thorough programming and cost analysis process, the design team recommended renovating the 1950s 14,500 SF two-story wing, deconstructing the oldest and least efficient single-story part of the facility, and constructing a new 21,330 SF two-story addition in its place. The solution significantly increased the facility's efficiency, as discussed earlier. Additionally, the revised concept enabled the renovated facility's main entrance to be located on the historic Palm Walk, the campus's main pedestrian spine, resulting in a more accessible facility and vibrant pedestrian campus. The revised concept also facilitated the removal of turf grass, replaced by native landscaping irrigated by rainwater harvested from the facility's roofs and stored in sub-grade cisterns.

When selecting materials, the first priority was to do more with less. Recycling the original Health Services Building allowed the team to reuse 76% of the existing structure. The team also eliminated extraneous finishes, exposing systems that celebrate the building while minimizing maintenance.

On the exterior, the design uses regional materials appropriate for the harsh Tempe environment and native to the campus: Brick, natural metal panels, exposed weathered steel, and stained concrete. Overhangs and screens of recycled composite wood are incorporated to protect glazing and preserve the building envelope. The screens act as armatures for vines and create a "living" building, becoming lusher over time while mitigating the thermal loads.

Materials were also selected to reinforce the building's sense of wellness and health. The interior palette employs natural materials, such as stained FSC (Forest Stewardship Council) certified wood screens and ceilings panels, natural earthen plaster, oiled steel plate, and ground fly-ash concrete with local earth-toned aggregate. The material selection creates calming, biophilic spaces that deinstitutionalize the facility and draw students to its wellness programs.

The building is mechanically ventilated and conditioned with multiple-zone recirculating systems, and outdoor air intake ventilation rates that exceed ASHRAE 62.1-2007 requirements by 30%. The project minimizes exposure to environmental tobacco smoke by prohibiting smoking within the building and within 25' 0" of all entries, outdoor air intakes, and operable windows.

The student group GreenLight Solutions is currently working with the design and construction team, collecting comprehensive data on each building product to calculate the project's carbon footprint using the Athena Sustainable Materials Institute's EcoCalculator.

Additionally, the design imbues the new facility with a sense of health and wellness that leverages Tempe's natural environment by creating meaningful and useful connections to the outdoors. Working off the existing lobby, the interior public circulation is located along the east side, parallel to the Palm Walk. A series of two-story bays punctuate the linear circulation, providing intimate and private waiting areas for patients. These lower-scaled bays frame and provide easy access to a series of native landscaped courts that serve as exterior waiting areas.

Similarly, a tall steel trellis that will be covered with vines in the next couple of years on the north side of the entry pavilion also serves as an exterior waiting area while controlling direct sun penetration from the east orientation. Strategic glazing location and self-shading along the east elevation provide generous daylight within the entire public circulation zone and waiting areas.

The project engages and activates the historic Palm Walk – the main pedestrian avenue on campus – resulting in a more vibrant, cohesive campus fabric. Whereas the disjointed existing building provided little order for the Palm Walk, the transformed facility's main entry pavilion directly engages the pedestrian core, welcoming students and faculty under shady porches and the vine-planted trellis.

Andrew Herdeg, FAIA | Partner, Lake | Flato
Project Role: Design Partner-in-Charge

Ted Flato, FAIA | Founding Partner, Lake | Flato
Project Role: Design Advisor

Bill Sheely, AIA, ACHA | Partner, Orcutt | Winslow
Project Role: Partner-in-Charge

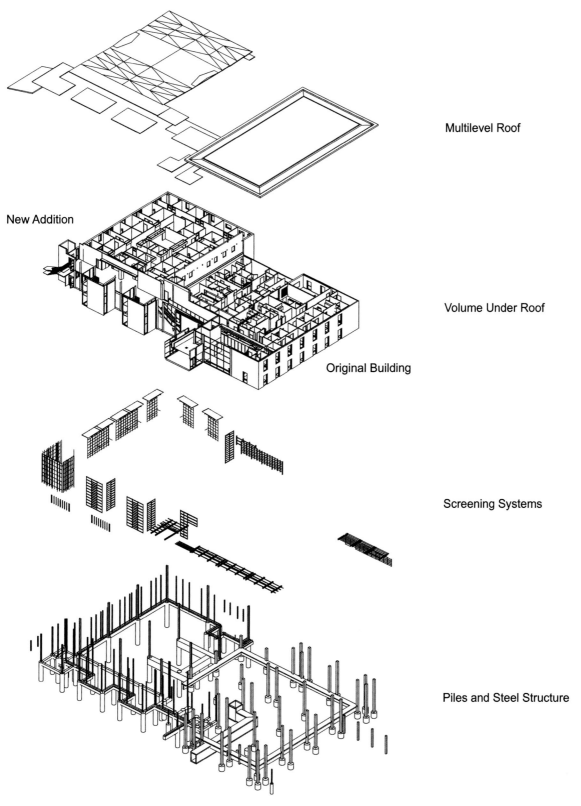

Multilevel Roof

New Addition

Volume Under Roof

Original Building

Screening Systems

Piles and Steel Structure

5.10
Major building components
(Not to scale.)

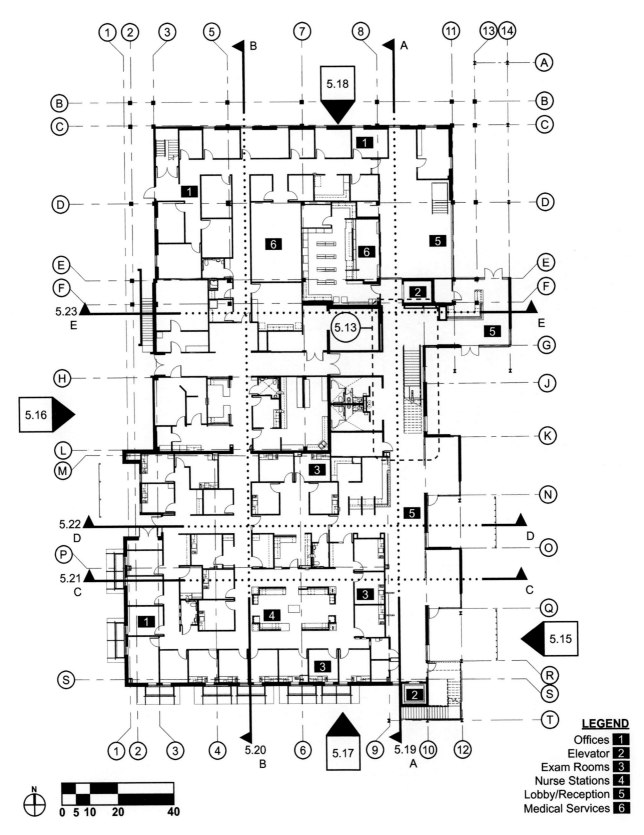

5.18

5.23

5.16

5.22

5.21

5.15

5.20
B

5.17

5.19

LEGEND
Offices 1
Elevator 2
Exam Rooms 3
Nurse Stations 4
Lobby/Reception 5
Medical Services 6

N
0 5 10 20 40

5.11
First floor plan

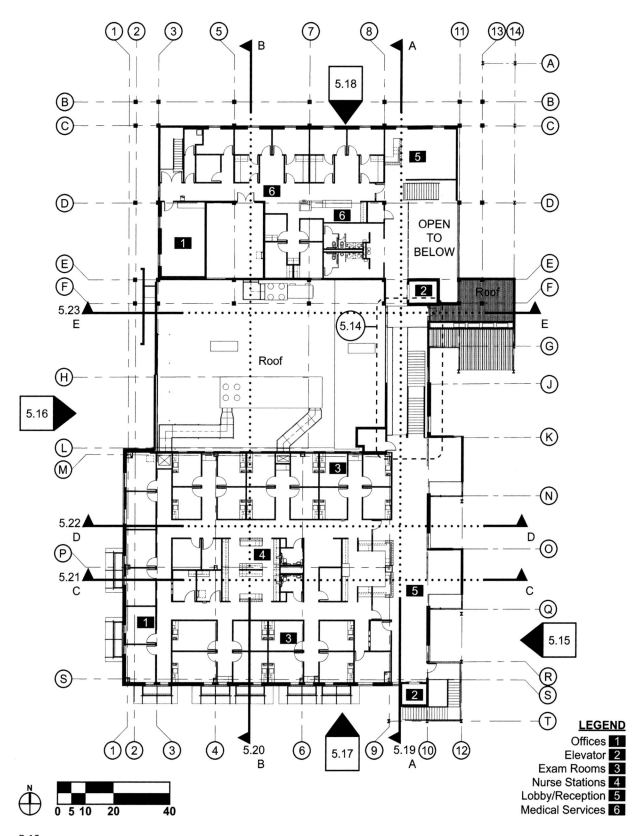

5.12
Second floor plan

LEGEND
Offices **1**
Elevator **2**
Exam Rooms **3**
Nurse Stations **4**
Lobby/Reception **5**
Medical Services **6**

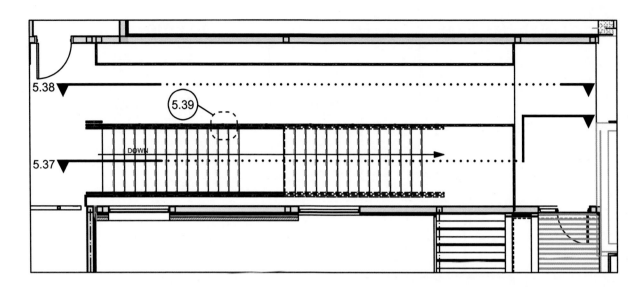

0   2   4   8 ft

5.13
Enlarged plan: first floor east stair

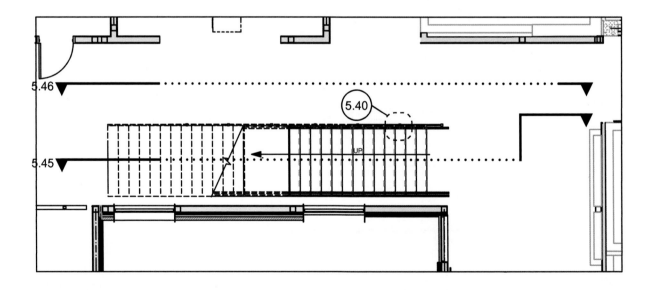

0   2   4   8 ft

5.14
Enlarged plan: second floor east stair

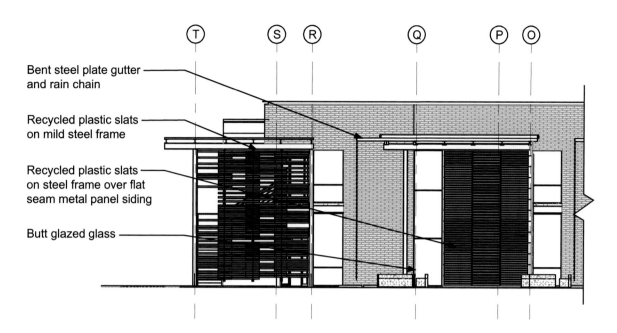

Bent steel plate gutter and rain chain

Recycled plastic slats on mild steel frame

Recycled plastic slats on steel frame over flat seam metal panel siding

Butt glazed glass

0 5 10 20 ft

5.15a
East elevation

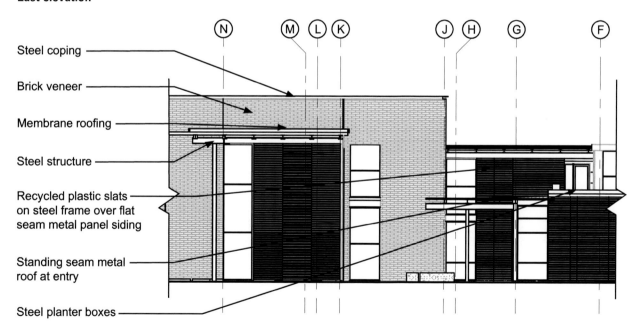

Steel coping

Brick veneer

Membrane roofing

Steel structure

Recycled plastic slats on steel frame over flat seam metal panel siding

Standing seam metal roof at entry

Steel planter boxes

0 5 10 20 ft

5.15b
East elevation

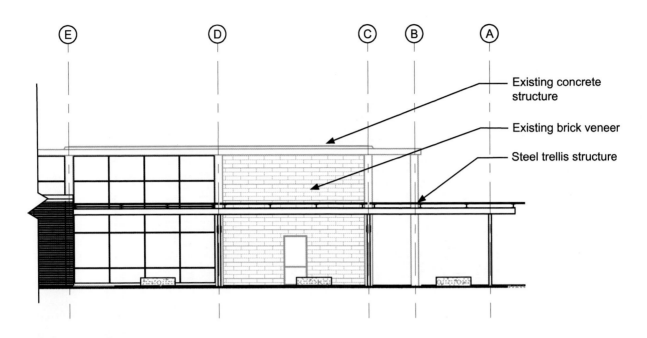

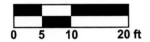

5.15c
East elevation

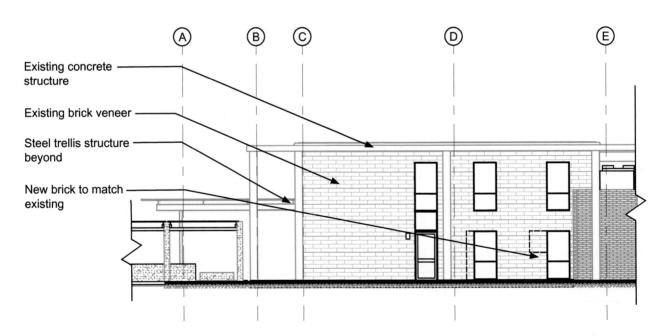

5.16a
West elevation

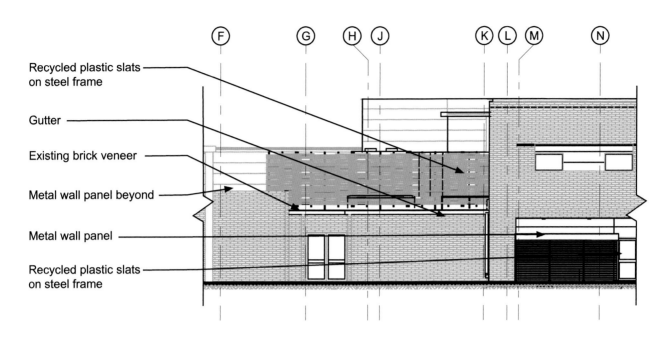

Recycled plastic slats on steel frame

Gutter

Existing brick veneer

Metal wall panel beyond

Metal wall panel

Recycled plastic slats on steel frame

0   5   10   20 ft

5.16b
West elevation

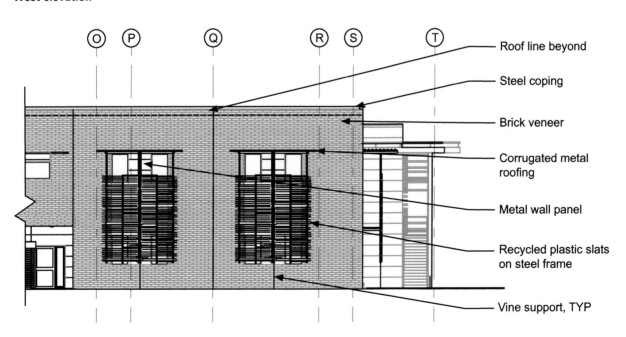

Roof line beyond

Steel coping

Brick veneer

Corrugated metal roofing

Metal wall panel

Recycled plastic slats on steel frame

Vine support, TYP

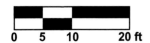

0   5   10   20 ft

5.16c
West elevation

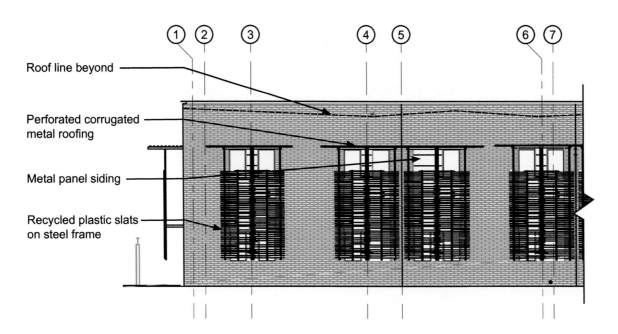

Roof line beyond

Perforated corrugated
metal roofing

Metal panel siding

Recycled plastic slats
on steel frame

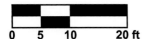

0 5 10   20 ft

5.17a
South elevation

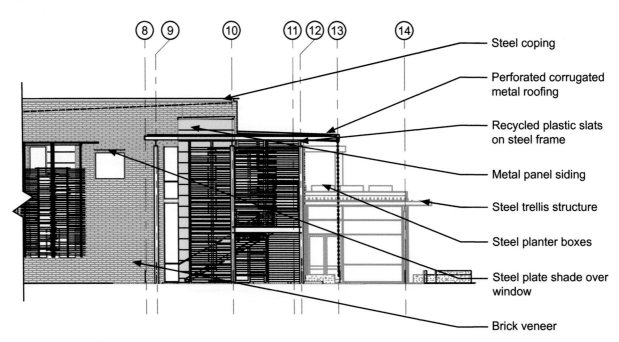

Steel coping

Perforated corrugated
metal roofing

Recycled plastic slats
on steel frame

Metal panel siding

Steel trellis structure

Steel planter boxes

Steel plate shade over
window

Brick veneer

0 5 10   20 ft

5.17b
South elevation

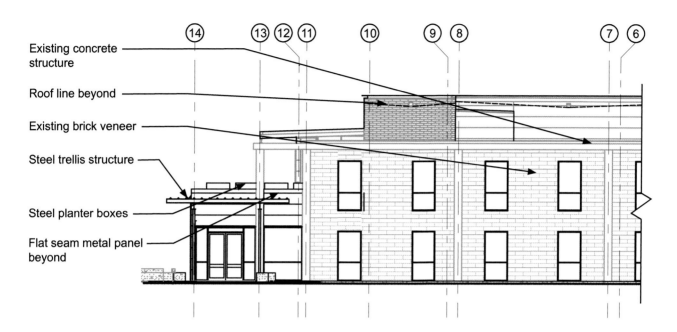

Existing concrete structure

Roof line beyond

Existing brick veneer

Steel trellis structure

Steel planter boxes

Flat seam metal panel beyond

0   5   10   20 ft

5.18a
North elevation

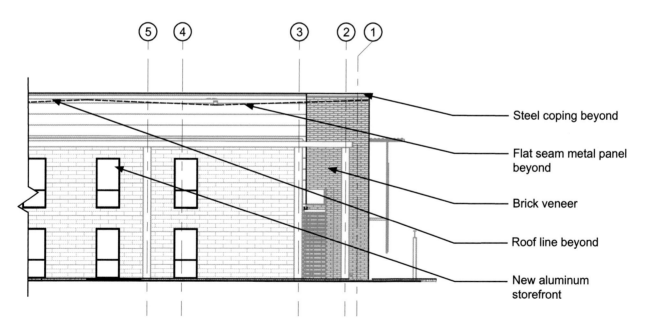

Steel coping beyond

Flat seam metal panel beyond

Brick veneer

Roof line beyond

New aluminum storefront

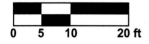

0   5   10   20 ft

5.18b
North elevation

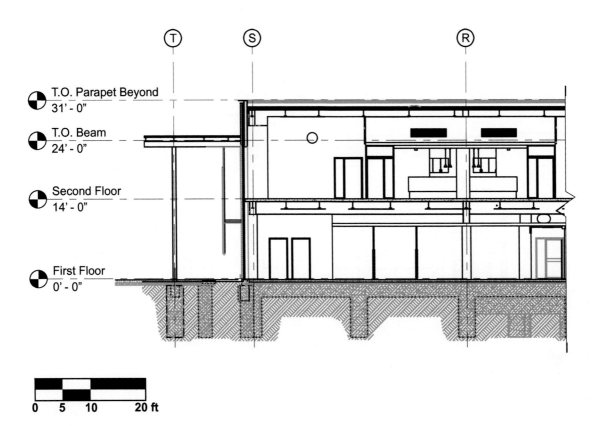

T.O. Parapet Beyond
31' - 0"

T.O. Beam
24' - 0"

Second Floor
14' - 0"

First Floor
0' - 0"

0   5   10   20 ft

5.19a
South/north building section A-A: lobbies

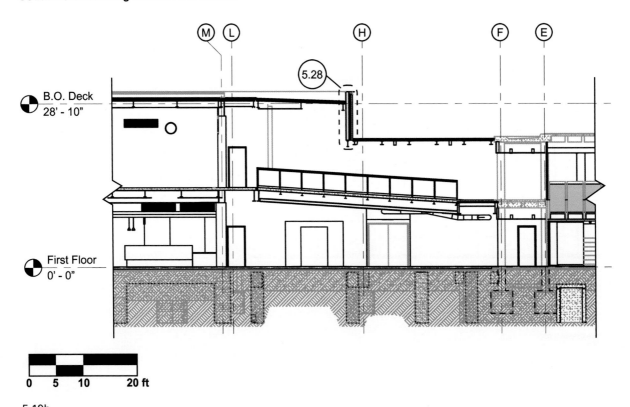

5.28

B.O. Deck
28' - 10"

First Floor
0' - 0"

0   5   10   20 ft

5.19b
South/north building section A-A: lobbies

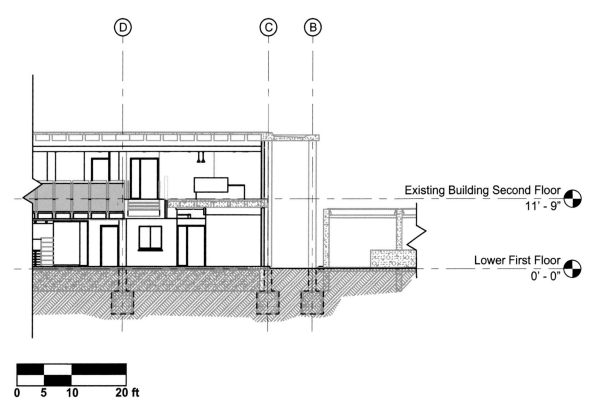

Ⓓ   Ⓒ   Ⓑ

Existing Building Second Floor
11' - 9"

Lower First Floor
0' - 0"

0   5   10   20 ft

5.19c
South/north building section A-A: lobbies

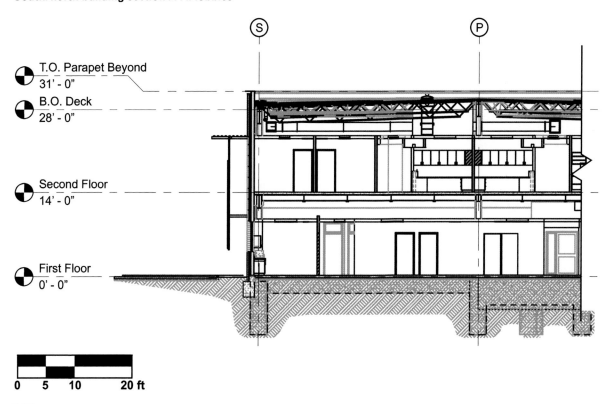

Ⓢ   Ⓟ

T.O. Parapet Beyond
31' - 0"

B.O. Deck
28' - 0"

Second Floor
14' - 0"

First Floor
0' - 0"

0   5   10   20 ft

5.20a
South/north building section B-B: exam rooms and corridor

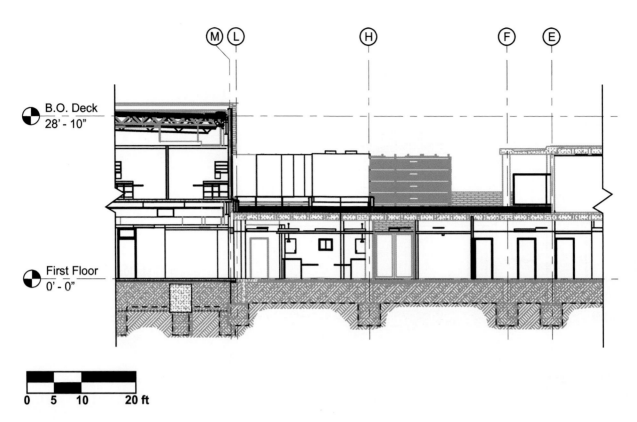

5.20b
South/north building section B-B: exam rooms and corridor

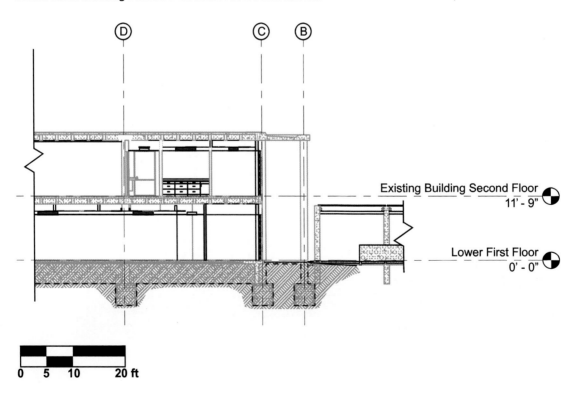

5.20c
South/north building section B-B: exam rooms and corridor

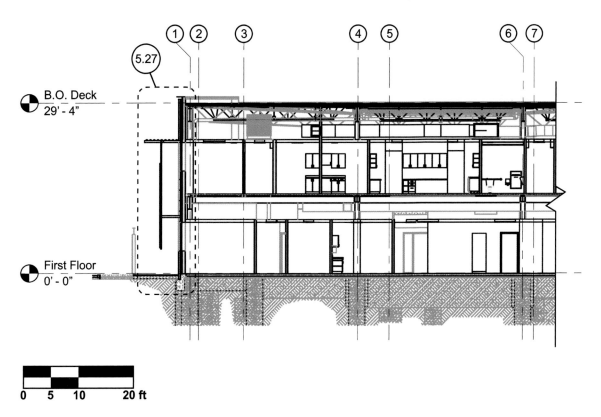

B.O. Deck
29' - 4"

First Floor
0' - 0"

0 5 10 20 ft

5.21a
West/east building section C-C: lobby and corridor

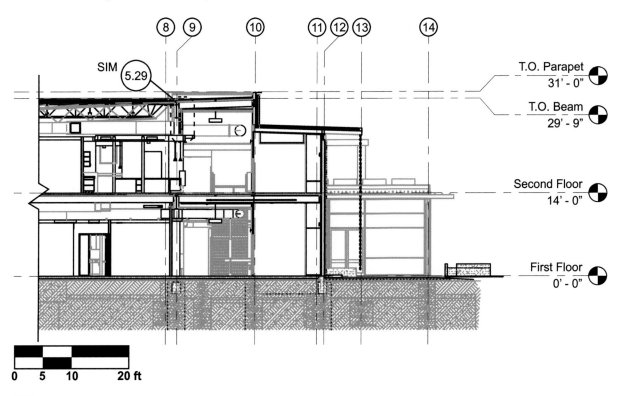

SIM

T.O. Parapet
31' - 0"

T.O. Beam
29' - 9"

Second Floor
14' - 0"

First Floor
0' - 0"

0 5 10 20 ft

5.21b
West/east building section C-C: lobby and corridor

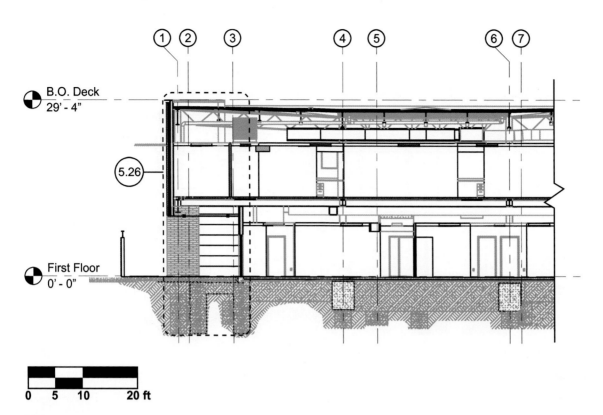

5.22a
West/east building section D-D: main corridor

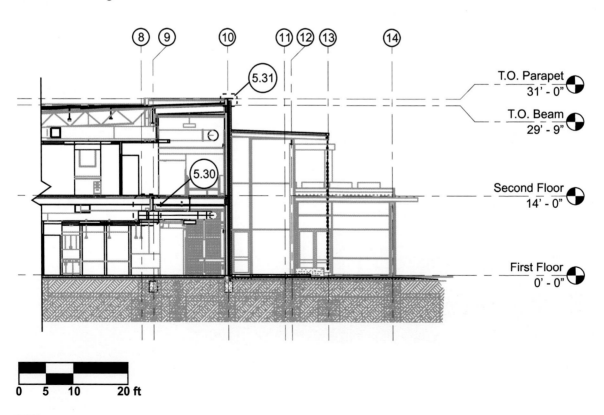

5.22b
West/east building section D-D: main corridor

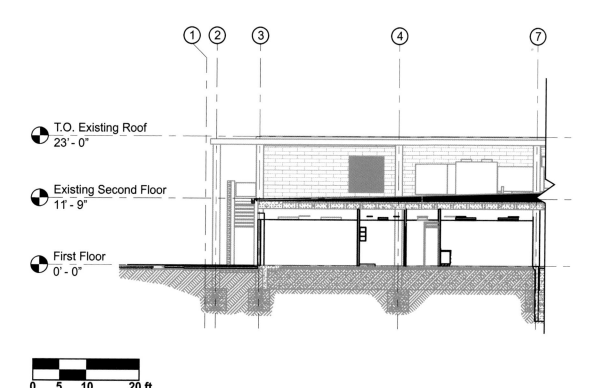

T.O. Existing Roof
23' - 0"

Existing Second Floor
11' - 9"

First Floor
0' - 0"

0   5   10   20 ft

5.23a
West/east building section E-E: lobby and medical services

Exposed steel structure

Tapered insulation

Exposed mechanical duct

Steel column

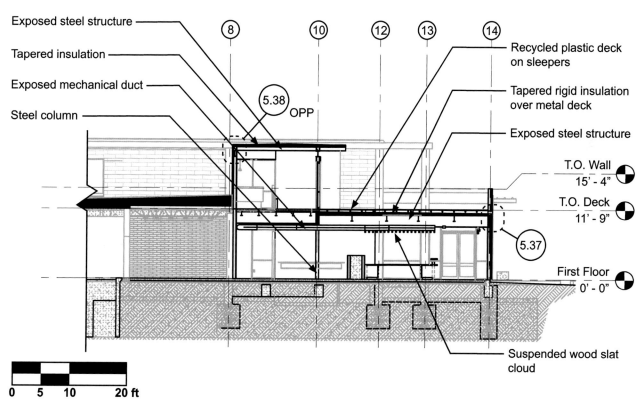

5.38 OPP

Recycled plastic deck
on sleepers

Tapered rigid insulation
over metal deck

Exposed steel structure

T.O. Wall
15' - 4"

T.O. Deck
11' - 9"

5.37

First Floor
0' - 0"

Suspended wood slat
cloud

0   5   10   20 ft

5.23b
West/east building section E-E: lobby and medical services

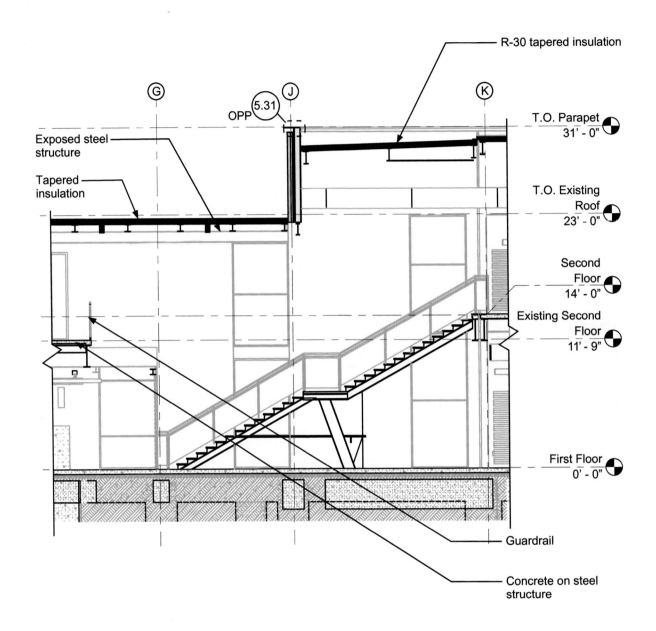

R-30 tapered insulation

Exposed steel structure

Tapered insulation

OPP 5.31

T.O. Parapet
31' - 0"

T.O. Existing Roof
23' - 0"

Second Floor
14' - 0"

Existing Second Floor
11' - 9"

First Floor
0' - 0"

Guardrail

Concrete on steel structure

0 2 4 8 ft

5.24
Enlarged building section: east stair

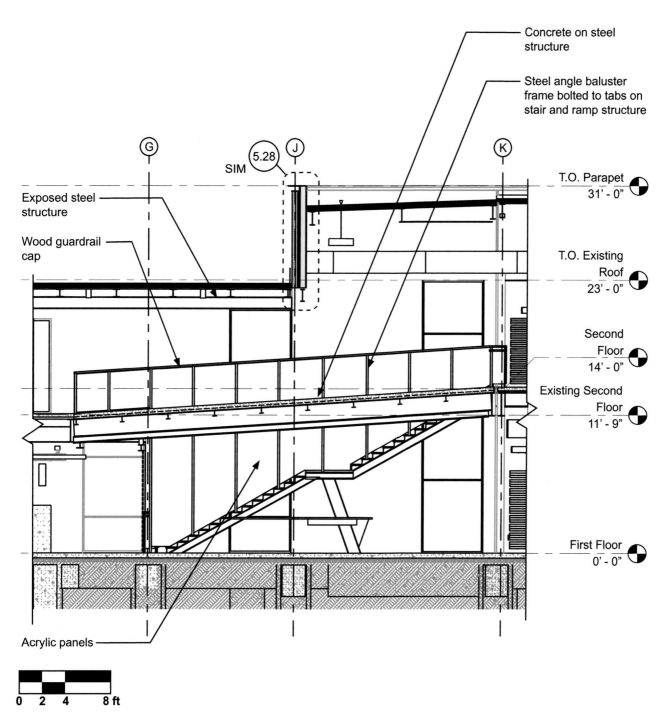

Concrete on steel
structure

Steel angle baluster
frame bolted to tabs on
stair and ramp structure

SIM

Exposed steel
structure

Wood guardrail
cap

T.O. Parapet
31' - 0"

T.O. Existing
Roof
23' - 0"

Second
Floor
14' - 0"

Existing Second
Floor
11' - 9"

First Floor
0' - 0"

Acrylic panels

0 2 4   8 ft

5.25
Enlarged building section: east ramp

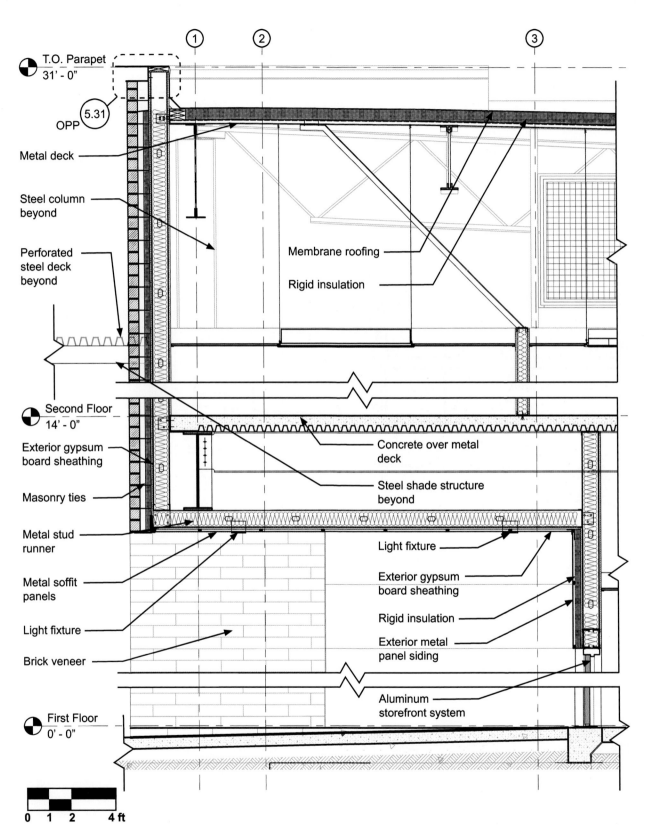

T.O. Parapet
31' - 0"

OPP (5.31)

Metal deck

Steel column
beyond

Perforated
steel deck
beyond

Membrane roofing

Rigid insulation

Second Floor
14' - 0"

Exterior gypsum
board sheathing

Masonry ties

Metal stud
runner

Metal soffit
panels

Light fixture

Brick veneer

Concrete over metal
deck

Steel shade structure
beyond

Light fixture

Exterior gypsum
board sheathing

Rigid insulation

Exterior metal
panel siding

Aluminum
storefront system

First Floor
0' - 0"

0 1 2 4 ft

5.26
Wall section: southeast lobby

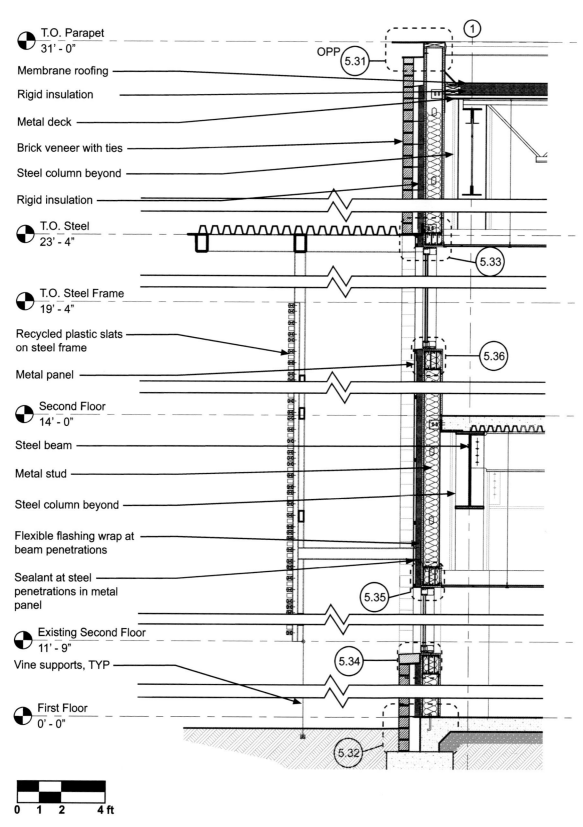

T.O. Parapet
31' - 0"

OPP (5.31)

Membrane roofing

Rigid insulation

Metal deck

Brick veneer with ties

Steel column beyond

Rigid insulation

T.O. Steel
23' - 4"

(5.33)

T.O. Steel Frame
19' - 4"

Recycled plastic slats
on steel frame

(5.36)

Metal panel

Second Floor
14' - 0"

Steel beam

Metal stud

Steel column beyond

Flexible flashing wrap at
beam penetrations

Sealant at steel
penetrations in metal
panel

(5.35)

Existing Second Floor
11' - 9"

Vine supports, TYP

(5.34)

First Floor
0' - 0"

(5.32)

0 1 2   4 ft

5.27
Wall section: southeast building screen

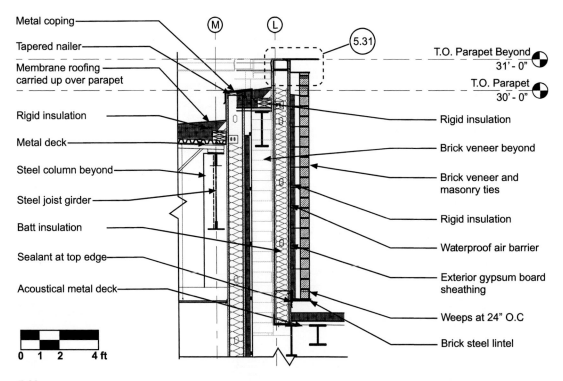

Metal coping

Tapered nailer

Membrane roofing carried up over parapet

Rigid insulation

Metal deck

Steel column beyond

Steel joist girder

Batt insulation

Sealant at top edge

Acoustical metal deck

M   L   5.31

T.O. Parapet Beyond
31' - 0"

T.O. Parapet
30' - 0"

Rigid insulation

Brick veneer beyond

Brick veneer and masonry ties

Rigid insulation

Waterproof air barrier

Exterior gypsum board sheathing

Weeps at 24" O.C

Brick steel lintel

0 1 2   4 ft

5.28
Wall section: mid roof

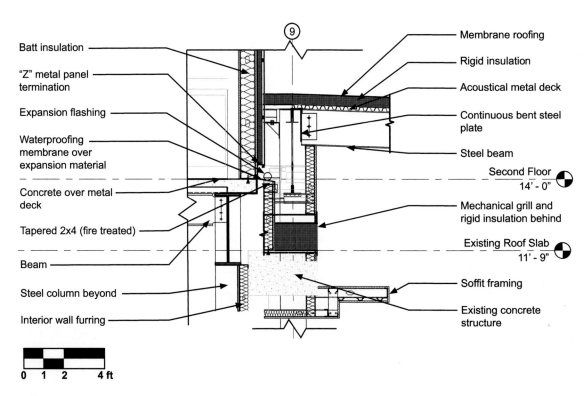

Batt insulation

"Z" metal panel termination

Expansion flashing

Waterproofing membrane over expansion material

Concrete over metal deck

Tapered 2x4 (fire treated)

Beam

Steel column beyond

Interior wall furring

9

Membrane roofing

Rigid insulation

Acoustical metal deck

Continuous bent steel plate

Steel beam

Second Floor
14' - 0"

Mechanical grill and rigid insulation behind

Existing Roof Slab
11' - 9"

Soffit framing

Existing concrete structure

0 1 2   4 ft

5.29
Wall section: soffit at second floor lobby

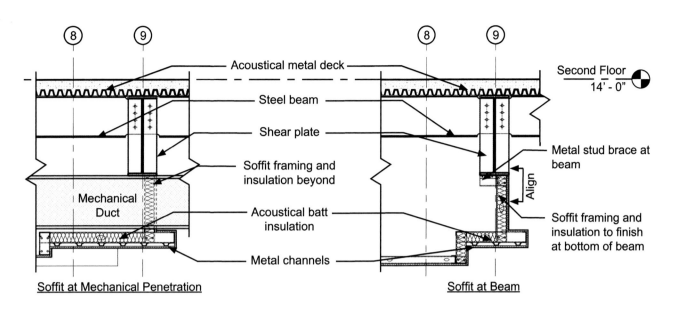

Acoustical metal deck

Steel beam

Shear plate

Soffit framing and insulation beyond

Acoustical batt insulation

Metal channels

Mechanical Duct

Second Floor
14' - 0"

Metal stud brace at beam

Align

Soffit framing and insulation to finish at bottom of beam

Soffit at Mechanical Penetration

Soffit at Beam

0   1   2   4 ft

5.30
Wall section: soffits in first floor lobby

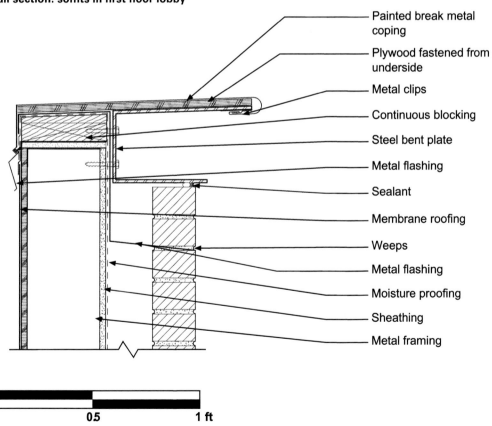

Painted break metal coping

Plywood fastened from underside

Metal clips

Continuous blocking

Steel bent plate

Metal flashing

Sealant

Membrane roofing

Weeps

Metal flashing

Moisture proofing

Sheathing

Metal framing

0   0.5   1 ft

5.31
Section detail: parapet cap

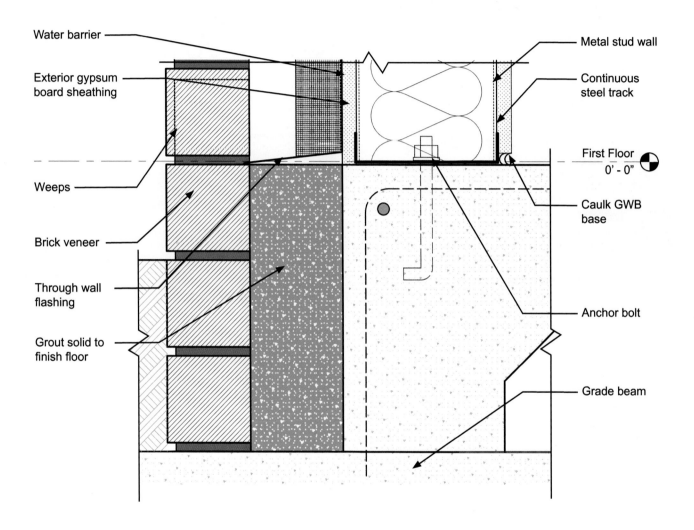

Water barrier

Exterior gypsum board sheathing

Weeps

Brick veneer

Through wall flashing

Grout solid to finish floor

Metal stud wall

Continuous steel track

First Floor
0' - 0"

Caulk GWB base

Anchor bolt

Grade beam

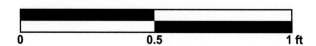

0   0.5   1 ft

5.32
Section detail: brick at grade beam

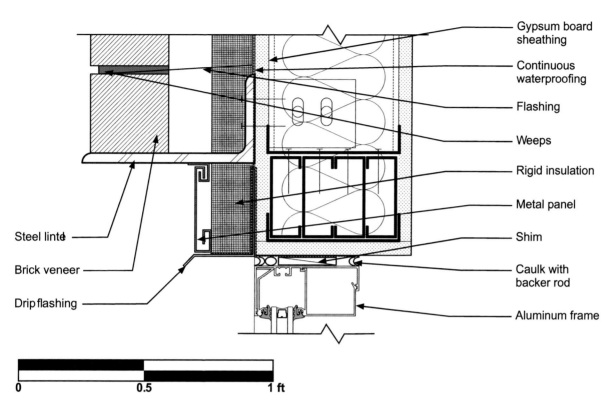

Gypsum board sheathing

Continuous waterproofing

Flashing

Weeps

Rigid insulation

Metal panel

Shim

Caulk with backer rod

Aluminum frame

Steel lintel

Brick veneer

Drip flashing

0   0.5   1 ft

5.33
Section detail: window head at brick/metal

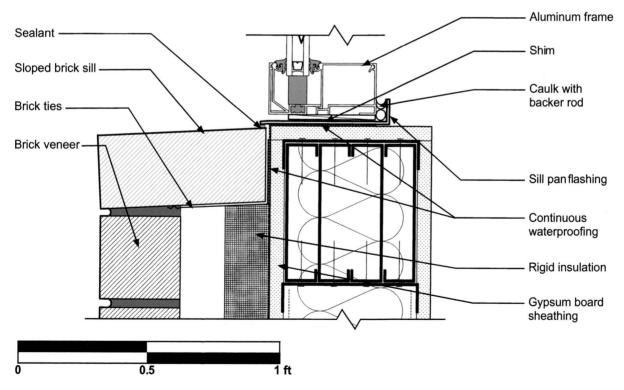

Sealant

Sloped brick sill

Brick ties

Brick veneer

Aluminum frame

Shim

Caulk with backer rod

Sill pan flashing

Continuous waterproofing

Rigid insulation

Gypsum board sheathing

0   0.5   1 ft

5.34
Section detail: window sill at brick

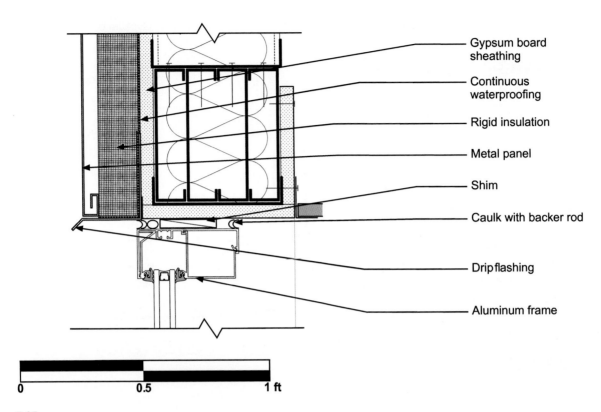

Gypsum board sheathing

Continuous waterproofing

Rigid insulation

Metal panel

Shim

Caulk with backer rod

Drip flashing

Aluminum frame

0   0.5   1 ft

5.35
Section detail: window head at metal panel

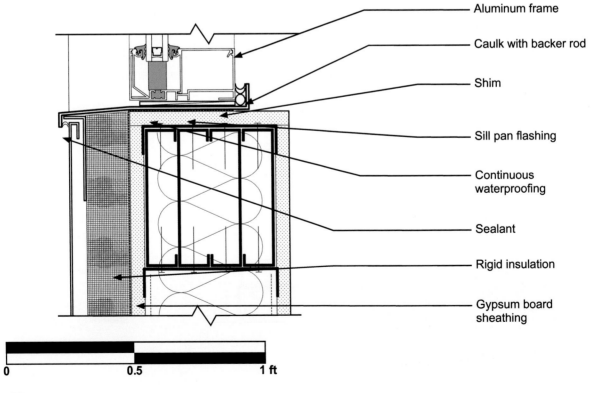

Aluminum frame

Caulk with backer rod

Shim

Sill pan flashing

Continuous waterproofing

Sealant

Rigid insulation

Gypsum board sheathing

0   0.5   1 ft

5.36
Section detail: window sill at metal panel

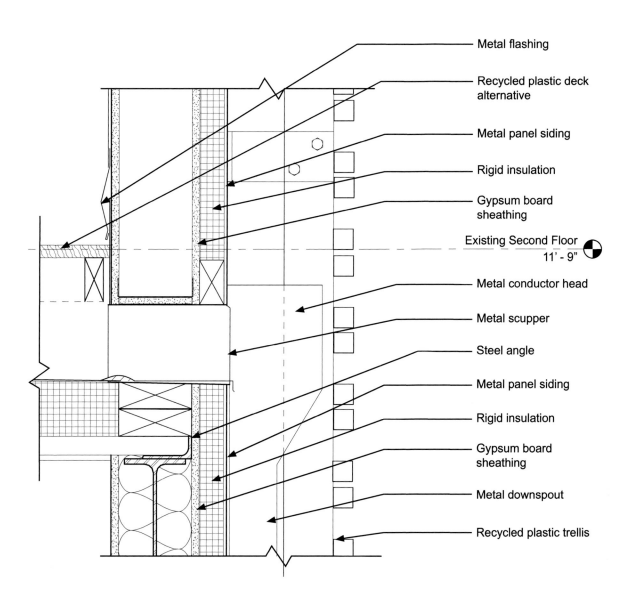

Metal flashing

Recycled plastic deck alternative

Metal panel siding

Rigid insulation

Gypsum board sheathing

Existing Second Floor
11' - 9"

Metal conductor head

Metal scupper

Steel angle

Metal panel siding

Rigid insulation

Gypsum board sheathing

Metal downspout

Recycled plastic trellis

0   0.5   1 ft

5.37
Section detail: scupper at terrace

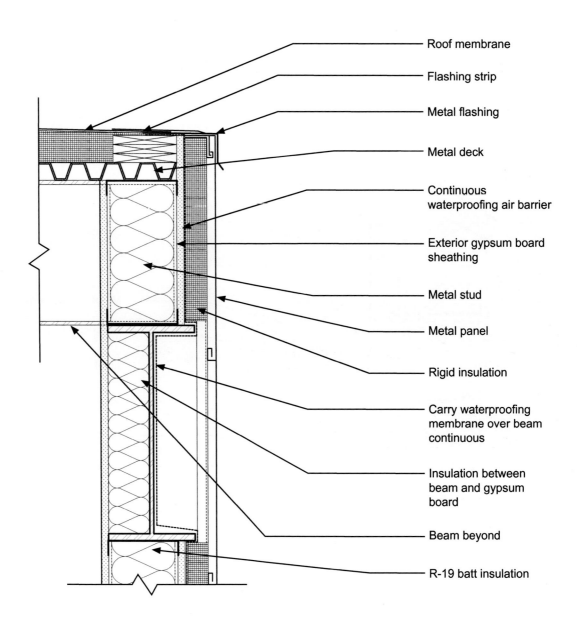

Roof membrane

Flashing strip

Metal flashing

Metal deck

Continuous waterproofing air barrier

Exterior gypsum board sheathing

Metal stud

Metal panel

Rigid insulation

Carry waterproofing membrane over beam continuous

Insulation between beam and gypsum board

Beam beyond

R-19 batt insulation

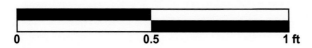

0   0.5   1 ft

5.38
Section detail: metal panel at roof

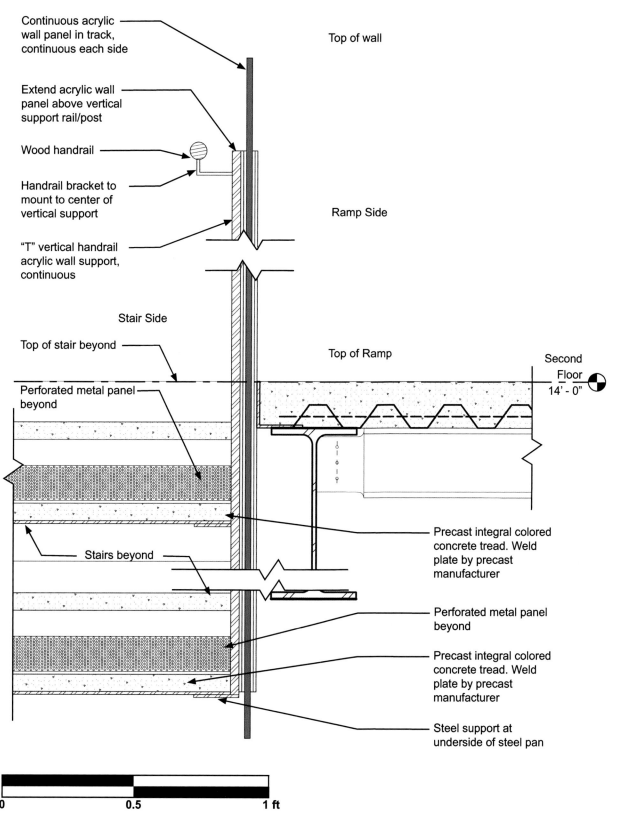

Continuous acrylic wall panel in track, continuous each side

Extend acrylic wall panel above vertical support rail/post

Wood handrail

Handrail bracket to mount to center of vertical support

"T" vertical handrail acrylic wall support, continuous

Top of wall

Ramp Side

Stair Side

Top of stair beyond

Perforated metal panel beyond

Stairs beyond

Top of Ramp

Second Floor 14' - 0"

Precast integral colored concrete tread. Weld plate by precast manufacturer

Perforated metal panel beyond

Precast integral colored concrete tread. Weld plate by precast manufacturer

Steel support at underside of steel pan

0   0.5   1 ft

5.39
Section detail: acrylic stairwall

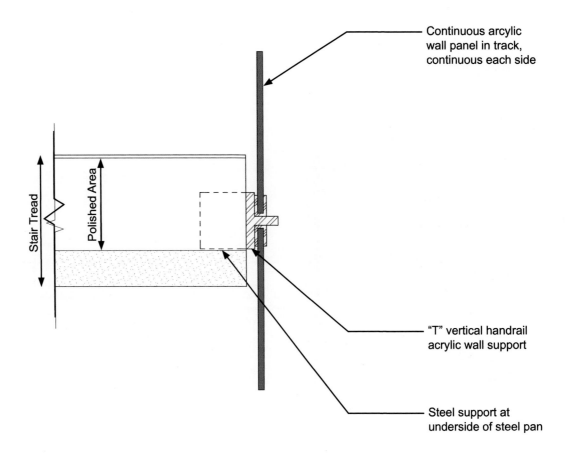

Continuous arcylic
wall panel in track,
continuous each side

"T" vertical handrail
acrylic wall support

Steel support at
underside of steel pan

0   0.5   1 ft

5.40
Plan detail: acrylic stairwall

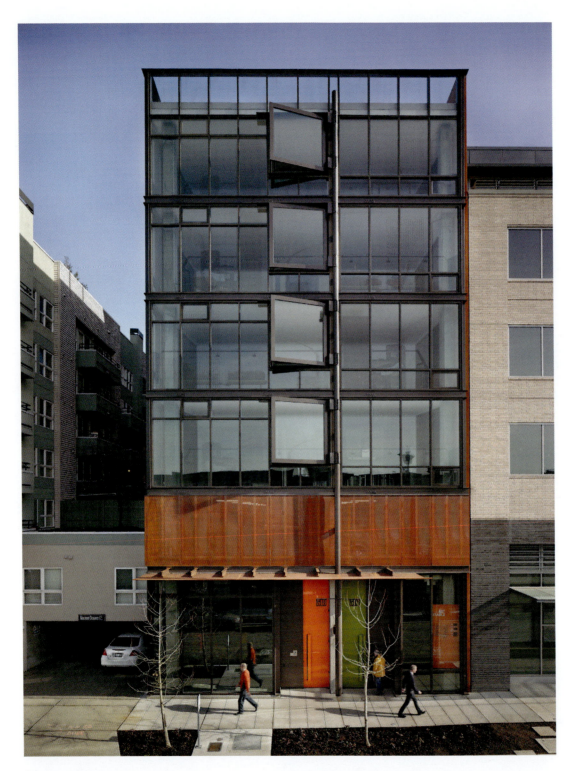

6.1
View of front façade

Credit: Benjamin Benschneider

6: Art Stable

Seattle, WA, Olson Kundig

Architect's Design Intent and Reasoning Behind Material and Tectonic Choices

Art Stable is an urban infill project in the rapidly developing South Lake Union neighborhood of Seattle. Built on the site of a former horse stable, the seven-story mixed-use building carries its working history into the future with highly adaptable live/work units.

The client brief called for a building that would hold a series of mixed-use units for art-oriented residents. Designed to accommodate changes to the building's program over time, the units are zoned for both residential and commercial use. The units are designed around the making and displaying of art; key features of the building – its large operable windows and an integrated davit crane – are designed to facilitate the movement of large art objects or supplies into and out of the building.

Both front and back elevations of Art Stable are active. The front end of each unit maximizes daylighting with floor-to-ceiling windows for the "living" side, while the alley-facing end is the "working" side, fully embodying the live/work concept of the building. The alley-facing rear façade features an 80' 5" tall hinge, davit crane and five steel-clad doors that cover nearly a third of the façade. Each of these hand-cranked doors is 9' 0" × 9' 0". The window and crane system references a warehousing tradition in how it moves oversize objects into the building while the street-facing façade is covered by large hinged windows, allowing for natural cross-ventilation in the units.

The rear façade is broken into three roughly equal sections: structural (a concrete shear wall), functional (the doors) and glazing (receiving northeast light). Olson Kundig's design team, led by architect Tom Kundig, collaborated with engineers to devise the hinge system which manually opens the five large steel-clad art doors. The davit crane on top of the building can lift oversize objects from the alley directly into the units. Users can open the doors up to 75 degrees by turning large, custom-designed hand wheels. Each wheel connects to a threaded rod that passes through the building envelope and connects to a pivot bolt on the exterior of the building. The threading on the rod ensures that the doors can be held open at the desired angle, and eliminates the possibility of them being blown open or shut. On the street-facing

6.2
View of front façade detail
Credit: Benjamin Benschneider

façade of the building, oversized hinged windows open with the same technique, providing natural ventilation.

At only 40′ 0″ wide, the building has a compact footprint. Unusual for an urban infill project, there is a gap not only in front of and behind the building (i.e., the street-facing side and the alley-facing side), but also on a third side facing north. Acknowledging that northern light is ideal for making or viewing art, a third set of windows on the north façade takes advantage of the space between Art Stable and its neighboring building to draw in additional daylight.

The shell and core of the building are built to last over 100 years. Units within the building are designed to accommodate flexibility in use and changes over time. The building itself was designed with durability and longevity in mind, as future needs might call for it to be converted from residential to workplace, commercial, or an as-yet-unknown use.

6.3
View of northeast corner and closed art doors

Credit: Benjamin Benschneider

6.4
View of northeast corner and open art doors

Credit: Benjamin Benschneider

6.5
View of art doors
Credit: Chris Rogers

6.6
Interior view of art door
Credit: Benjamin Benschneider

6.7
Interior view of loft
Credit: Benjamin Benschneider

6.8
Interior view of loft
Credit: Benjamin Benschneider

Art Stable

The concrete structure is designed to take heavy loads, and structural and mechanical systems are exposed. Geothermal loops were inserted into the building's structural piles, resulting in an innovative and highly energy efficient radiant heating and cooling system. At the time of construction, this was one of the first uses of this type of geothermal system in this country. The building is wired so that electricity can eventually extend to the roof for photovoltaic panels. The structure is designed to be durable and long-lasting with enough flexibility that it could accommodate a mix of different uses long into the future.

The building contains one floor of street-level retail, which totals 2,000 square feet. The street-level entry doors are 14' 0" high and painted with oven-baked chartreuse and orange car enamel. Parking is on the second floor – the parking entrance is through the alley, at grade. Locating the parking on the second floor allowed the garage to be naturally ventilated, and allowed commercial space to sit along the street-level to activate the pedestrian zone. Above, five floors of residential space contain a total of five living units. The penthouse unit is two stories and contains a roof terrace.

The use of simple, no-to-low-maintenance materials including concrete, steel and glass draws upon the warehouse typology of the formerly industrial neighborhood, now a vibrant urban neighborhood, home to world-class technology, commercial and bioscience firms. Weathered steel panels clad the building's exterior while glass and metal windows comprise the majority of the façade to maximize natural daylighting. Interior build-outs are determined by each unit's owners, who can punch windows into the north façade of the building, providing a personalized balance between privacy and transparency. A collective of hard-working spaces, the building draws upon the architectural concepts of prospect and refuge, transposed to an urban setting.

Kirsten R. Murray, FAIA
Principal/Owner

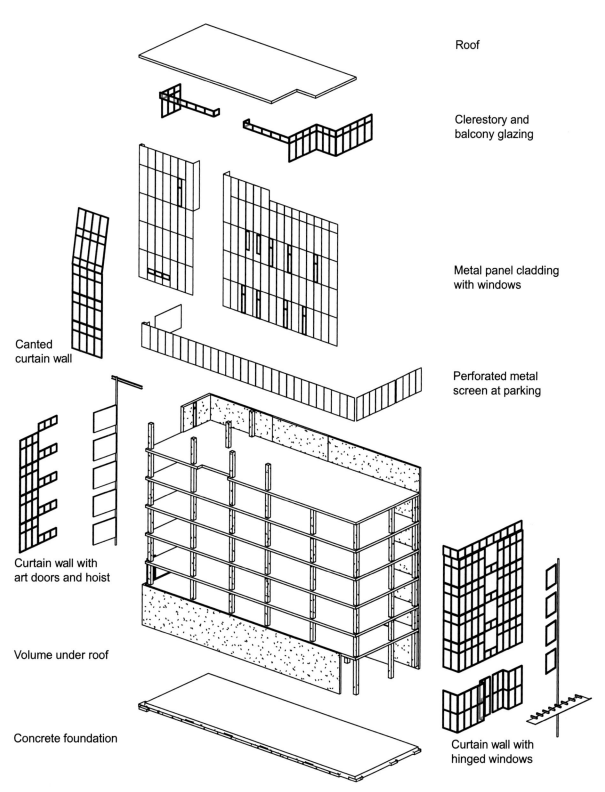

Roof

Clerestory and
balcony glazing

Metal panel cladding
with windows

Canted
curtain wall

Perforated metal
screen at parking

Curtain wall with
art doors and hoist

Volume under roof

Concrete foundation

Curtain wall with
hinged windows

6.9
Major building components
(Not to scale.)

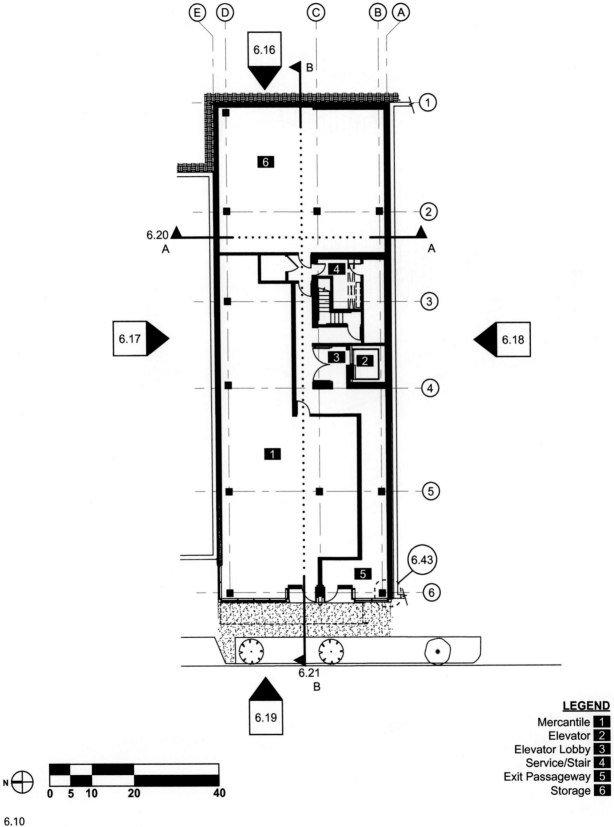

6.10
First floor plan – mercantile

LEGEND
Mercantile 1
Elevator 2
Elevator Lobby 3
Service/Stair 4
Exit Passageway 5
Storage 6

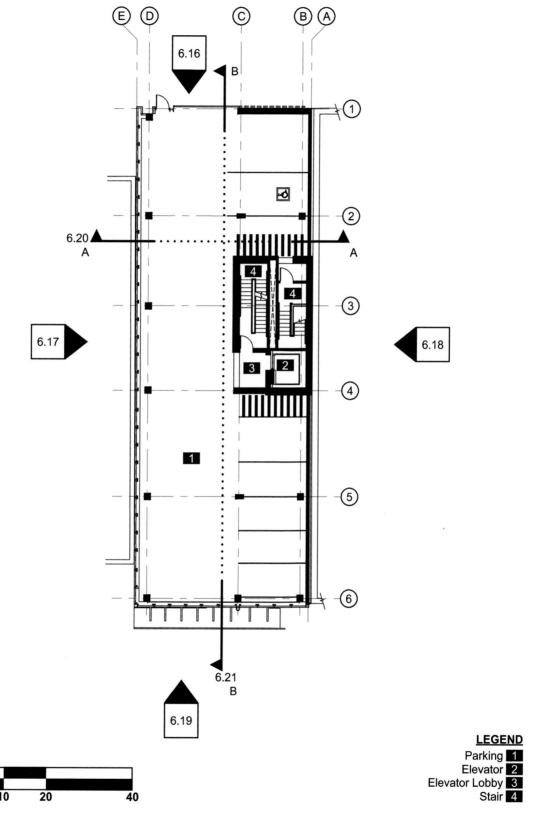

6.16

6.20

6.17

6.18

6.21

6.19

N

0 5 10   20   40

6.11
Second floor plan – parking

LEGEND
Parking 1
Elevator 2
Elevator Lobby 3
Stair 4

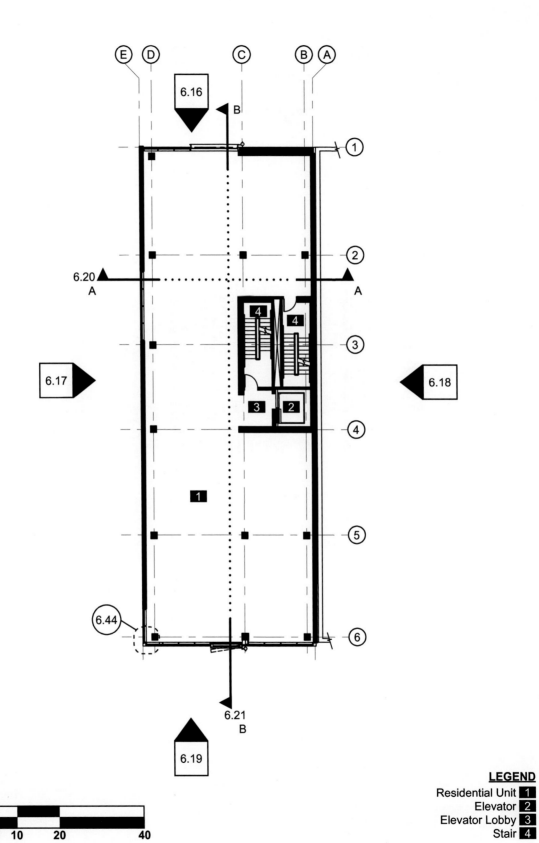

LEGEND

Residential Unit 1
Elevator 2
Elevator Lobby 3
Stair 4

6.12
Third, fourth, and fifth floor plan – residential

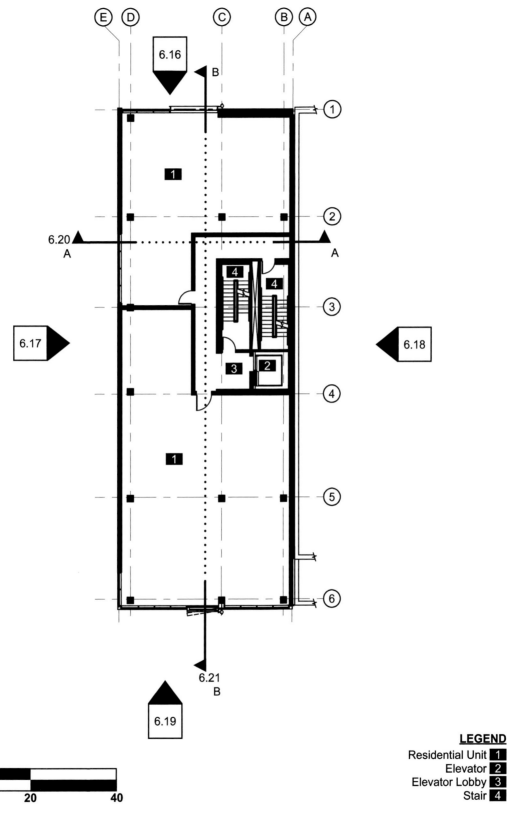

6.16

B

E D C B A

6.20 A — A

6.17

6.18

4 4

3 2

6.21 B

6.19

N

0 5 10 20 40

6.13
Sixth floor plan – residential

LEGEND
Residential Unit 1
Elevator 2
Elevator Lobby 3
Stair 4

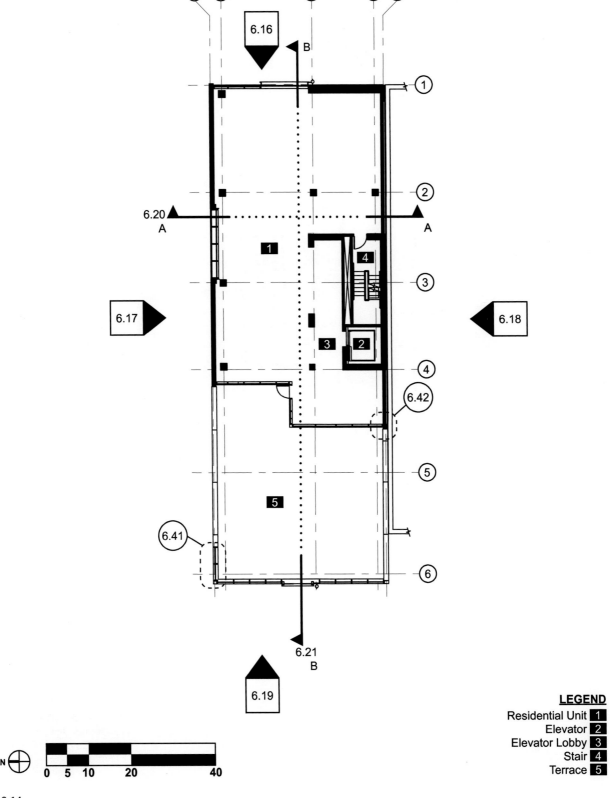

6.16

B

6.20

A

A

1

2

3

4

6.42

5

6.41

6

6.17

6.18

6.21

B

6.19

1

2

3

4

5

N

0 5 10   20   40

6.14
Seventh floor plan – residential

LEGEND

Residential Unit 1
Elevator 2
Elevator Lobby 3
Stair 4
Terrace 5

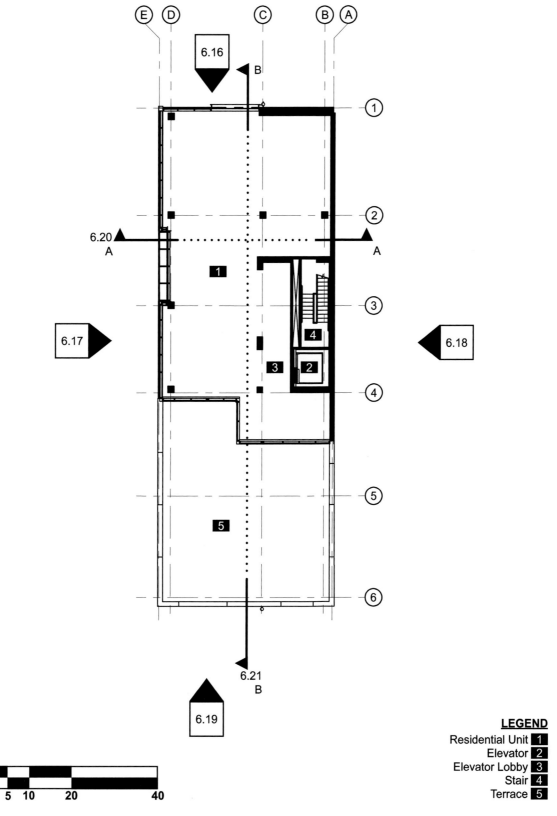

6.15
Seventh floor clerestory plan – residential

N

0 5 10 20 40

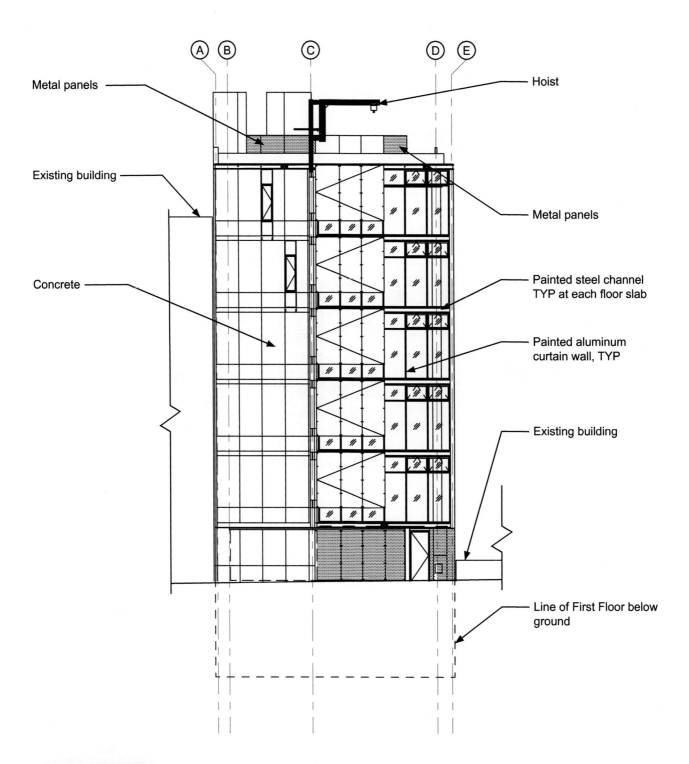

Metal panels

Existing building

Concrete

Ⓐ Ⓑ Ⓒ Ⓓ Ⓔ

Hoist

Metal panels

Painted steel channel
TYP at each floor slab

Painted aluminum
curtain wall, TYP

Existing building

Line of First Floor below
ground

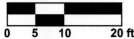

0   5   10   20 ft

6.16
East elevation

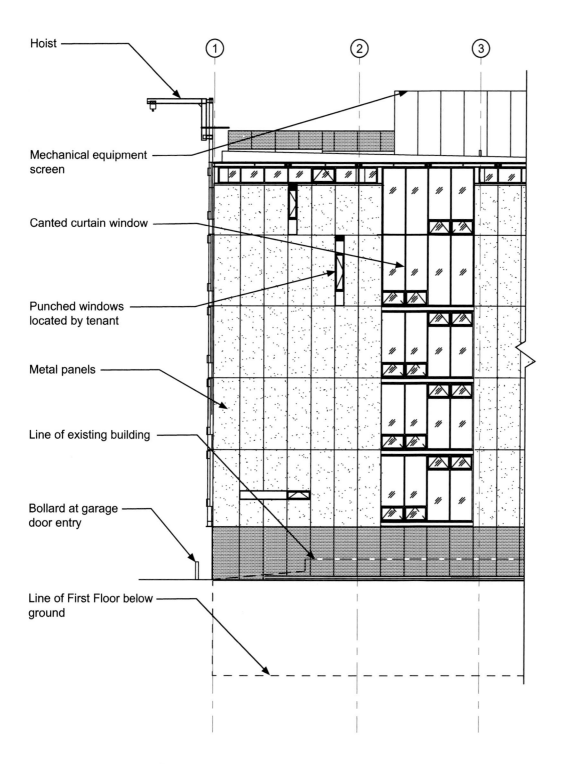

Hoist

Mechanical equipment screen

Canted curtain window

Punched windows located by tenant

Metal panels

Line of existing building

Bollard at garage door entry

Line of First Floor below ground

0   5   10   20 ft

6.17a
North elevation

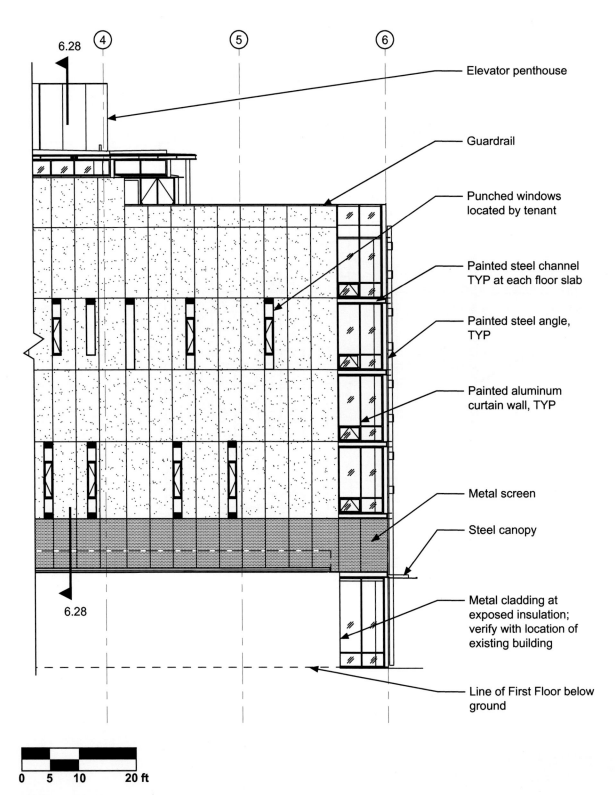

Elevator penthouse

Guardrail

Punched windows located by tenant

Painted steel channel TYP at each floor slab

Painted steel angle, TYP

Painted aluminum curtain wall, TYP

Metal screen

Steel canopy

Metal cladding at exposed insulation; verify with location of existing building

Line of First Floor below ground

6.28

6.28

0   5   10   20 ft

6.17b
North elevation

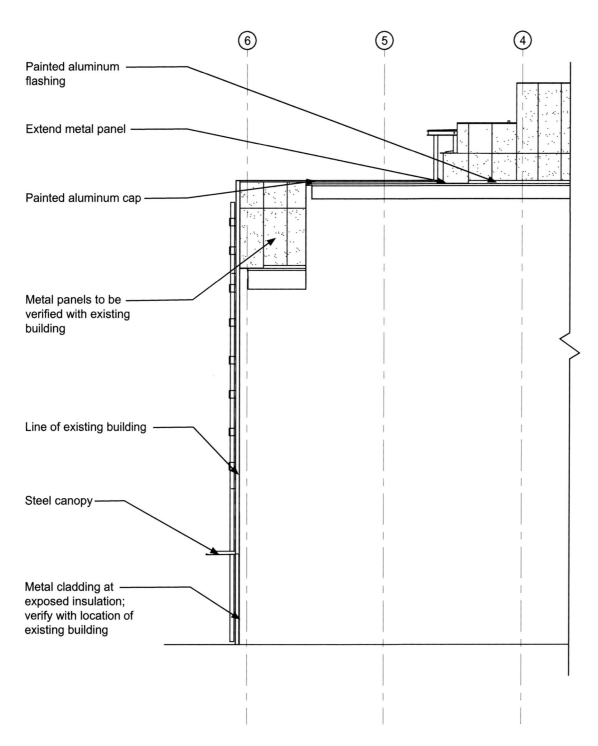

Painted aluminum
flashing

Extend metal panel

Painted aluminum cap

Metal panels to be
verified with existing
building

Line of existing building

Steel canopy

Metal cladding at
exposed insulation;
verify with location of
existing building

⑥   ⑤   ④

0   5   10   20 ft

6.18a
South elevation

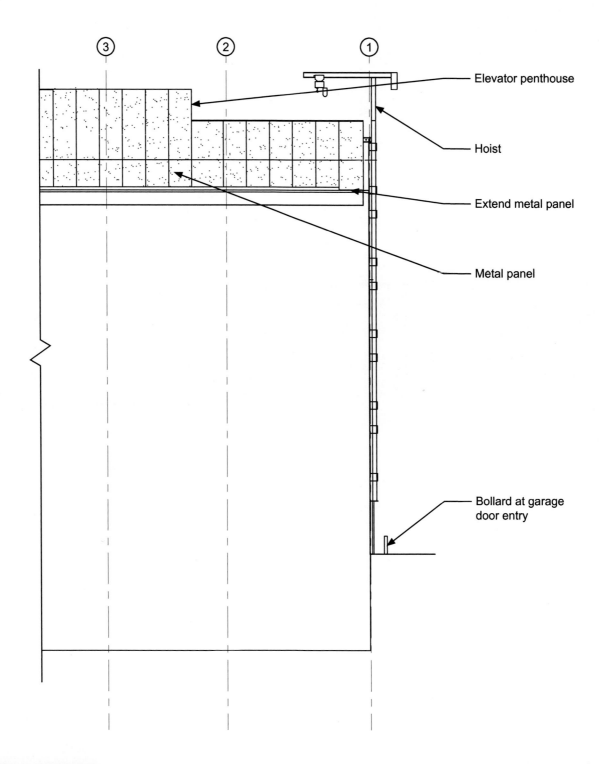

Elevator penthouse

Hoist

Extend metal panel

Metal panel

Bollard at garage door entry

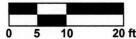

0   5   10   20 ft

6.18b
South elevation

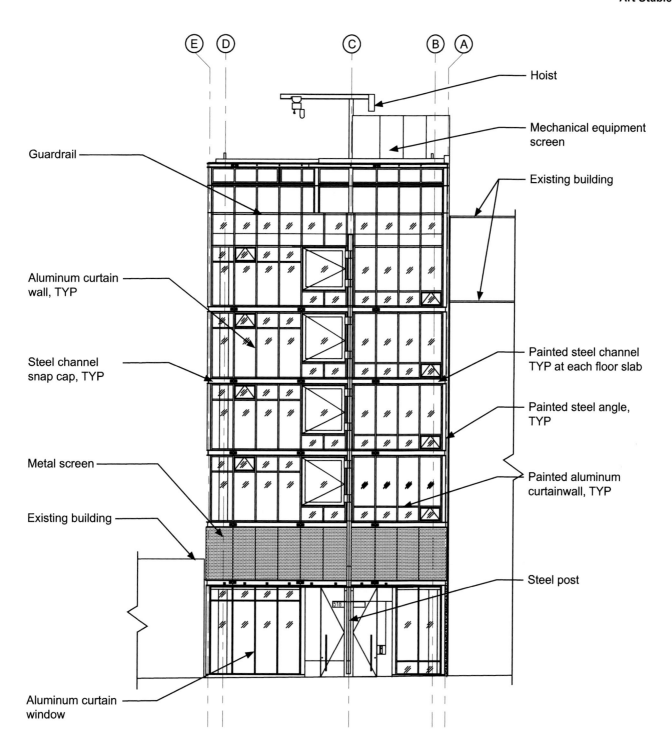

Hoist

Mechanical equipment screen

Existing building

Guardrail

Aluminum curtain wall, TYP

Steel channel snap cap, TYP

Painted steel channel TYP at each floor slab

Painted steel angle, TYP

Painted aluminum curtainwall, TYP

Metal screen

Existing building

Steel post

Aluminum curtain window

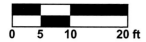

0   5   10   20 ft

6.19
West elevation

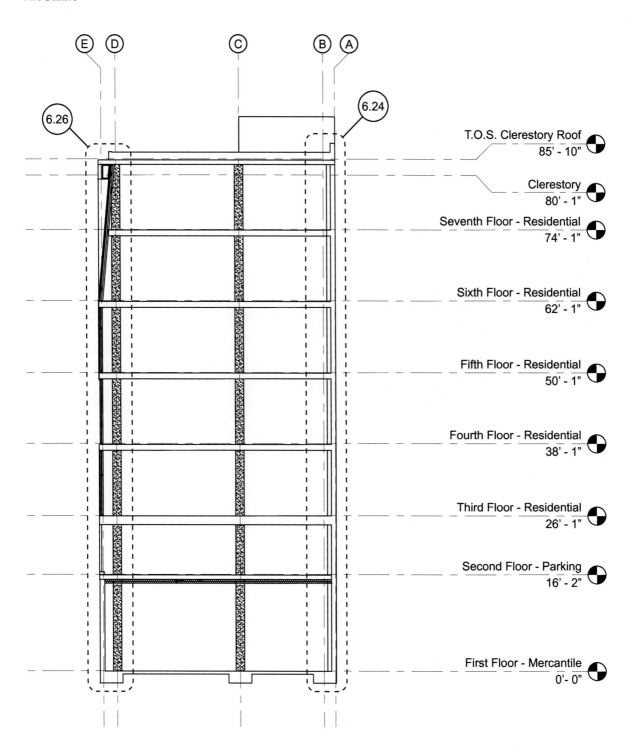

Ⓔ Ⓓ Ⓒ Ⓑ Ⓐ

(6.26)

(6.24)

T.O.S. Clerestory Roof
85' - 10"

Clerestory
80' - 1"

Seventh Floor - Residential
74' - 1"

Sixth Floor - Residential
62' - 1"

Fifth Floor - Residential
50' - 1"

Fourth Floor - Residential
38' - 1"

Third Floor - Residential
26' - 1"

Second Floor - Parking
16' - 2"

First Floor - Mercantile
0'- 0"

0   5   10   20 ft

6.20
North/south building section A-A

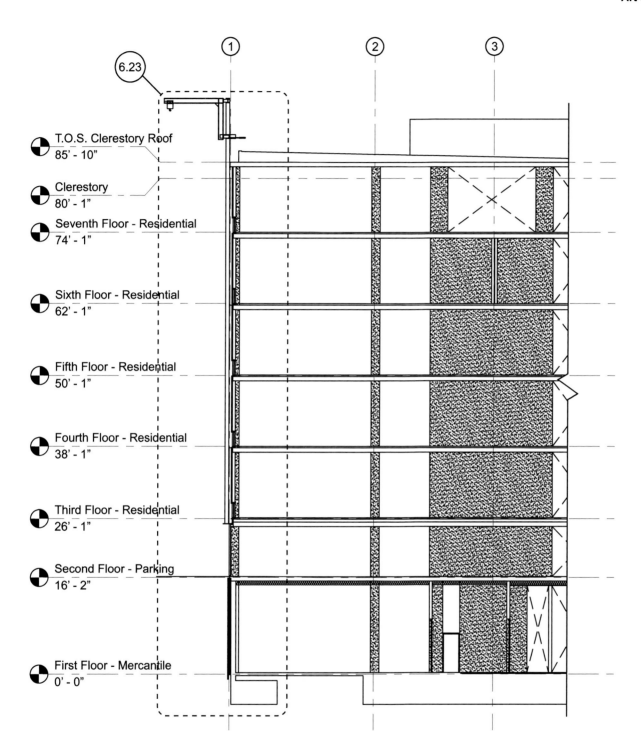

6.23

T.O.S. Clerestory Roof
85' - 10"

Clerestory
80' - 1"

Seventh Floor - Residential
74' - 1"

Sixth Floor - Residential
62' - 1"

Fifth Floor - Residential
50' - 1"

Fourth Floor - Residential
38' - 1"

Third Floor - Residential
26' - 1"

Second Floor - Parking
16' - 2"

First Floor - Mercantile
0' - 0"

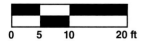

0   5   10   20 ft

6.21a
East/west building section B-B

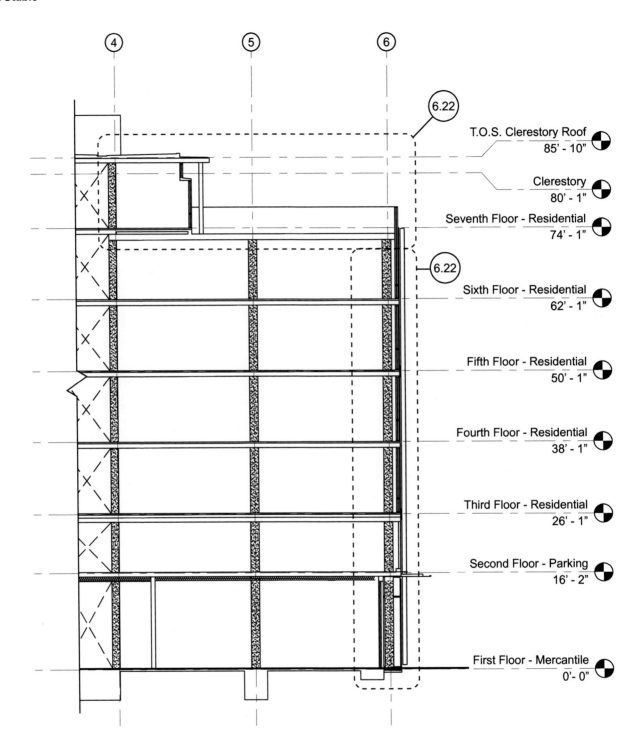

T.O.S. Clerestory Roof
85' - 10"

Clerestory
80' - 1"

Seventh Floor - Residential
74' - 1"

Sixth Floor - Residential
62' - 1"

Fifth Floor - Residential
50' - 1"

Fourth Floor - Residential
38' - 1"

Third Floor - Residential
26' - 1"

Second Floor - Parking
16' - 2"

First Floor - Mercantile
0' - 0"

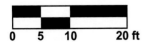

0   5   10   20 ft

6.21b
East/west building section B-B

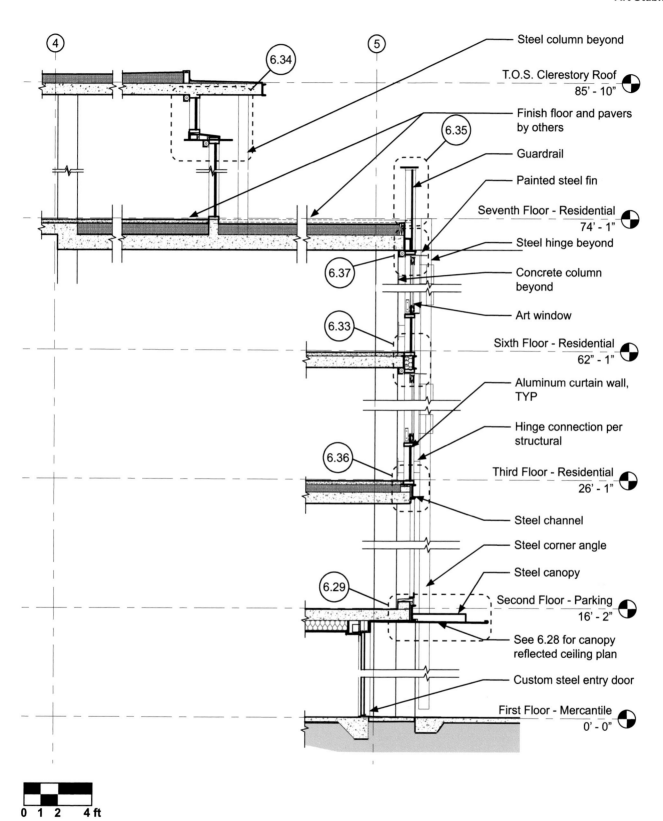

④ ⑤

6.34

6.35

6.37

6.33

6.36

6.29

— Steel column beyond

T.O.S. Clerestory Roof
85' - 10"

— Finish floor and pavers
by others

— Guardrail

— Painted steel fin

Seventh Floor - Residential
74' - 1"

— Steel hinge beyond

— Concrete column
beyond

— Art window

Sixth Floor - Residential
62" - 1"

— Aluminum curtain wall,
TYP

— Hinge connection per
structural

Third Floor - Residential
26' - 1"

— Steel channel

— Steel corner angle

— Steel canopy

Second Floor - Parking
16' - 2"

— See 6.28 for canopy
reflected ceiling plan

— Custom steel entry door

First Floor - Mercantile
0' - 0"

0 1 2   4 ft

6.22
Wall section: west wall

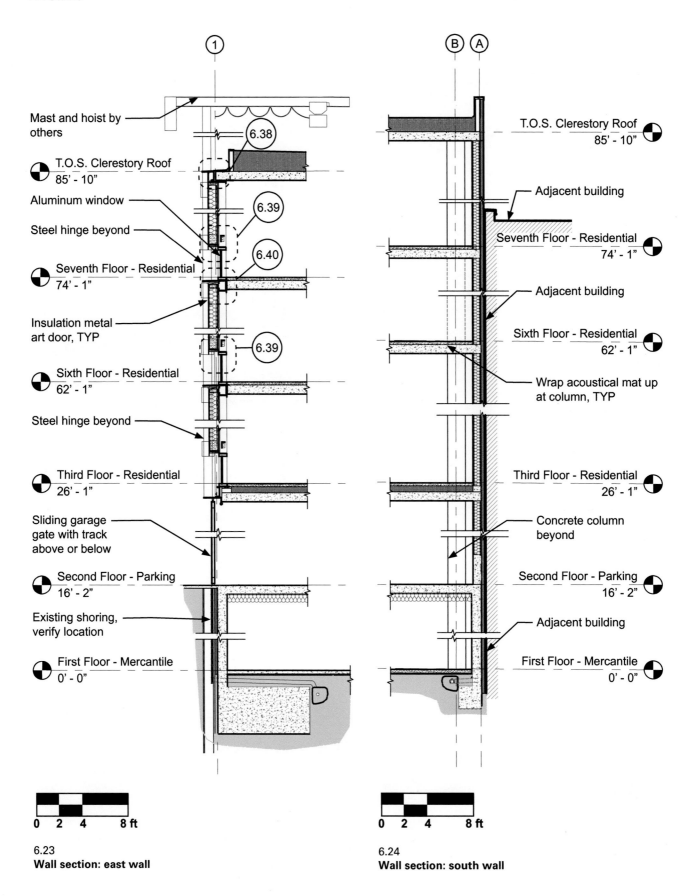

6.23
Wall section: east wall

Mast and hoist by others

⊕ T.O.S. Clerestory Roof
85' - 10"

Aluminum window

Steel hinge beyond

6.38

6.39

6.40

⊕ Seventh Floor - Residential
74' - 1"

Insulation metal art door, TYP

6.39

⊕ Sixth Floor - Residential
62' - 1"

Steel hinge beyond

⊕ Third Floor - Residential
26' - 1"

Sliding garage gate with track above or below

⊕ Second Floor - Parking
16' - 2"

Existing shoring, verify location

⊕ First Floor - Mercantile
0' - 0"

0 2 4   8 ft

6.24
Wall section: south wall

T.O.S. Clerestory Roof
85' - 10" ⊕

Adjacent building

Seventh Floor - Residential
74' - 1" ⊕

Adjacent building

Sixth Floor - Residential
62' - 1" ⊕

Wrap acoustical mat up at column, TYP

Third Floor - Residential
26' - 1" ⊕

Concrete column beyond

Second Floor - Parking
16' - 2" ⊕

Adjacent building

First Floor - Mercantile
0' - 0" ⊕

0 2 4   8 ft

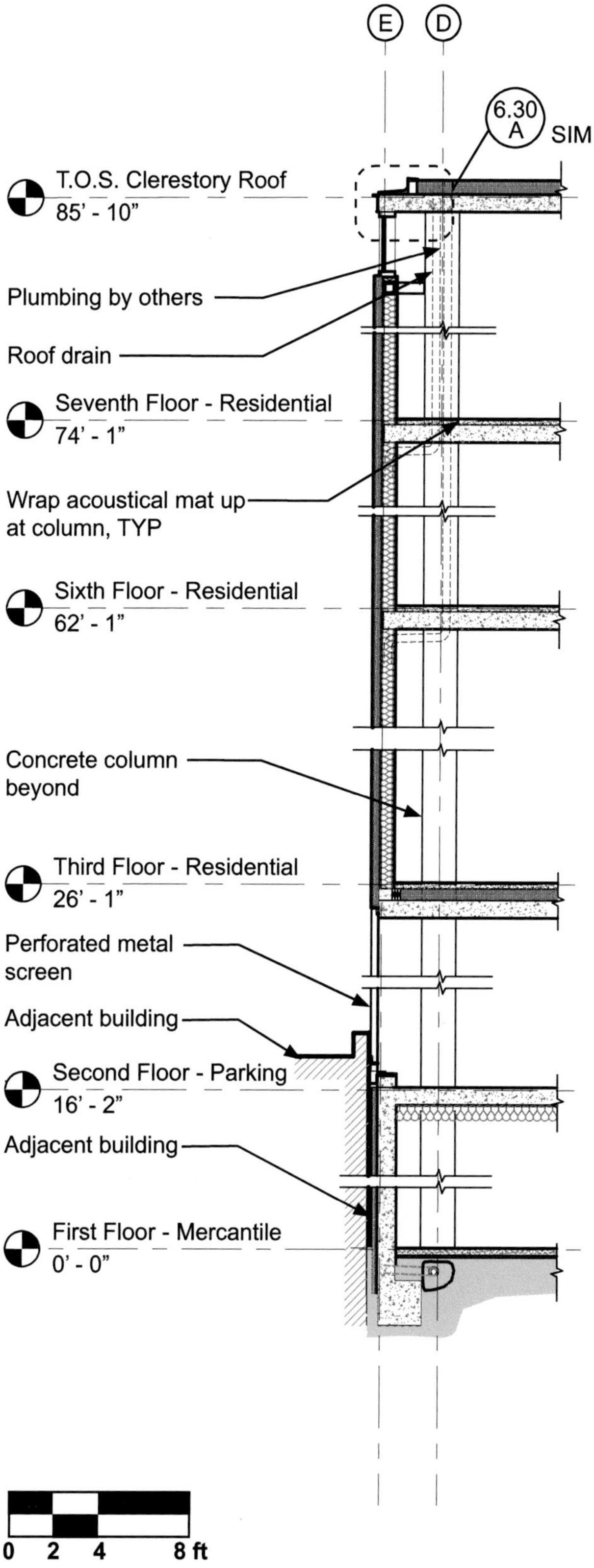
E
D
6.30
A
SIM
T.O.S. Clerestory Roof
85' - 10"
Plumbing by others
Roof drain
Seventh Floor - Residential
74' - 1"
Wrap acoustical mat up at column, TYP
Sixth Floor - Residential
62' - 1"
Concrete column beyond
Third Floor - Residential
26' - 1"
Perforated metal screen
Adjacent building
Second Floor - Parking
16' - 2"
Adjacent building
First Floor - Mercantile
0' - 0"
0 2 4 8 ft

6.25
Wall section: north wall

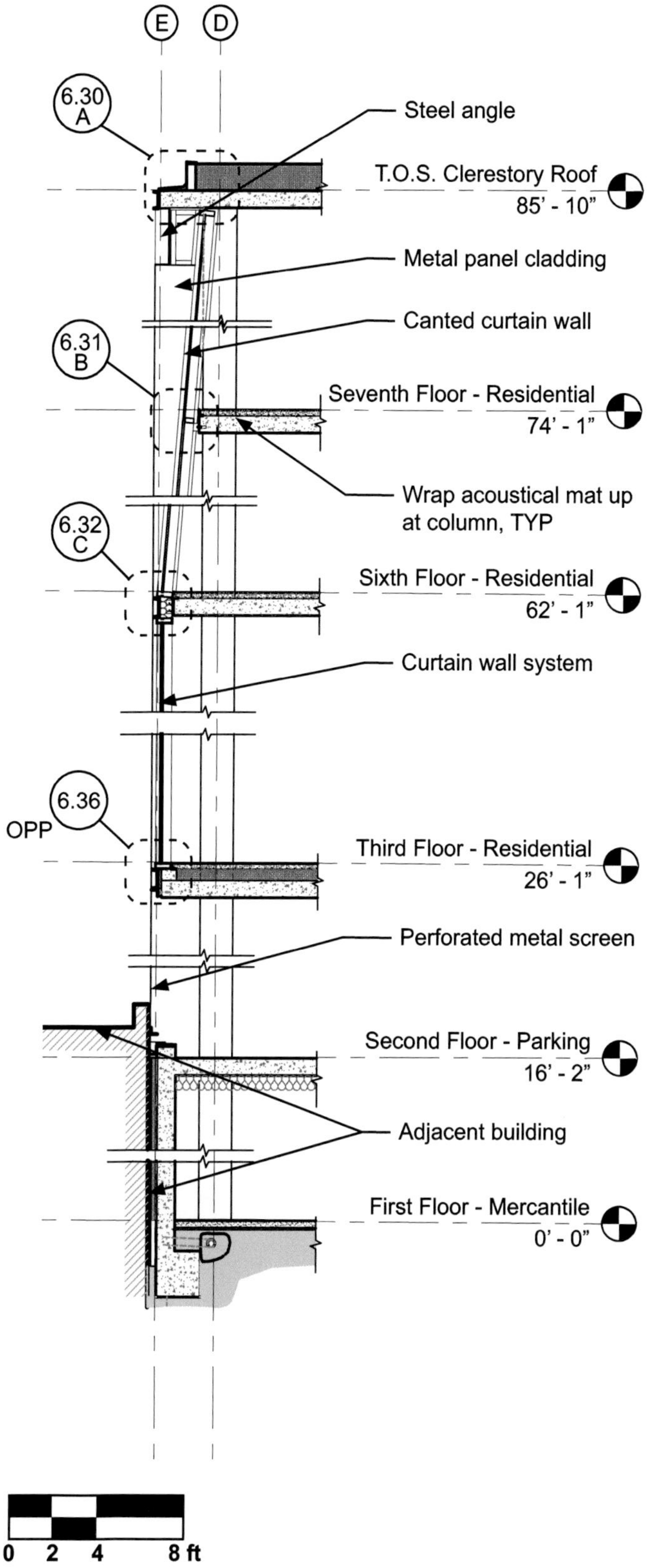
E
D
6.30
A
Steel angle
T.O.S. Clerestory Roof
85' - 10"
Metal panel cladding
Canted curtain wall
6.31
B
Seventh Floor - Residential
74' - 1"
Wrap acoustical mat up at column, TYP
6.32
C
Sixth Floor - Residential
62' - 1"
Curtain wall system
6.36
OPP
Third Floor - Residential
26' - 1"
Perforated metal screen
Second Floor - Parking
16' - 2"
Adjacent building
First Floor - Mercantile
0' - 0"
0 2 4 8 ft

6.26
Wall section: north cant window

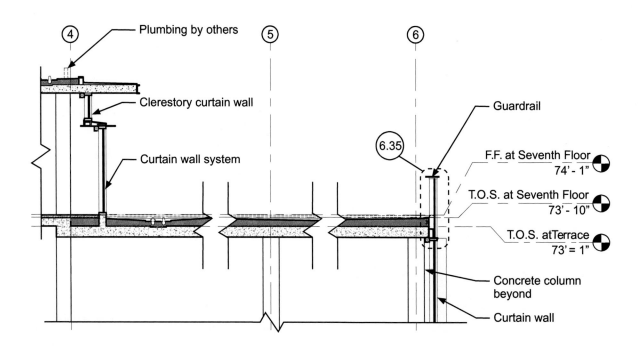

0 2 4   8 ft

6.27
Wall section: terrace

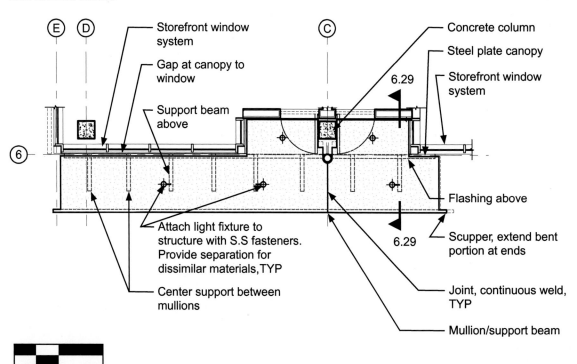

0 2 4   8 ft

6.28
Enlarged plan: entry canopy

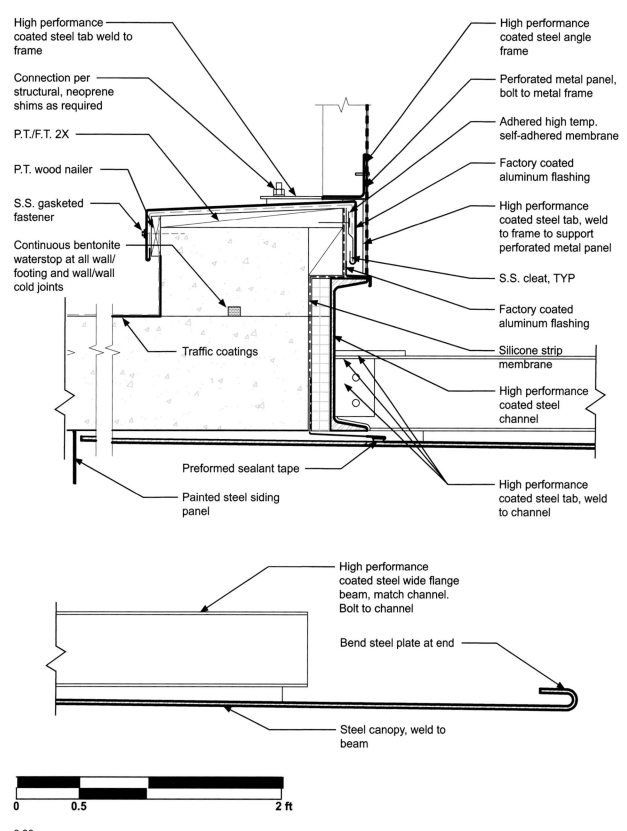

High performance coated steel tab weld to frame

Connection per structural, neoprene shims as required

P.T./F.T. 2X

P.T. wood nailer

S.S. gasketed fastener

Continuous bentonite waterstop at all wall/ footing and wall/wall cold joints

Traffic coatings

Preformed sealant tape

Painted steel siding panel

High performance coated steel angle frame

Perforated metal panel, bolt to metal frame

Adhered high temp. self-adhered membrane

Factory coated aluminum flashing

High performance coated steel tab, weld to frame to support perforated metal panel

S.S. cleat, TYP

Factory coated aluminum flashing

Silicone strip membrane

High performance coated steel channel

High performance coated steel tab, weld to channel

High performance coated steel wide flange beam, match channel. Bolt to channel

Bend steel plate at end

Steel canopy, weld to beam

0   0.5   2 ft

6.29
Section detail: awning section at roof

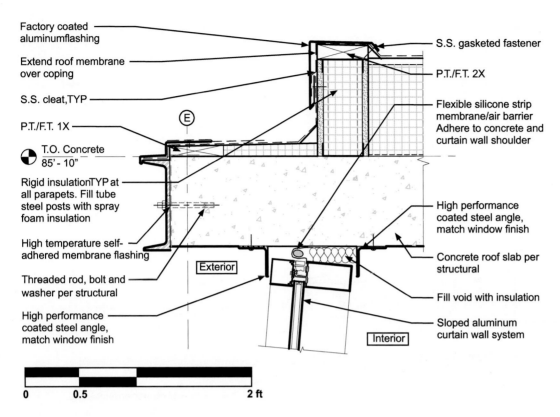

Factory coated aluminumflashing

Extend roof membrane over coping

S.S. cleat,TYP

P.T./F.T. 1X

T.O. Concrete
85' - 10"

Rigid insulationTYP at all parapets. Fill tube steel posts with spray foam insulation

High temperature self-adhered membrane flashing

Threaded rod, bolt and washer per structural

High performance coated steel angle, match window finish

S.S. gasketed fastener

P.T./F.T. 2X

Flexible silicone strip membrane/air barrier Adhere to concrete and curtain wall shoulder

High performance coated steel angle, match window finish

Concrete roof slab per structural

Fill void with insulation

Sloped aluminum curtain wall system

Exterior

Interior

(E)

0   0.5   2 ft

6.30
Section detail: head at cant glazing

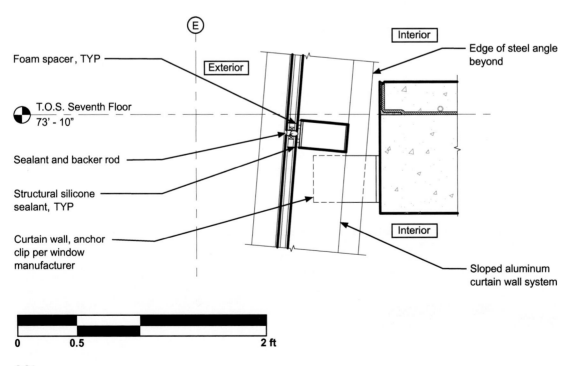

Foam spacer, TYP

T.O.S. Seventh Floor
73' - 10"

Sealant and backer rod

Structural silicone sealant, TYP

Curtain wall, anchor clip per window manufacturer

Interior

Exterior

Interior

(E)

Edge of steel angle beyond

Sloped aluminum curtain wall system

0   0.5   2 ft

6.31
Section detail: cant glazing at seventh floor

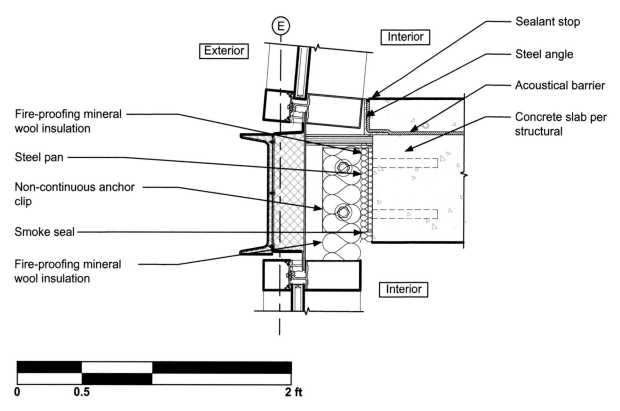

Sealant stop

Steel angle

Acoustical barrier

Concrete slab per structural

Fire-proofing mineral wool insulation

Steel pan

Non-continuous anchor clip

Smoke seal

Fire-proofing mineral wool insulation

Interior

Exterior

Interior

E

0   0.5   2 ft

6.32
Section detail: sill/head at cant glazing at sixth floor

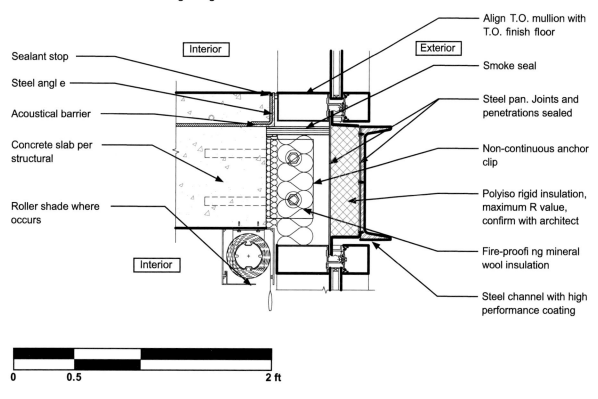

Align T.O. mullion with T.O. finish floor

Smoke seal

Steel pan. Joints and penetrations sealed

Non-continuous anchor clip

Polyiso rigid insulation, maximum R value, confirm with architect

Fire-proofing mineral wool insulation

Steel channel with high performance coating

Sealant stop

Steel angle

Acoustical barrier

Concrete slab per structural

Roller shade where occurs

Interior

Exterior

Interior

0   0.5   2 ft

6.33
Section detail: sill/head at fourth, fifth, and sixth floors

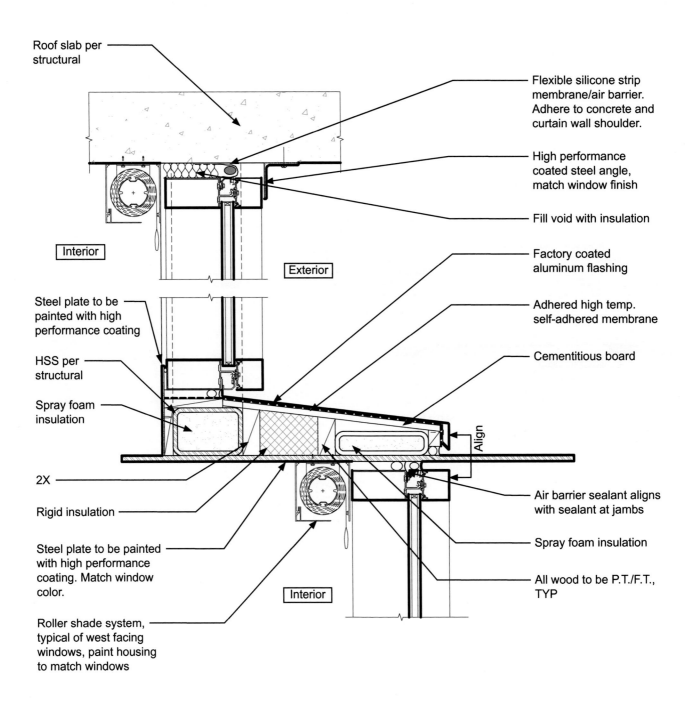

Roof slab per structural

Flexible silicone strip membrane/air barrier. Adhere to concrete and curtain wall shoulder.

High performance coated steel angle, match window finish

Fill void with insulation

Interior

Exterior

Factory coated aluminum flashing

Steel plate to be painted with high performance coating

Adhered high temp. self-adhered membrane

HSS per structural

Cementitious board

Spray foam insulation

Align

2X

Air barrier sealant aligns with sealant at jambs

Rigid insulation

Spray foam insulation

Steel plate to be painted with high performance coating. Match window color.

Interior

All wood to be P.T./F.T., TYP

Roller shade system, typical of west facing windows, paint housing to match windows

0   0.5   2 ft

6.34
Section detail: sill/head at clerestory

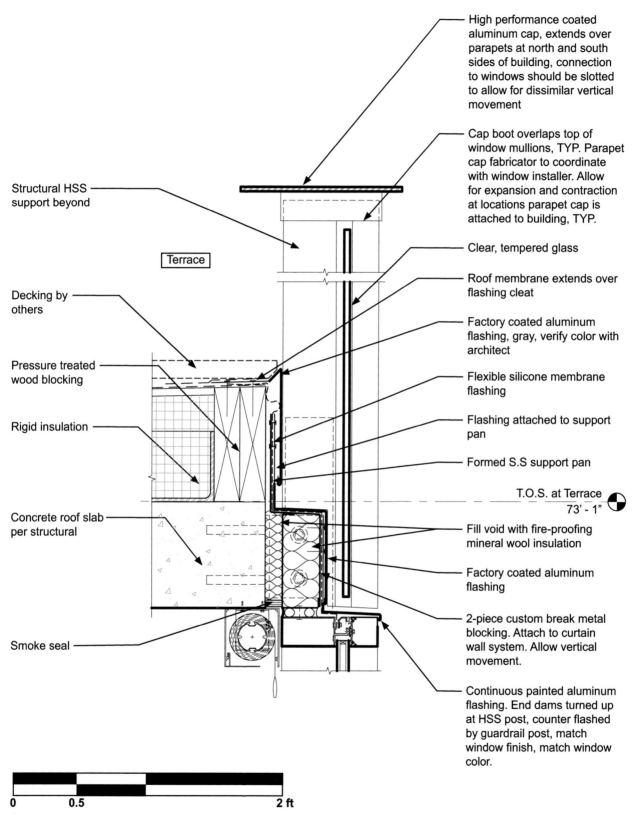

High performance coated aluminum cap, extends over parapets at north and south sides of building, connection to windows should be slotted to allow for dissimilar vertical movement

Cap boot overlaps top of window mullions, TYP. Parapet cap fabricator to coordinate with window installer. Allow for expansion and contraction at locations parapet cap is attached to building, TYP.

Structural HSS support beyond

Terrace

Clear, tempered glass

Roof membrane extends over flashing cleat

Decking by others

Factory coated aluminum flashing, gray, verify color with architect

Pressure treated wood blocking

Flexible silicone membrane flashing

Flashing attached to support pan

Rigid insulation

Formed S.S support pan

T.O.S. at Terrace
73' - 1"

Concrete roof slab per structural

Fill void with fire-proofing mineral wool insulation

Factory coated aluminum flashing

2-piece custom break metal blocking. Attach to curtain wall system. Allow vertical movement.

Smoke seal

Continuous painted aluminum flashing. End dams turned up at HSS post, counter flashed by guardrail post, match window finish, match window color.

0   0.5   2 ft

6.35
Section detail: head at terrace guardrail

Art Stable

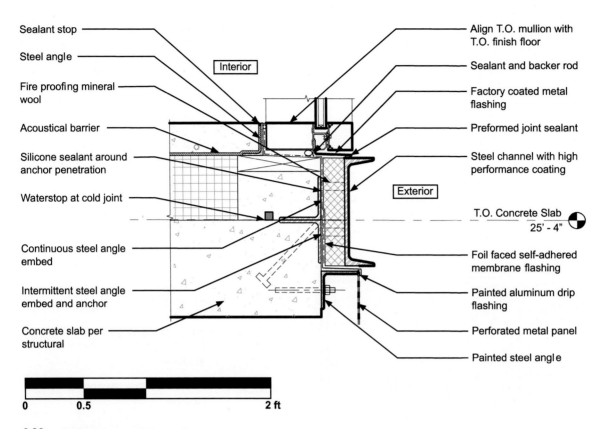

Sealant stop

Steel angle

Fire proofing mineral wool

Acoustical barrier

Silicone sealant around anchor penetration

Waterstop at cold joint

Continuous steel angle embed

Intermittent steel angle embed and anchor

Concrete slab per structural

Interior

Exterior

Align T.O. mullion with T.O. finish floor

Sealant and backer rod

Factory coated metal flashing

Preformed joint sealant

Steel channel with high performance coating

T.O. Concrete Slab
25' - 4"

Foil faced self-adhered membrane flashing

Painted aluminum drip flashing

Perforated metal panel

Painted steel angle

0   0.5   2 ft

6.36
Section detail: sill at third floor

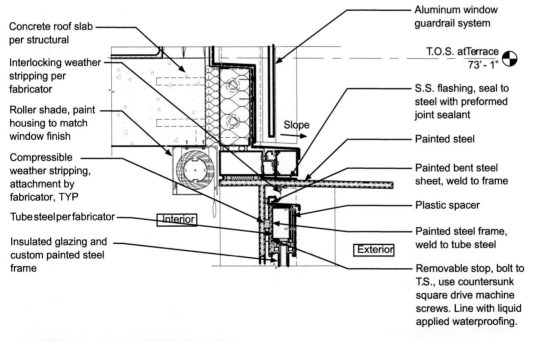

Concrete roof slab per structural

Interlocking weather stripping per fabricator

Roller shade, paint housing to match window finish

Compressible weather stripping, attachment by fabricator, TYP

Tube steel per fabricator

Insulated glazing and custom painted steel frame

Interior

Exterior

Slope

Aluminum window guardrail system

T.O.S. at Terrace
73' - 1"

S.S. flashing, seal to steel with preformed joint sealant

Painted steel

Painted bent steel sheet, weld to frame

Plastic spacer

Painted steel frame, weld to tube steel

Removable stop, bolt to T.S., use countersunk square drive machine screws. Line with liquid applied waterproofing.

0   0.5   2 ft

6.37
Section detail: art window head, TYP

216

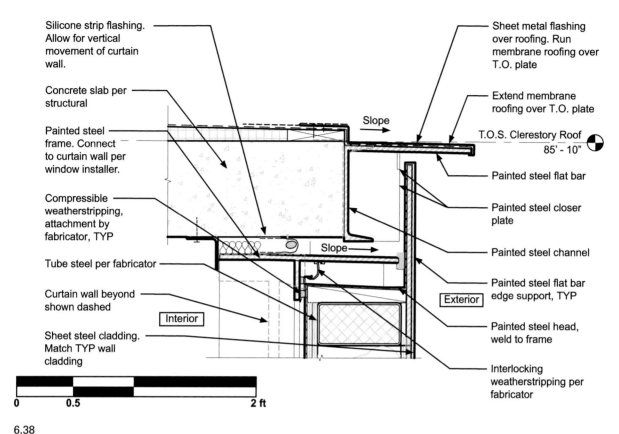

Silicone strip flashing. Allow for vertical movement of curtain wall.

Concrete slab per structural

Painted steel frame. Connect to curtain wall per window installer.

Compressible weatherstripping, attachment by fabricator, TYP

Tube steel per fabricator

Curtain wall beyond shown dashed

Sheet steel cladding. Match TYP wall cladding

Sheet metal flashing over roofing. Run membrane roofing over T.O. plate

Extend membrane roofing over T.O. plate

T.O.S. Clerestory Roof
85' - 10"

Painted steel flat bar

Painted steel closer plate

Painted steel channel

Painted steel flat bar edge support, TYP

Painted steel head, weld to frame

Interlocking weatherstripping per fabricator

Slope

Slope

Interior

Exterior

0   0.5   2 ft

6.38
Section detail: art door head at roof

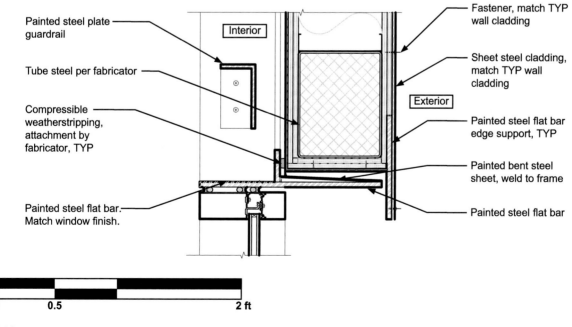

Painted steel plate guardrail

Tube steel per fabricator

Compressible weatherstripping, attachment by fabricator, TYP

Painted steel flat bar. Match window finish.

Fastener, match TYP wall cladding

Sheet steel cladding, match TYP wall cladding

Painted steel flat bar edge support, TYP

Painted bent steel sheet, weld to frame

Painted steel flat bar

Interior

Exterior

0   0.5   2 ft

6.39
Section detail: art door sill, TYP

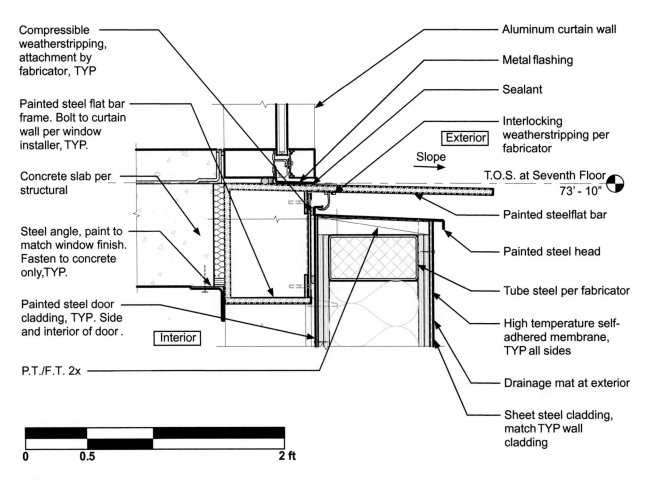

Compressible weatherstripping, attachment by fabricator, TYP

Painted steel flat bar frame. Bolt to curtain wall per window installer, TYP.

Concrete slab per structural

Steel angle, paint to match window finish. Fasten to concrete only, TYP.

Painted steel door cladding, TYP. Side and interior of door.

Interior

P.T./F.T. 2x

Aluminum curtain wall

Metal flashing

Sealant

Exterior

Interlocking weatherstripping per fabricator

Slope

T.O.S. at Seventh Floor
73' - 10"

Painted steel flat bar

Painted steel head

Tube steel per fabricator

High temperature self-adhered membrane, TYP all sides

Drainage mat at exterior

Sheet steel cladding, match TYP wall cladding

0   0.5   2 ft

6.40
Section detail: art door head, TYP

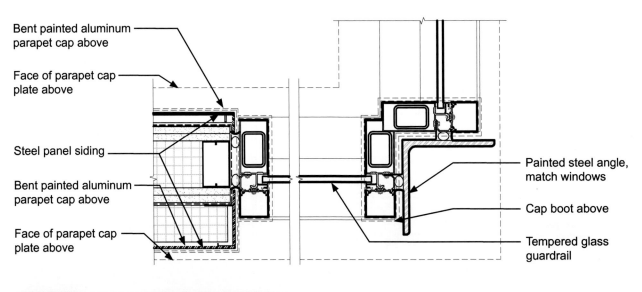

Bent painted aluminum parapet cap above

Face of parapet cap plate above

Steel panel siding

Bent painted aluminum parapet cap above

Face of parapet cap plate above

Painted steel angle, match windows

Cap boot above

Tempered glass guardrail

0   0.5   2 ft

6.41
Plan detail: guardrail wall

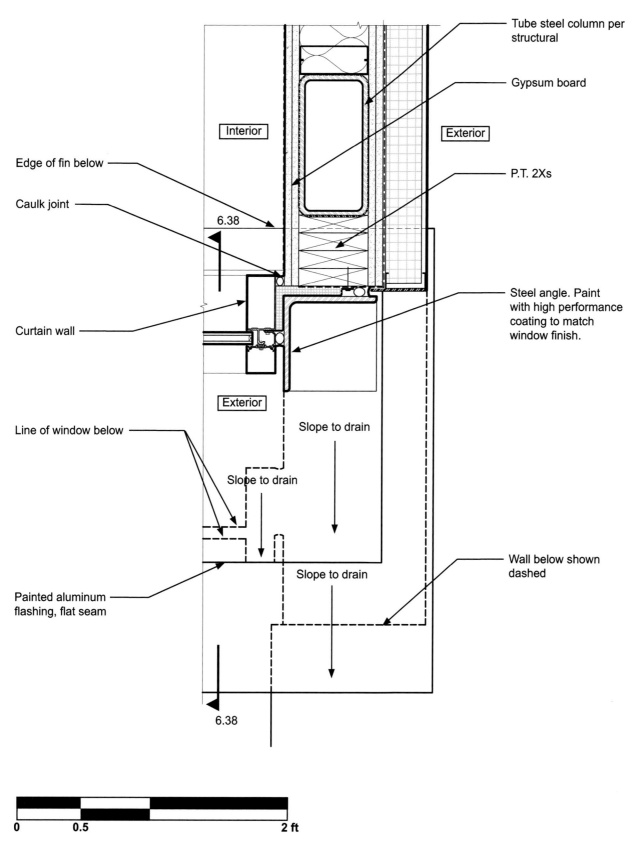

Tube steel column per structural

Gypsum board

Interior

Exterior

Edge of fin below

P.T. 2Xs

Caulk joint

6.38

Steel angle. Paint with high performance coating to match window finish.

Curtain wall

Exterior

Line of window below

Slope to drain

Slope to drain

Slope to drain

Wall below shown dashed

Painted aluminum flashing, flat seam

0   0.5   2 ft

6.38

6.42
Plan detail: jamb at southwest corner of clerestory

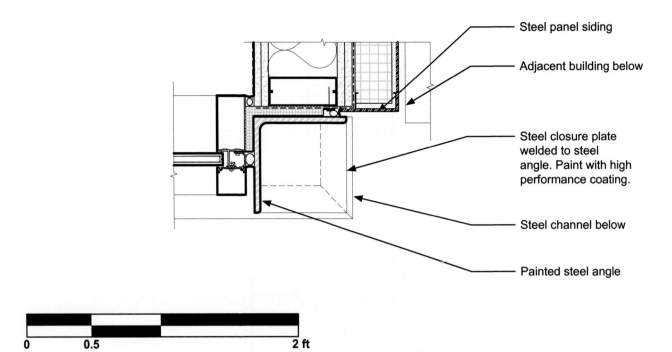

Steel panel siding

Adjacent building below

Steel closure plate welded to steel angle. Paint with high performance coating.

Steel channel below

Painted steel angle

0   0.5   2 ft

6.43
Plan detail: jamb at southwest corner

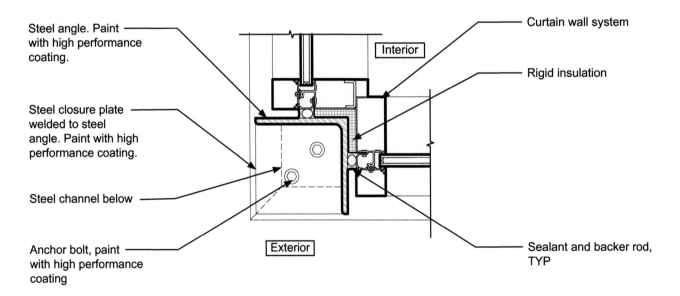

Steel angle. Paint with high performance coating.

Steel closure plate welded to steel angle. Paint with high performance coating.

Steel channel below

Anchor bolt, paint with high performance coating

Interior

Exterior

Curtain wall system

Rigid insulation

Sealant and backer rod, TYP

0   0.5   2 ft

6.44
Plan detail: jamb at angle

7.1

Aerial view of main entrance and courtyard

Credit: James and Connor Steinkamp

7: Shanghai Nature Museum

Shanghai, China, Perkins + Will

Architect's Design Intent and Reasoning Behind Material and Tectonic Choices

This project for the Shanghai Natural History Museum is consistent with Chinese garden design in that it approaches the spirit of nature, but does not imitate it. Through its relationship to the site, it represents the harmony of man and nature and is an abstraction of the basic elements of Chinese art and design.

The museum sits within the Jing An sculpture park. The shape and building organization are inspired by the nautilus shell, one of the purest geometric forms found in nature. The nautilus was also chosen as an organizational strategy to provide the opportunity for a sequential exhibit experience in the museum. A spiraling landscaped plane rises out of the park recalling the harmonious forms and proportions of the nautilus shell. This plane terminates in a roof deck that provides views of the park and surrounding city. Within this spiraling plane is an oval courtyard that contains a stepped garden composed of rock formations and water features which recalls the Chinese tradition of the "Mountain Water Garden." Adjacent to the courtyard is an atrium exhibit space on the lowest level. This volume peaks at 30 meters in height with its ceiling rising with the sloped roof. Taking advantage of the ultraviolet sensitivity of the exhibits, 70% of the building is placed below grade, which reduces its museum's visual scale within the park. Additionally, the Museum entry is located in the center of the park, rather than on the street, further integrating the structure within the park, rather than isolating it. A point-supported cable façade maximizes transparency and strengthens the buildings relationship to the park.

The museum has three levels above-grade, which accommodate such spaces as the entry corridor, office facilities, and an IMAX theater, as well as some exhibit space. The two large levels with additional mezzanines spiral to a depth of 16 meters below grade and house the majority of the primary exhibit halls. The central atrium and adjacent central courtyard act as a way-finding device to offset the potential for disorientation in the three underground levels.

The landscaping concept integrates the museum into the landscape of the existing sculpture park while also reinforcing its message. Plant groupings of wild and untamed species and rock formations act as metaphors of the primordial forest.

7.2
**Aerial view of main entrance
and green wall**

Credit: James and Connor
Steinkamp

7.3
View of stone façade wall

Credit: James and Connor
Steinkamp

7.4
View of main entrance

Credit: James and Connor Steinkamp

7.5
Night view of main entrance

Credit: James and Connor Steinkamp

7.6
Interior view of screen wall at courtyard

Credit: James and Connor Steinkamp

7.7
Detail view of screen wall

Credit: James and Connor Steinkamp

7.8
View from green roof to main entrance

Credit: James and Connor Steinkamp

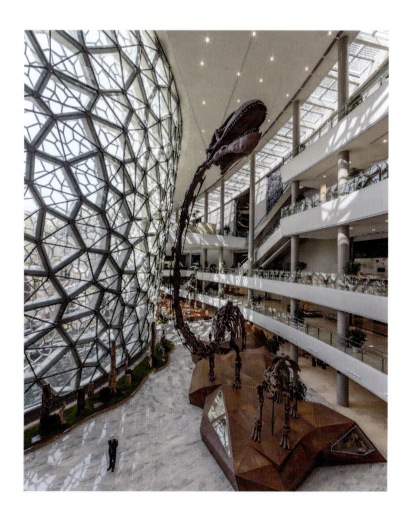

7.9
Interior view of atrium and screen wall

Credit: James and Connor Steinkamp

7.10
View of intersection of green wall and stone façade wall
Credit: James and Connor Steinkamp

The Museum is a bioclimatic building, which responds to the sun using an appropriately oriented intelligent building skin to maximize daylight and minimize solar gain. The pond in the oval courtyard provides evaporative cooling while the temperature of the earth provides heating and cooling by using a geothermal system. The geothermal field, as well as integrated photovoltaics in the skylight glass help offset the energy demands of the Museum. Rainwater is collected from the vegetated roof and stored in the pond along with recycled grey water. The green roof therefore does a number of things – helps with storm water management, provides a direct link to the park in which it sits by extending its landscape up, and utilizes the surface as an additional façade, as the building sits within a forest of high rises, whose residents view it from above. All of the energy features of the Museum are part of the exhibits, which explains the story of the Museum.

The Cell Wall is the iconic feature of the Shanghai Natural History Museum, and is the main design feature from the initial competition phase. Composed of three layers, each with its own unique geometrical pattern and organic form, the wall is organized in a sloped elliptical cone shape envelope. At the core is the main layer, the structural cell layer, which emphasizes the organic cells as structural building blocks of nature, while the outer aluminum screen layer is a smaller scale version of the geometry which provides further solar shading. The inner layer, the waterproof envelope of the building, is a triangular breakdown of the structural geometry composed of glass and aluminum mullion curtain-wall, supported from the structural at the nodes.

In resolving complex organic geometry at the scale of the building's Cell Wall, the seemingly random patterning of the mesh structure is actually composed of a series of repeated shapes which interlock to form the overall diaphragm. This strategy simplifies construction by minimizing the number of unique component members in the three layers of the wall and allows for the utilization of readily-available building materials.

The façades express the Museum's message and content. The structural network and sunscreen lining the curved inner façade facing the oval courtyard, are an abstraction of patterns found in traditional Chinese garden pavilions and also suggest human cell organization. The north wall suggests the layering of tectonic plates. The east wall is a living wall, bringing the horizontal plane of the park onto the vertical surface, forming an arcade and representing the vegetation of the earth's surface. These features focus our awareness on the fundamental elements of the natural world: plants, earth and water.

Ralph Johnson,
Global Design Director at Perkins+Will

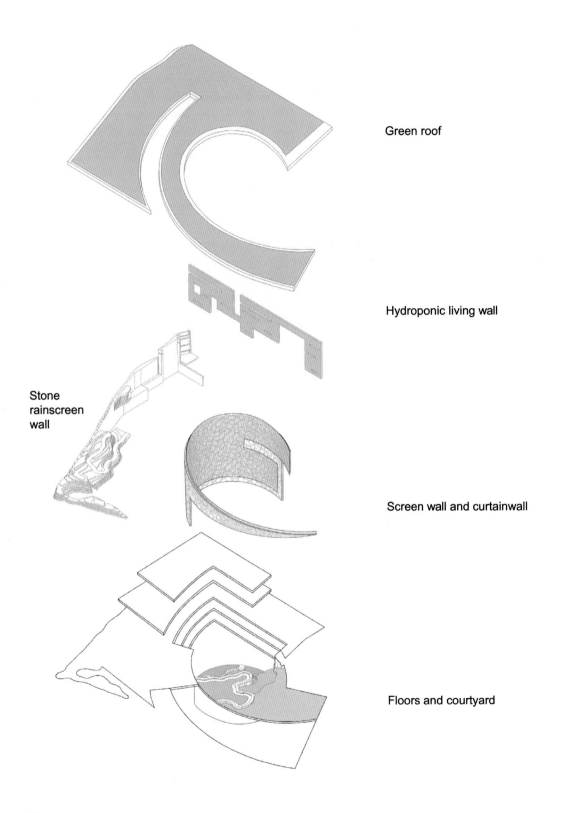

Green roof

Hydroponic living wall

Stone
rainscreen
wall

Screen wall and curtainwall

Floors and courtyard

7.11
Major building components
(Not to scale.)

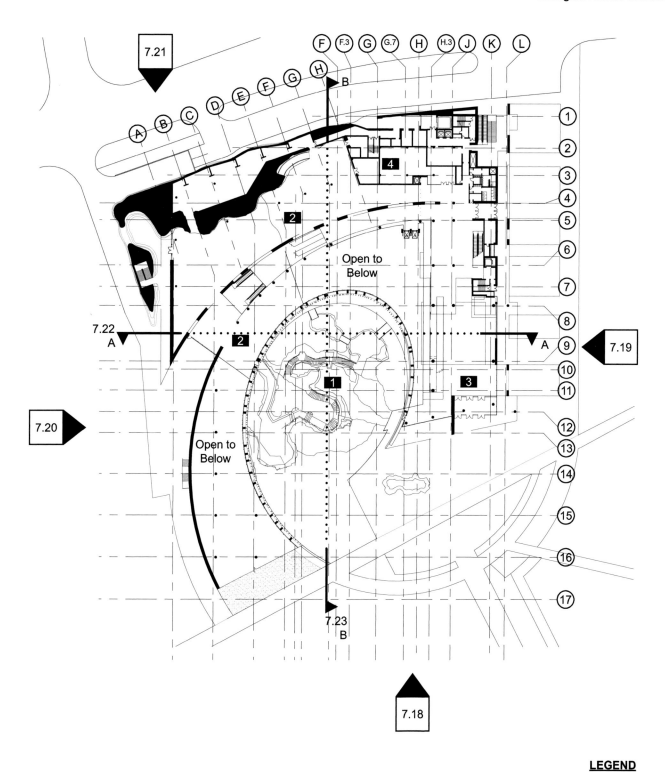

7.21

Ⓕ Ⓕ.3 Ⓖ Ⓖ.7 Ⓗ Ⓗ.3 Ⓙ Ⓚ Ⓛ

Ⓐ Ⓑ Ⓒ Ⓓ Ⓔ Ⓕ Ⓖ Ⓗ

B

4

2

Open to
Below

①
②
③
④
⑤
⑥
⑦
⑧
⑨
⑩
⑪
⑫
⑬
⑭
⑮
⑯
⑰

7.22
A

2

Open to
Below

1

3

A

7.19

7.20

7.23
B

7.18

0 5 10   20 M

7.12
Ground floor plan

<u>LEGEND</u>
Courtyard ▮1▮
Exhibit Hall ▮2▮
Lobby ▮3▮
Gift Shop ▮4▮

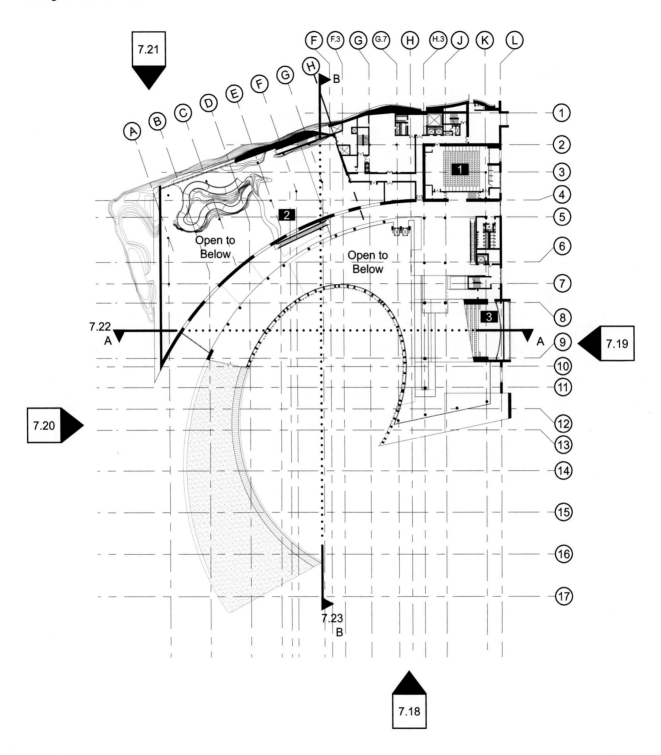

Open to Below

Open to Below

0 5 10 20 M

7.13
Second floor plan

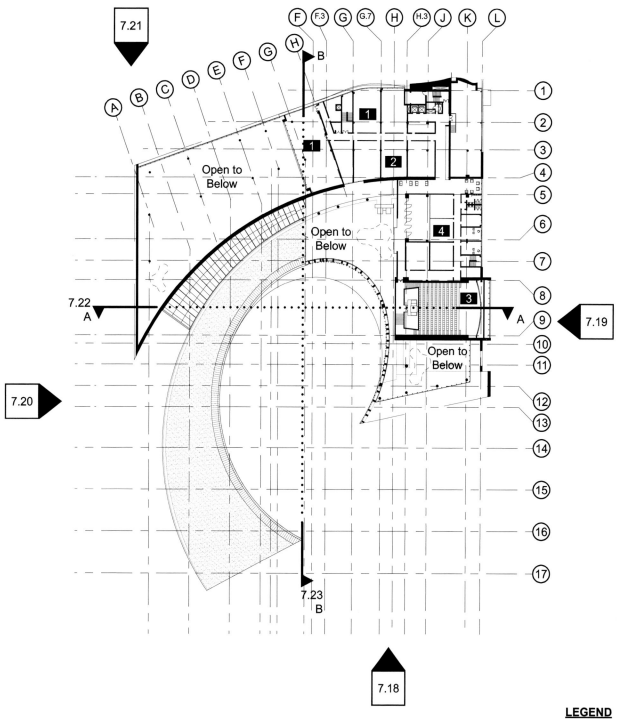

Open to Below

Open to Below

Open to Below

7.21

7.22
A

7.20

7.23
B

7.19

7.18

N

0 5 10   20 M

7.14
Third floor plan

LEGEND
Research **1**
Offices **2**
Theater **3**
Meeting **4**

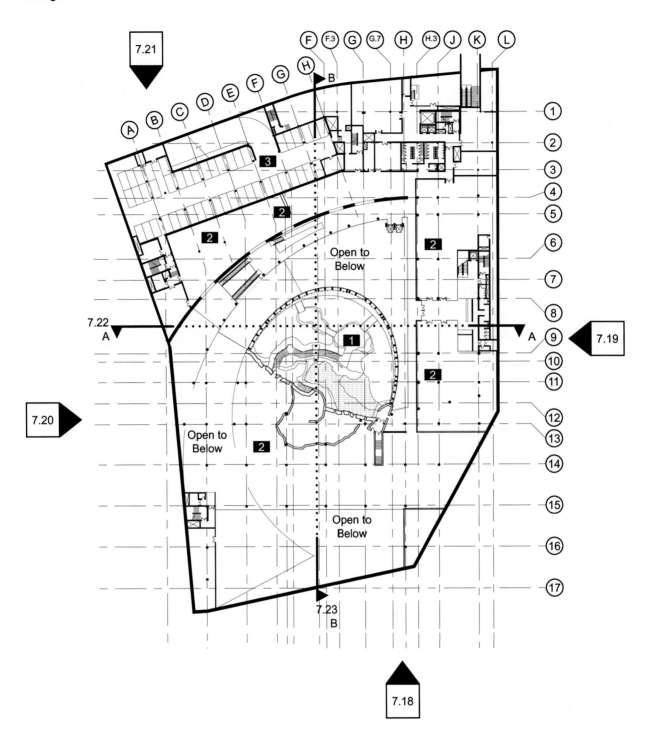

7.21

F F.3 G G.7 H H.3 J K L

H
G
B
F
A B C D E F

3

2

2

Open to
Below

2

1

Open to
Below

2

Open to
Below

7.22
A

7.20

7.19

7.23
B

7.18

1
2
3
4
5
6
7
8
9
10
11
12
13
14
15
16
17

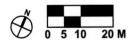

0 5 10   20 M

LEGEND
Courtyard 1
Exhibit Hall 2
Parking 3

7.15
Basement level one floor plan

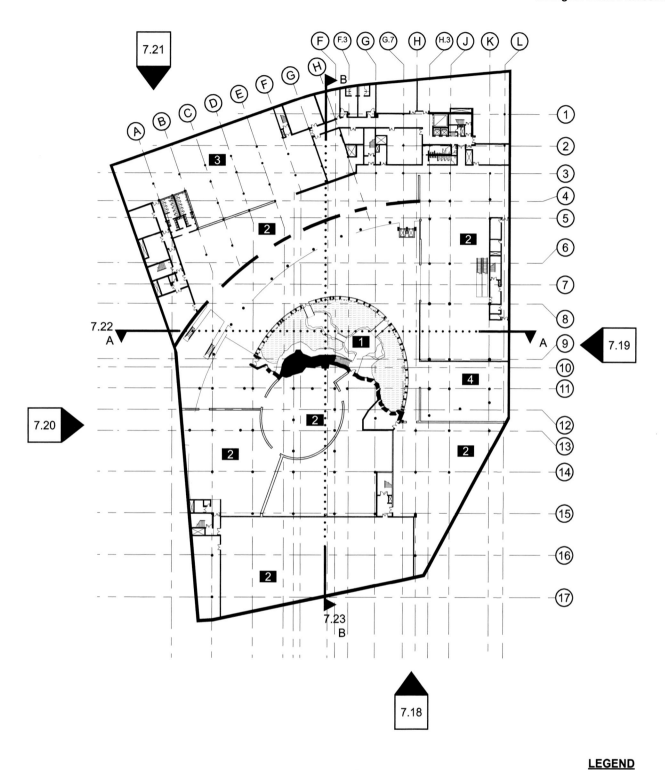

7.21

Ⓕ Ⓕ.3 Ⓖ Ⓖ.7 Ⓗ Ⓗ.3 Ⓙ Ⓚ Ⓛ

Ⓕ Ⓖ Ⓗ
B

Ⓐ Ⓑ Ⓒ Ⓓ Ⓔ Ⓕ Ⓖ Ⓗ

① ② ③ ④ ⑤ ⑥ ⑦ ⑧ ⑨ ⑩ ⑪ ⑫ ⑬ ⑭ ⑮ ⑯ ⑰

7.22
A

7.19

7.20

7.23
B

7.18

3 2 1 2 2 2 2 4 2

N
0 5 10 20 M

7.16
Basement level two floor plan

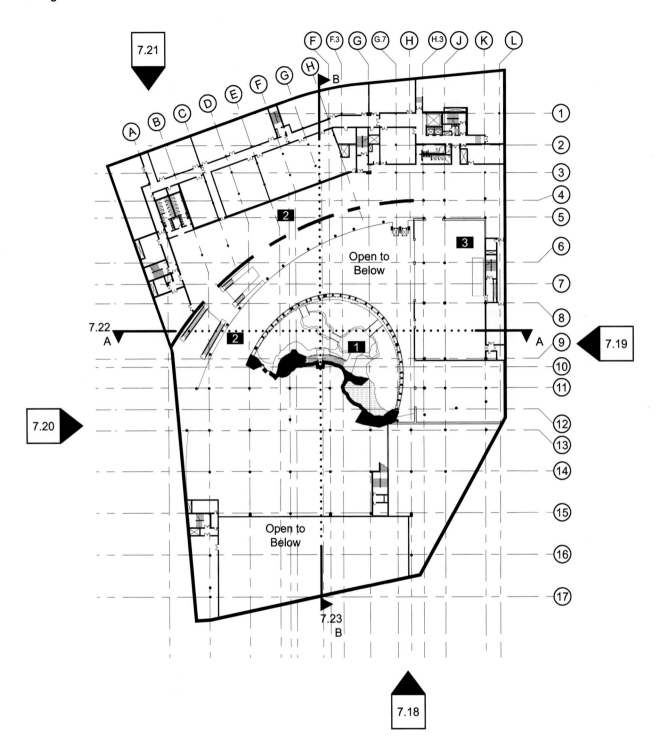

7.21

7.22
A

7.20

7.19

7.18

7.23
B

2

3

Open to
Below

1

Open to
Below

0 5 10   20 M

7.17
Basement level two mezzanine floor plan

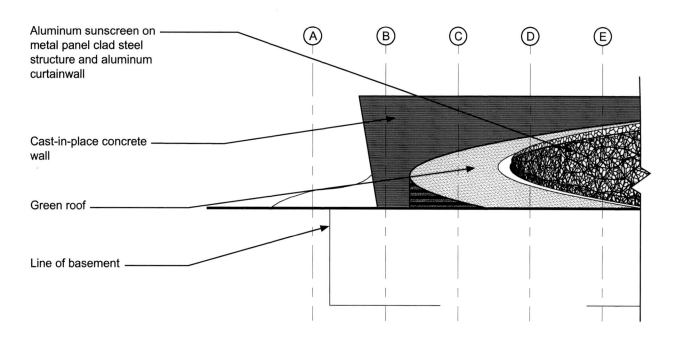

Aluminum sunscreen on metal panel clad steel structure and aluminum curtainwall

Cast-in-place concrete wall

Green roof

Line of basement

0 5 10 20 M

7.18a
South entry elevation

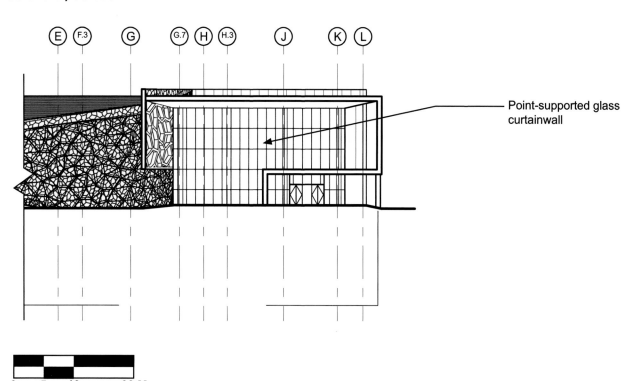

Point-supported glass curtainwall

0 5 10 20 M

7.18b
South entry elevation

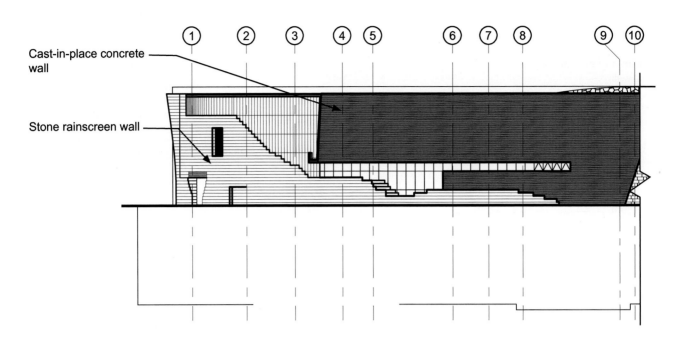

Cast-in-place concrete wall

Stone rainscreen wall

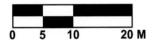

0 5 10 20 M

7.19a
East elevation

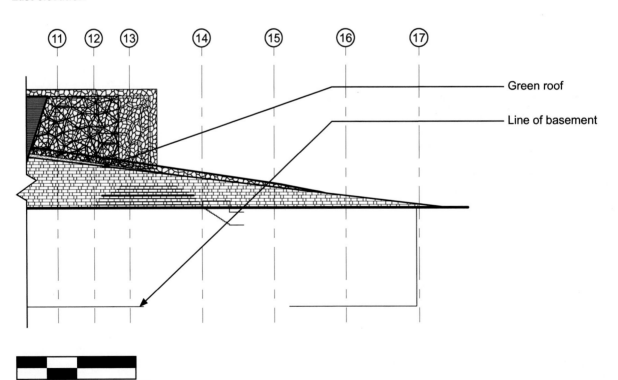

Green roof

Line of basement

0 5 10 20 M

7.19b
East elevation

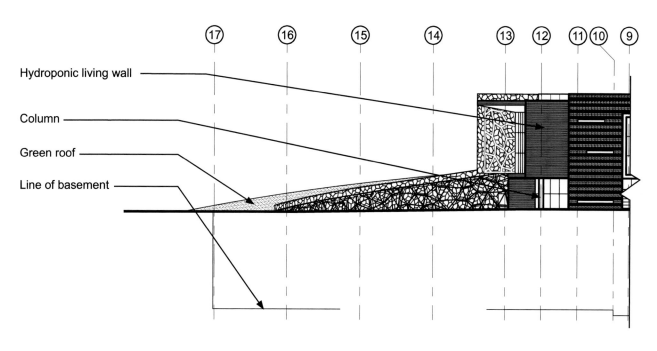

Hydroponic living wall

Column

Green roof

Line of basement

0   5   10   20 M

7.20a
West elevation

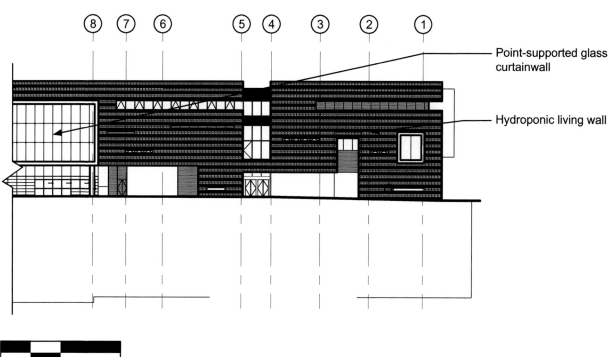

Point-supported glass
curtainwall

Hydroponic living wall

0   5   10   20 M

7.20b
West elevation

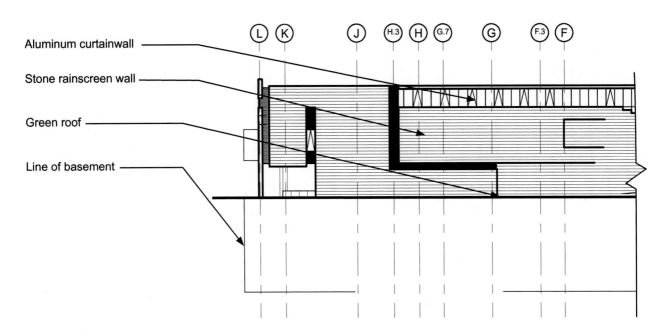

Aluminum curtainwall

Stone rainscreen wall

Green roof

Line of basement

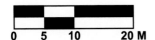

0   5   10   20 M

7.21a
North entry elevation

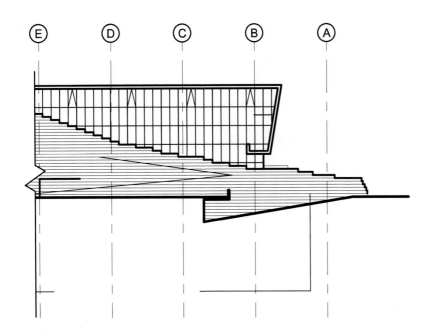

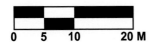

0   5   10   20 M

7.21b
North entry elevation

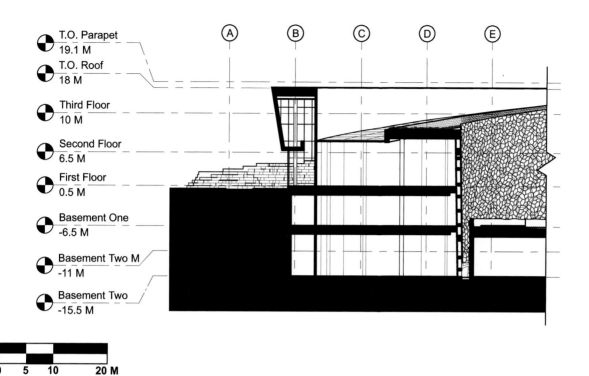

T.O. Parapet
19.1 M

T.O. Roof
18 M

Third Floor
10 M

Second Floor
6.5 M

First Floor
0.5 M

Basement One
-6.5 M

Basement Two M
-11 M

Basement Two
-15.5 M

0 5 10 20 M

7.22a
East–west building section A-A

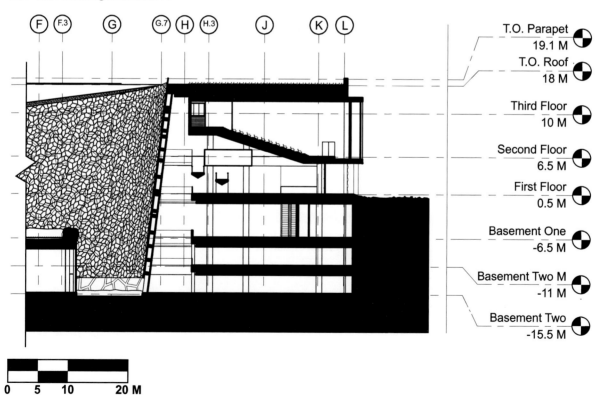

T.O. Parapet
19.1 M

T.O. Roof
18 M

Third Floor
10 M

Second Floor
6.5 M

First Floor
0.5 M

Basement One
-6.5 M

Basement Two M
-11 M

Basement Two
-15.5 M

0 5 10 20 M

7.22b
East–west building section A-A

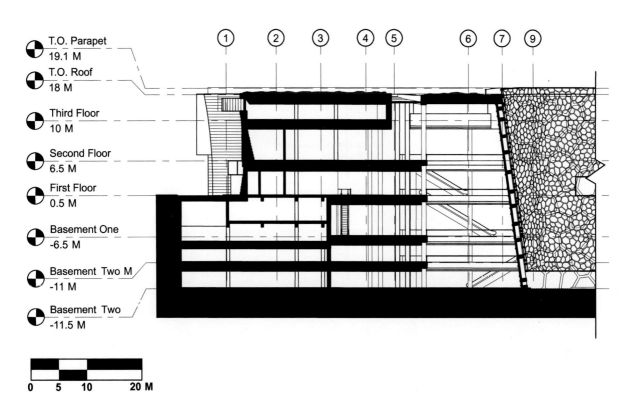

T.O. Parapet
19.1 M

T.O. Roof
18 M

Third Floor
10 M

Second Floor
6.5 M

First Floor
0.5 M

Basement One
-6.5 M

Basement Two M
-11 M

Basement Two
-11.5 M

0 5 10 20 M

7.23a
North–south building section B-B

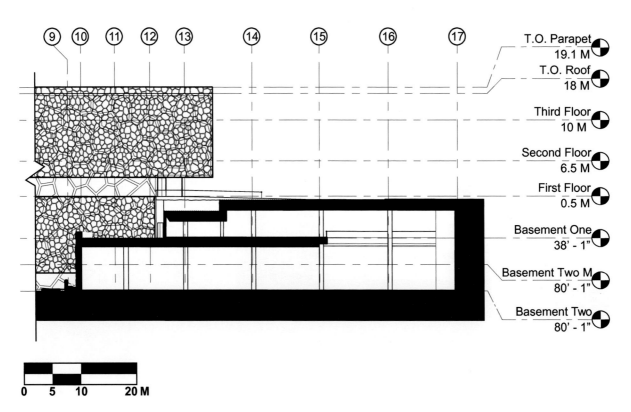

T.O. Parapet
19.1 M

T.O. Roof
18 M

Third Floor
10 M

Second Floor
6.5 M

First Floor
0.5 M

Basement One
38' - 1"

Basement Two M
80' - 1"

Basement Two
80' - 1"

0 5 10 20 M

7.23b
North–South building section B-B

Aluminum
Sunscreen

Aluminum Clad
Steel Structure

Aluminum
Curtainwall

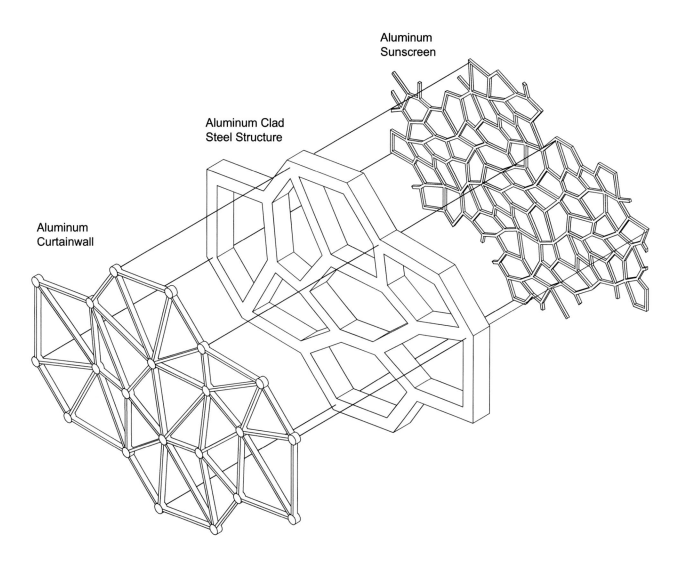

7.24
Exploded axonometric at screen wall
(Not to scale.)

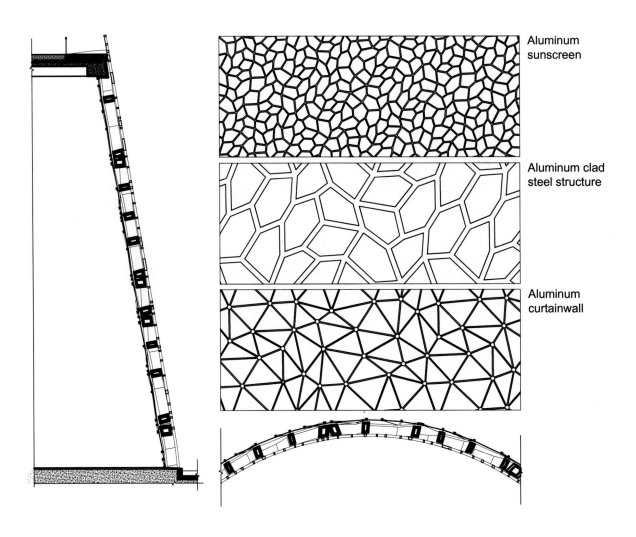

Aluminum
sunscreen

Aluminum clad
steel structure

Aluminum
curtainwall

7.25
Wall section and enlarged plan: screen wall
(Not to scale.)

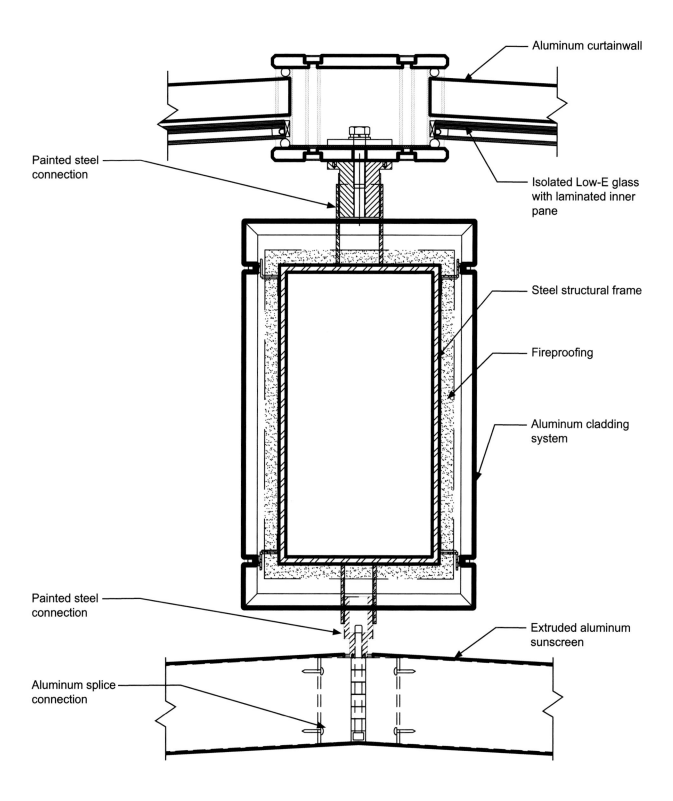

Aluminum curtainwall

Isolated Low-E glass with laminated inner pane

Painted steel connection

Steel structural frame

Fireproofing

Aluminum cladding system

Painted steel connection

Extruded aluminum sunscreen

Aluminum splice connection

7.26
Plan detail: screen wall
(Not to scale.)

Guide

How to Determine Assembly

Construction detailing expresses an architect's ideas on the use of materials to create space, relate to the building's surroundings, and the typology of a building. Students must study existing buildings to understand how and why architects do this to create a tectonic language of their own. This guide is intended to help students begin their thought process and analyze their own ideas on materiality and tectonics while learning from others.

1 Study the buildings in this book.

    a   How are materials around the buildings used?

    b   What is the use of materials for the buildings, and how are they are detailed, what are they saying about each design?

    c   How do they integrate, or not integrate, into their surroundings?

    d   Why do you think this was done?

2 Study the surroundings for your building design.

    a   How are materials around your building site used?

    b   What is the use of materials for your building design, and how do you think they should be detailed, what are they saying about your design idea?

    c   How do you integrate, or not integrate, into the surroundings for your building design?

    d   Why did you make these decisions and how does it relate to the building surroundings and your design ideas?

3 Make decisions on what materials to use and why. Have a reason related to your design intent and the surroundings for your building design.

4 What is the impact of these decisions on the building design?

    a   How will these materials be assembled during construction?

5 How will the building meet the ground?

    a   What will people experience as they interact with the building?

    b   How will the materials and assemblies wear and fare over time?

6 What happens when different materials meet?

7 How do material sizes and assemblies impact design and vice versa?

8 How will the building turn the corner?

9 How does the building, not just the materials, interact with its surroundings?

10 What is the environmental impact of your material and assemblies choices?

11 How does the space feel from the inside based on your material and assemblies choices?

12 How does the building meet the sky?

Many of these questions and suggestions are similar to questions asked in design studios about overall design ideas and form. However, an important aspect is how materials and building construction assemblies are part of those design decisions. This book provides a holistic look at various projects because design is a holistic process that must include consideration of space, form, materials, and assemblies.

Afterword

> Detailing is very important. It is the architect's sole means of turning dreams into built reality, the language by which we instruct workers in how to assemble a building to achieve the results we desire. Skill in detailing is also the architect's best insurance against getting sued for buildings that leak, crack, or otherwise misbehave.
>
> Edward Allen, FAIA[1]

I use this quote to open my lecture course on building construction assemblies each semester because it eloquently describes the importance of comprehensive tectonic ideas and their connection to architectural design. The understanding of architecture and its relationship to building construction detailing instills the idea that building construction assemblies and architectural form are one in the same,[2] and that understanding the "... complete system binding all of the parts ..."[3] must be a part of architecture education. Students will use this book to realize that building construction detailing can express design ideas and show the relationship of the detail to the overall building design.[4]

Once students have studied projects like the Tenley-Friendship Library they will begin to understand that building construction detailing lends itself not just to aesthetic choices, but also ethical ones.[5] The use of a book metaphor for a library is not a new one, however, the material choices and details used to express an opaque "cover" to protect knowledge, while also having a "clear book cover" to encourage entry shows students how details can reinforce design concepts.[6] Hatiloo Theater worked with a tight budget for a client that wanted to use their building design to express their identity and become part of a community. The result was a durable and flexible building with details that could evolve over time as the client budget expanded. Even projects like the Maritime and Seafood Industry Museum demonstrate how the development of stricter, and necessary, regulations need not restrict the importance of the relationship between building construction detailing and architectural form. The slow evolution, or some might argue devolution, of architectural detailing from artistic expression to merely legal and economic means to construct a building does not mean beauty cannot be developed from thoughtful and well-designed "joints."[7]

This "joining" of both building materials, and design ideas must also be developed in relation to specific project needs and influences. Detailing and design for the Arizona

State University Health Services Building (ASU HSB) is, and should be, markedly different than that of the Waveland Business Incubator. The ASU HSB is located in a dry, arid climate as opposed to the wet, humid climate where the Waveland Business Incubator is located. Also, the size and scale of the ASU HSB is much larger than the Waveland Business Incubator. However, both are very sustainable projects and were designed with much thought and detailing based on the specific needs of each project, their clients, and the users. Based on this idea one detail does not fit all projects, and the variety of differences between these two projects, from scale, function, climate, and client all show that architects, and with this book our students, should use the inherent nature of architectural thinking to resolve the specific needs of the project through thoughtful detailing.[8]

Even though there is an argument for the negative influence of technology (both professionally linked, and personally linked) on our students, and the profession, there are ways that detailing can harness these advances and use them to develop the profession and expand the importance of building construction detailing to what it once was.[9] The Shanghai Nature Museum utilizes this technology to develop the form of the building, and also the intricate structure-skin-shading device along the courtyard to shade the building. In contrast, Art Stable uses technology and the craft of local artisans to express the function of that project through the design of the oversized hinge to facilitate the movement of large-scaled art in and out of the building. Olson Kundig, in particular, is known for its interest and ability to forgo the ". . . illusion that quotation is a sufficient substitute for the detail as a system of articulation in architectural language" and embraces building construction detailing as a way to express the design concept instead of using building form alone.[10] The development of the davit crane expresses the history of the neighborhood of the project, and the function of the new building that Olson Kundig designed.

Students will continue to struggle with the same issues that all architects face: the continued economic and cultural pressures of clients,[11] the formal pressures of architectural "styles,"[12] and the time to adequately complete the design they wish to achieve. However, as Marco Frascari notes in relation to Princeton professor Jean Labatut, "The detail tells the tale," and can inform all parts of an architectural design.[13]

This is why holistic project presentation is important to the creation and development of this book because architecture requires a holistic process to create beautiful and successful buildings.[14] The efforts to create this book were inspired by this thought and utilize projects to not just show a holistic design idea, but also a more thorough view of a variety of project typologies and scales. Students can learn from studying these existing buildings and can develop a strategy of their own to design building construction details and assemblies to express their design ideas. Similar to learning about how world-renowned architects designed and detailed their buildings in books like Kenneth Frampton's *Studies in Tectonic Culture*, users of this book can hear directly from contemporary architecture firms and the reasoning behind building construction detailing decisions.

The intent was to improve upon independent details focused only on one specific part of a building construction assembly. Additionally, addressing the prevalence of limited information, lack of context, and size of the image in other technical literature will improve the understanding of students and other readers of this book when they are reading architectural drawings and trying to comprehend their contents that express how a building was constructed. *Comprehensive Tectonics: Technical Building Assemblies from the Ground to the Sky* aims to eliminate the struggle that I have seen in my students who try to use other technical literature as they have no reference for how to input and utilize the information provided. The use of the case studies in the book, along with the *Guide: How to Determine Assembly* will provide students the ability to better understand building construction assemblies and their impact on design.

> The joint, that is the fertile detail, is the place where both the construction and the construing of architecture take place.[15]

> Marco Frascari

Notes

1   Allen, Edward. 205. "Some Comments Concerning Technical Teaching in Schools of Architecture," *ACSA News* (May 2005).

2   Frampton, Kenneth. 1995. "Chapter 1 – Introduction: Reflections on the Scope of the Tectonic." In *Studies in Tectonic Culture: The Poetics of Construction in Nineteenth and Twentieth Century Architecture*, edited by John Cave, 2. Cambridge, MA: MIT Press.

3   Ibid, 4.

4   Nesbitt, Kate. 1996. "Introduction: The Exercise of Detailing." In *Theorizing a New Agenda for Architecture: An Anthology of Architectural Theory*, edited by Kate Nesbitt, 494. New York, NY: Princeton Architectural Press.

5   Frascari, Marco. 1996. "The Tell-the-Tale Detail." In *Theorizing a New Agenda for Architecture: An Anthology of Architectural Theory*, edited by Kate Nesbitt, 500. New York, NY: Princeton Architectural Press.

6   Gregotti, Virttorio. 1996. "The Exercise of Detailing." In *Theorizing a New Agenda for Architecture: An Anthology of Architectural Theory*, edited by Kate Nesbitt, 496. New York, NY: Princeton Architectural Press.

7   Frascari, 503.

8   Frascari, 501.

9   Gregotti, 497.

10   Ibid.

11   Ibid.

12   Frampton, 2.

13   Frascari, 500–501.

14   Frascari, 501.

15   Frascari, 511.

Image and Drawing Credits

Images

Waveland Business Incubator, Waveland, MS

1   Allison Anderson, unabridged Architecture
2   Eugenia Uhl, Eugenia Uhl Photography

Hatiloo Theatre, Memphis, TN

1   Archimania
2   Hank Mardukas, Hank Mardukas Photography

Maritime & Seafood Industry Museum, Biloxi, MS

1   Francis Dzikowski, Francis Dzikowski Photography
2   OTTO

Tenley-Friendship Library, Washington, DC

1   Mark Herboth, Mark Herboth Photography LLC

Arizona State University Health Services Building, Tempe, AZ

1   Lake | Flato Architects, Orcutt Winslow, and Bill Timmerman

Art Stable, Seattle, WA

1   Benjamin Benschneider, Benjamin Benschneider Photography
2   Chris Rogers, Point32

Shanghai Nature Museum, Shanghai, China

1   James and Connor Steinkamp, Steinkamp Photography

Drawings

Waveland Business Incubator, Waveland, MS

1   unabridged Architecture

Hatiloo Theatre, Memphis, TN

1   Archimania

Maritime & Seafood Industry Museum, Biloxi, MS

1   H3 Hardy Collaboration Architecture

Tenley-Friendship Library, Washington, DC

1   The Freelon Group (now part of Perkins + Will)

Arizona State University Health Services Building, Tempe, AZ

1   Lake | Flato Architects, Orcutt Winslow, and Bill Timmerman

Art Stable, Seattle, WA

1   Olson Kundig Architects

Shanghai Nature Museum, Shanghai, China

1   Perkins + Will – Chicago

Glossary of Terms and Materials

1x nominal name for a ¾" wood board

1x2 nominal name for a ¾" thick by 1½" deep wood board

2x nominal name for a 1½" thick wood stud

2x4 nominal name for a 1½" thick by 3½" deep wood stud

2x6 nominal name for a 1½" thick by 5½" deep wood stud

ACT shorthand for Acoustical Ceiling Tile, a standard ceiling for commercial and office spaces in buildings.

ADA acronym for the Americans with Disabilities Act. The Americans with Disabilities Act is a civil right that regulates universal accessibility for people with disabilities in building design and other aspects of the built environment.

AFF shorthand for Above Finish Floor that is typical of the building construction industry.

Acoustical barrier material used to block noise and provide an acoustical dampener between floors and rooms. Typically consists of some type of insulation.

Acoustical batt insulation batt insulation specifically created to be used to provide an acoustical barrier.

Acoustical mat another term for acoustical insulation used for an acoustical barrier.

Acoustical sealant sealant used to fill joints between materials to help provide an acoustical barrier between walls and floors.

Air barrier (see also Protective membrane) material used to prevent air infiltration in an exterior wall assembly. Typically consists of some type of membrane or felt paper.

Anchor bolt galvanized steel bolt that is cast into concrete footings to allow the attachment of wood stud sill plates and steel structural base plates.

Anodized aluminum a specific finish for aluminum that protects the aluminum and looks like unpainted aluminum.

Argon a gas sometimes used in double, or triple, pane windows between the panes of glass to increase the insulating value of the window.

ASL shorthand for Above Sea Level.

BO acronym for Bottom Of, for example, Bottom of Steel for the location of the bottom of a steel structural frame.

BOS acronym for Bottom of Steel.

BOW   acronym for Bottom of Window, could also indicate the location of the window head.

Baluster   vertical element in a stair railing or guardrail.

Batt insulation   fluffy insulation that is most traditionally made of fiberglass and often comes with a kraft paper or reflective membrane on one side. Typically installed between wood or metal studs, but also can also be used as an acoustical barrier.

Batten   exterior wood strip used to cover the joint between exterior wood board siding. For example, board and batten.

Bearing plate   steel plate that another structural member rests, or bears, on. Often is another steel structural member such as a beam or open-web joist.

Bentonite waterstop   waterstop made out of Bentonite clay to utilize the absorptive properties of Bentonite clay. Most often used with a cold joint in site-cast concrete.

Blocking   typically wood studs cut to shape for the specific area where blocking is needed. Blocking helps to fill area where materials come together, or to facilitate the fastening of materials together, such as windows to walls.

Blown cellulose insulation   a loose type of insulation that is typically made up of recycled newspapers and can be blown into attics and walls. Can be installed either wet or dry, depending on the location where the insulation is needed.

Bollards   vertical posts typically made of steel to protect areas where cars might run into parts of a building.

Bracing   added structural element that can be made of steel or wood, depending on the structure being braced.

Brake metal   sheet metal bent on a brake, a metal bending machine, to create custom metal components.

Brick ties (see also Masonry ties)   galvanized steel elements that anchor brick veneer cladding to a backup wall. Backup walls can be wood or metal studs, CMU walls, site-cast concrete walls, pre-cast concrete walls, and even steel structures. The type of brick or masonry tie varies depending on the backup wall that is supporting the brick veneer.

Brick veneer   one wythe, or layer of brick that is not structural, but is instead a cladding made of brick. Must be supported through brick ties, a backup wall, and a slab or shelf angles at all levels.

Bubble skylight   skylight that has a curved shape as opposed to a flat shape.

Building wrap   another term for membrane, a building wrap is used over sheathing to prevent air and moisture from penetrating the exterior wall or roof of a building assembly.

Burnished   a specific finish for site-cast concrete that is left exposed, it is the term for polishing the concrete for a smooth and shiny finish when complete.

Butyl tape   a sticky, membrane like tape that is used to seal joints between flashing and other materials.

Butt joints   a joint where two materials butt up against one another and the exterior surfaces tend to align for a smooth joint.

Butt-glazed   when two pieces of glazing butt up to one another to align on the surface and form a smooth joint. Often sealed with clear sealant to create an air and water barrier.

C-Channel   C-shaped structural channel.

CL abbreviation for Center Line. Used to show alignment of attachments, organization of dimensions for construction detailing.

Cable rail Railing made out of thin steel cables. Typically used when a low-profile and less visible railing is wanted.

Cant or cant strip angled wood blocking used at the intersection of a roof and parapet wall to prevent water buildup at that location. Protected by flashing and roof membrane.

Cast-in-place concrete also called site-cast concrete, this is a concrete structure that is created on site where it is cast in formwork that is built on site, hence the name cast-in-place.

Catch basin Part of exterior drainage system that catches rain water to facilitate drainage away from a building.

Caulk or caulk joint Interior sealant used in areas where there will not be much expansion and contraction of the materials sealed by the caulk.

Caulk and backer rod caulk used in conjunction with a backer rod that is installed in a joint to be sealed by the caulk. The backer rod is a spongy material that will not bod with the caulk, but does allow a surface for the caulk to be installed on to facilitate the creation of a sealed joint where the caulk is applied. Caulk is used only in interior applications as it does not have the ability to expand and contract enough for exterior use.

Cavity space in an exterior wall that allows for airflow and drainage of any external moisture that may get into an exterior wall assembly.

Cementitious board exterior wall board made primarily of cement and used as a more durable and longer-lasting alternative to wood board siding.

Chamfered curved or angled edge used to prevent damage to the edge.

Clad covered by a material; typically refers to a structure or structural element.

Cladding skin of a building which can be made of a wide variety of different materials and systems that can range from brick veneer to curtain walls.

Cleat fasteners a specific type of fastener that is shaped like a Z.

Clerestory a high window that is typically not for views but instead primarily for bringing in light.

Closed cell spray foam insulation a type of spray foam insulation that has a higher R-value than open cell spray foam insulation, and is more rigid and durable due to the closed cells of the insulation that encapsulate the air.

CMU (concrete masonry unit) a masonry unit created out of concrete that is also often referred to as cinder block or concrete block. Typical sizes are 8″ wide × 8″ high × 16″ long but it does come in a variety of other size and many different surface textures.

Cold joint joint between different concrete pours for cast-in-place, or site-cast concrete.

Compressible filler sometimes also called an expansion joint, this is a spongy material that fills joints between concrete slabs or sidewalks, and concrete walls. It is named as such because the material needs to be able to compress based on the expansion and contraction of the materials on either side of the joint being filled.

Concrete joints the lines of the concrete formwork showing the joints of the material when it was created by the formwork.

Concrete stem wall   the low wall that rises from the concrete footing as part of the foundation. This wall can connect to the slab-on-grade or continue to rise out of the ground to allow connection to an exterior wall.

Conductor head   part of a roof drainage system that connects a scupper to a downspout.

Control joint   a pre-formed joint in a concrete slab that controls where the slab will crack if subjected to pressures such as creep, temperature, or other stresses.

Coping cap, coping, or parapet cap   a flashing element at the top of a parapet wall that prevents the entrance of water into the parapet wall. It works in conjunction with base flashing and counter flashing to maintain an air and water barrier where a roof meets a parapet wall.

Corner bead   a metal or plastic component used on corners of gypsum board or plaster walls to protect the corners and to facilitate the addition of joint compound.

Corrugated metal deck   a piece of sheet metal formed into corrugations that is used for the base to pour a concrete slab on top of a steel structure.

Cover board   similar to protection board, a cover board covers a membrane or other sensitive material that needs to be protected as part of a wall or roof assembly.

Cricket   a flashing component used to divert water around a vertical component, such as a chimney.

Curtain wall   a type of cladding system made primarily of glass supported by an aluminum or steel frame that is hung from the building structure.

Dampproofing   a type of membrane, typically liquid-applied, that is used to resist water penetration for an exterior wall.

Deck (decking)   the floor of a structural support system, such as a corrugated metal deck, a concrete deck, and a plywood deck.

Decorative score joints   preformed joints in site-cast concrete to emulate concrete joints and possibly to match the pattern and rhythm of other materials in the assembly, such as storefront or curtain wall systems.

Drainage gap   similar to a weep hole, a drainage gap allows any moisture that has accumulated in a cavity to drain out of an exterior wall to prevent moisture build-up and damage.

Drainage mat   a material added in various locations to facilitate the drainage of any moisture that accumulates in an exterior wall. Most commonly used on basement walls to aid in the prevention of moisture penetration from ground water, but is also used in exterior wall assemblies that are above ground.

Drip or drip edge   most often a metal flashing element that extends out of a wall to facilitate the dripping of water away from an exterior wall to prevent the wicking of the water back into the wall assembly.

Edge bead   similar to a corner bead, an edge bead can be used in gypsum board assemblies, but can also be used to create a reveal where two materials join together.

Embeds or embed   various items cast into both site-cast (cast-in-place) and pre-cast concrete. These items are embedded during the casting process so that they are part of the concrete element and can facilitate connections to other materials, such as steel structure. They can also be used to house light fixtures to other items that would be hard, or even impossible, to install once the concrete is cured.

Glossary of Terms and Materials

End dams flashing at the ends of openings in exterior walls such as windows and doors. This flashing is to prevent any moisture that builds up in the wall above those openings from dropping down further into the wall. The moisture is instead removed from the wall with flashing, weeps, and drips over the opening.

Expansion joint similar to a compressible filler, an expansion joint allows for the expansion and contraction of materials that come together at that joint. Most commonly seen at certain intervals of masonry material such as concrete sidewalks, and masonry walls made of brick or CMU.

Exterior grade sheathing sheathing made of a panel product that has been treated to resist exterior forces such as moisture from rain and snow to condensation.

Extruded aluminum aluminum that is melted to a point that it can be pushed through a die, or extruded, to create various shapes that create aluminum frames for doors, windows, curtain walls, and storefront systems.

FF abbreviation for Finish Floor, which indicates the surface of the final surface finish whether it be carpet or wood flooring. This is in contrast to the surface of the structure which could be significantly lower depending on the final surface finish.

FO (Finished Opening) the level of the final opening after all surface finishes have been applied, such as gypsum board and paint or wall covering.

Façade another term for exterior wall surface that comes from a French word that means face.

Fascia one part of an eave, the fascia is the vertical component, while the soffit is the horizontal component. It often helps to enclose the eave while the soffit allows for ventilation of the roof space.

Fastener this encompasses many various types of items from nails to screws to bolts that help to attach a variety of materials and systems together.

Fiber-cement panel similar to the cementitious board, it is also made up primarily of cement but has added cellulose fibers to increase the strength and durability of the material.

Fill this instance refers to soil fill where a space may have either been excavated for a project, or did not originally have soil in that location.

Fire caulk a caulk with fire-resistant properties that helps to seal a wall or floor assembly to help slow down the spread of fire and smoke to aid in the fire resistance of the assembly.

Fire proofing mineral wool insulation this is one type of insulation that is made of mineral wool, which has fire resistant properties, as well as acoustic properties.

Fire safing or safing material used to prevent fire from spreading through openings in floor slabs for items such as pipes and ducts. Also used where curtain walls are attached to structures to prevent fire from spreading from floor to floor along the façade. Mineral wool is typically in a batt insulation format when used in these instances, but can also be used as a compressed insulating board.

Fire spray foam another option for fire proofing in the form of spray foam insulation that has fire resistant properties in addition to insulating qualities.

Fire stopping materials that impede the spread of fire and smoke and are used in fire wall and floor assemblies to achieve certain fire ratings.

Finish ceiling   level of ceiling where the final finish has been applied, such as gypsum board and paint.

Finish plaster coating   final coat of plaster to complete a plaster finish system.

Finish slab   level of slab where the final floor finish is the slab itself with no additional flooring added on top of the slab.

Flashing   made of various metals, plastics, or rubbery materials flashing can be both external and internal (**see Through wall flashing**). External flashing prevents the penetration of water into a wall or roof assembly, while internal flashing aids in removing moisture that has gathered in the cavity of an exterior wall assembly.

Flat seam metal panel   as opposed to a standing seam metal panel, this product flattens the seams between the metal panels. The seams are still visible, but no longer protrude from the surface of the wall on which they are installed.

Flush   aligned with.

Footing   part of a foundation, footings are made of cast-in-place concrete and work with other items like piles or concrete stems to connect to the rest of the structure or transfer the load of the building to the earth in which the footing is placed.

FRC (see also GFCR)   shorthand for Fiber Reinforced Concrete.

Furring (see also Hat channels)   a smaller stud that can be made of metal, wood, or plastic that is used to attach finish materials to concrete and masonry surfaces. They are sometimes called hat channels as the metal or plastic versions can be formed in a way that looks like a hat in plan.

GC   shorthand for General Contractor.

GFRC (see also FRC)   shorthand for Glass Fiber Reinforced Concrete.

Galvanized   a zinc coating that protects steel from rusting, so is often used for flashing and fasteners that will be exposed to moisture.

Glazing   a term for the glass pieces in construction assemblies such as curtain walls, windows, doors, and storefront systems.

Grade   another term for the level of the existing earth in relation to a built project.

Grade beam   a beam that generally runs along grade and connects typically isolated foundation elements such as column footings and piles and transfers load from the wall it is supporting to those isolated foundation elements.

Green roof   a roof designed to support vegetation and the elements required to maintain the vegetation.

Grout   similar to mortar, but more plastic due to higher water content, grout is typically a filler where mortar is meant to bond masonry together. As an example, grout is used between flooring tiles.

GWB (Gypsum Wall Board or Gypsum Board)   also referred to as drywall and sheetrock, gypsum wall board is used as a standard finish for wood and metal stud walls and ceilings. It is composed of gypsum plaster that is hardened and sandwiched between two layers of paper that accepts the wall finish.

HSS   shorthand for Hollow Structural Section.

HVAC   acronym for Heating, Ventilation, and Air Conditioning.

Glossary of Terms and Materials

Hat channels (see Furring)

Head   typically refers to the top of an opening such as a window head or door head.

Heavy gauge   refers to a thicker sheet of steel. The thicker the gauge, the more load the steel can take.

Hydroponic living wall   similar to a green roof, this is a wall that is designed to support vegetation using hydroponic systems.

Insulation   various materials and systems that prevent the flow of heat energy through the building envelope.

Insulated glass   glass that typically is double paned and may contain argon gas or another gas between the two panes to slow the transfer of heat energy through the glass.

Ipe   a type of Brazilian hardwood that is both insect and rot-resistant.

Jamb   typically refers to the sides of openings such as a window jamb or a door jamb.

Joint sealant (see Sealant)

Joint tape (see Butyl tape)

Keyway   a recess cast into concrete footings to aid in the physical connection of the concrete stem wall cast on top of the concrete footing in a separate concrete pour.

Ledger   point at which a structural element can bear and be attached to a load bearing wall, such as a CMU wall.

Lintel   structural element that transfers the load of a wall over an opening to either side of the opening. Lintels can be made of different materials from steel to pre-cast concrete.

Low-E glass   a type of glass that blocks certain UV rays from the sun that increase heat gain through the window. This type of glass is used in conjunction with insulated glass to make a more energy efficient window or door.

Marine grade plywood   similar to Exterior Grade Sheeting, this type of plywood is treated to stand up to more extreme moisture environments, such as those in marine environments that have more salt inherent in the moisture that impacts building assemblies.

Masonry ties (see Brick ties)

Max   short for maximum.

Membrane roof   also noted as Roof Membrane, this can consist of various materials and systems that protect the roof structure of a building. Membrane roofs tend to be on low-slope roofs as opposed to steep roofs. Possible materials include modified bitumen roofs and thermoplastic membrane roofs.

Metal stud runner   this is the horizontal member of metal stud walls and runs at the top and bottom of the stud wall to accept the C-studs that run vertically.

Mineral wool insulation (see Fire proofing mineral wool insulation)

Moisture proofing (see Dampproofing)

Mullion   the frame of a window that holds the glazing in place.

Nailer (see Blocking)

Non-combustible plywood   plywood sheathing treated for fire resistance.

OC   acronym for On Center, similar to Center Line.

OPP   shorthand for opposite.

Outrigger   horizontal structural element that works with and supports angled structural members and ties back into vertical structural members such as columns or walls.

Pan flashing installed at the bottom of windows and doors, this type of flashing has a turned up edge on the inside of the wall to encourage any moisture that enters the wall to flow back outside of the wall.

Parapet top of a wall at the roof that extends past the roofline. A parapet is composed of many items including coping, flashing, cant strip, and membrane.

Piles part of a foundation, piles are used when the building load must be transferred deeper into the earth than more shallow foundations are able to achieve.

Pin mounting a clean and simple way of mounting letters on a building for signage.

Plaster finish (see Finish plaster coating)

Plenum space in the ceiling between the finish ceiling and the structure that is open and can be used for returning the stale air from a space back to the HVAC equipment.

Precast concrete panel panels created off-site at a precast plant based on the project requirements and shipped to the project site.

Preformed sealant tape or preformed joint sealant a solid sealant, as opposed to the gunnable sealant that is associated with caulk and the movement joints between materials. Typically used to hold down and seal flashing in exterior wall assemblies.

Protection board a board to protect a membrane from other parts of the assembly, as well as from soil when the membrane is on a wall underground.

Protective membrane or membrane similar to a roof membrane, but this protects other parts of a building assembly and helps to prevent air and moisture penetration.

Purlin a sloped beam that supports the roof deck.

Rainscreen the outer skin of an exterior wall assembly that acts as a screen against the rain and other precipitation to protect the cavity and backup wall which has the membrane and vapor barrier installed on it.

Reflected ceiling plan a plan that shows the arrangement of items in a ceiling plane such as light fixtures, sprinklers, etc.

Reglet an opening cast into concrete elements to allow for the attachment of flashing.

Retaining wall a load bearing wall that retains soil and is designed to take the load of the soil and not crack or overturn due to the weight of the soil.

Reveal an intentional joint in a wall, floor, or ceiling that is part of the design of the building. This may be used to reflect a pattern in a surrounding material or system, such as a storefront, curtain wall, or concrete joint.

Ridge the highest point of a roof.

Rigid insulation a popular form of insulation that is rigid in formation, unlike batt, blown, or spray foam insulation. It is typically used in a tapered format to help with roof slope and drainage in low-slope roofs, and in cavity walls that have a concrete or masonry backup wall.

Ripped to cut down a 2× or other nominal wood stud down to a smaller size.

Rock wool insulation (see Mineral wool insulation)

SS abbreviation for Stainless Steel.

Scupper drain from low-slope roof that is an opening in the parapet wall and drains directly out instead of through a gutter and downspout.

Sealant various types of materials from solid to gunnable that help seal joints between materials as part of an exterior building assembly.

Glossary of Terms and Materials

Sealant and backer rod   similar to caulk and backer rod, however, sealant is used in exterior applications because sealant comes in versions that allow for more expansion and contraction for temperature differences.

Shear plate   a vertical plate attached to a steel structure to discourage shear at a connection point where shear might occur.

Sheathing   typically a panel product such as plywood or OSB (oriented strand board) that is attached to metal stud walls, floors, and roofs. It acts as a part of the structural action when attached to the exterior of walls and the tops of floors and roofs.

Shim   similar to blocking, shims are formed by small slivers of wood studs and are used to help plumb and level items such as windows and doors when they are installed.

Ship lap   exterior siding pattern that is most often formed by overlapping wood siding on an exterior wall, however, the pattern is emulated in various other exterior cladding materials to look like the original ship lap.

Shoring   a form of soil retention used to hold soil back during site excavation for the beginning of a building construction project.

Sill   typically the bottom of an opening such as a window sill or door sill.

SIM   shorthand for Similar

Sleeper   structural element most often made out of wood to support a wood deck on a concrete slab.

Slip connection   also known as a friction connection, a slip connection uses high strength bolts to form a friction connection to prevent slippage when the connection is loaded.

Slip track   a slotted deflection track that allows for building movement.

Soffit or soffit vent   one part of an eave, the soffit is the horizontal component, while the fascia is the vertical component. It allows for ventilation of the roof space and the fascia often helps to enclose the eave.

Sound attenuation batts or sound batt insulation   batt insulation that helps deter sound transmittance.

Spandrel   an opaque panel in a curtain wall or storefront system that can be made of glass or other material that conceals the building assembly behind the spandrel.

Spray foam insulation or spray on insulation   insulation that is sprayed in between wood or metal studs or on other floor and wall surfaces that then expands to fill the joints and cracks of the building assembly.

Steel pan   used for both the bottom of stairs that accepts concrete for a foot surface, and as part of flashing systems.

Storefront   a type of cladding system similar to a curtain wall, but tends to only run for one floor level at the bottom floor. Typically used for mercantile spaces, hence the name Storefront.

Stringer   Diagonal part of a stair that supports the treads, and sometimes risers, of a stair.

Structural base plate   steel plate welded to the bottom of steel columns to allow for the attachment of the column to concrete slabs and foundations.

Suspended ceiling   ceilings that are suspended from the structure above and can consist of ACT, gypsum board, or other materials.

Glossary of Terms and Materials

TO abbreviation for Top Of, for example, top of steel for the location of the top of a steel structural frame.

TOS acronym for Top of Steel.

TOW acronym for Top of Window.

Tempered glass a type of glass that has been processed to break into small granules when broken to prevent injury. Tempered glass is required by the International Building Code in various locations due to these properties.

Through wall flashing also known as internal flashing, this is flashing that is integrated into wall construction to prevent water from penetrating the wall in certain areas.

Treated wood products that are treated can either be fire treated to resist fire or pressure treated to resist rot.

TYP shorthand for Typical.

Type C and Type X two types of fire resistant gypsum board.

Vapor barrier different from a membrane that resists moisture but could allow vapor to penetrate, a vapor barrier is important to prevent the creation of condensation which can cause mold and other damage in building assemblies.

Waterproof air barrier Material used to prevent air and water infiltration in an exterior wall assembly. Typically consists of some type of membrane or felt paper.

Waterstop (see Bentonite waterstop)

Weather stripping two basic types of weatherstripping exist, brush-type and rubber gasket type. Both help prevent air and water penetration around doors and windows.

Weathering steel steel that creates a rusted appearance that actually creates a durable barrier that protects the rest of the steel under the rust as it continues to weather.

Weep holes or weeps small holes at the bottom of walls or above openings such as doors and windows that allows moisture that has collected in the wall cavity to exit.

Weld plate a steel plate embedded in concrete elements that allows the connection of other steel elements, such as beams and open-web joist through a welded connection.

Index

Index